Routledge Revivals

Birth Control in Germany 1871-1933

First published in 1988, *Birth Control in Germany* deals in detail with the dissemination and acceptance of ideas of birth control from 1871 -1933 and shows the variety of methods that were in use-condoms, pessaries, diaphragms, caps and most notably abortion. In common with many western societies, Germany experienced a notable decline in the birth rate as it entered into the 20th century. Demographers differ in their explanation for such changes in the birth rate. Some argue that fluctuating birth rates reflect society's efforts to match population and economy, while others argue that modern low levels can only be the result of radical innovations in popular behavior. The author argues that the latter can be shown to be the case in the German instance. He further says that attitudes quite similar to those found in liberal circles today were widespread among ordinary men and women in Germany, in contrast to, for example, the pro natalist ideologies dominant in France in the same period. This despite the regional, class and religious differentials which influence the German picture.

The book amounts to an important study of the sexual politics of pre–Nazi Germany, and study in modernization of a traditional society. This is an important historical work for scholars and researchers of German history, women's studies, health & reproductive history, European history, and gender studies.

Birth Control in Germany 1871-1933

James Woycke

First published in 1988
by Routledge

This edition first published in 2024 by Routledge
4 Park Square, Milton Park, Abingdon, Oxon, OX14 4RN

and by Routledge
605 Third Avenue, New York, NY 10017

Routledge is an imprint of the Taylor & Francis Group, an informa business

© 1988 James Woycke

All rights reserved. No part of this book may be reprinted or reproduced or utilised in any form or by any electronic, mechanical, or other means, now known or hereafter invented, including photocopying and recording, or in any information storage or retrieval system, without permission in writing from the publishers.

Publisher's Note
The publisher has gone to great lengths to ensure the quality of this reprint but points out that some imperfections in the original copies may be apparent.

Disclaimer
The publisher has made every effort to trace copyright holders and welcomes correspondence from those they have been unable to contact.

A Library of Congress record exists under ISBN: 0415003733

ISBN: 978-1-032-86153-1 (hbk)
ISBN: 978-1-003-52157-0 (ebk)
ISBN: 978-1-032-86158-6 (pbk)

Book DOI 10.4324/9781003521570

BIRTH CONTROL IN GERMANY 1871–1933

JAMES WOYCKE

ROUTLEDGE
London and New York

First published in 1988 by
Routledge
11 New Fetter Lane, London EC4P 4EE

Published in the USA by
Routledge
in association with Routledge, Chapman and Hall, Inc.
29 West 35th Street, New York NY 10001

© 1988 James Woycke

Printed and bound in Great Britain by
Biddles Ltd, Guildford and King's Lynn

All rights reserved. No part of this book may be reprinted or reproduced or utilised in any form or by any electronic, mechanical, or other means, now known or hereafter invented, including photocopying and recording, or in any information storage or retrieval system, without permission in writing from the publishers.

British Library Cataloguing in Publication Data

Woycke, James
   Birth control in Germany, 1871–1933.
   1. Birth control — Germany — History
   I., Title
   304.6'6'0943   HQ766.5.G3

ISBN 0-415-00373-3

Library of Congress Cataloging-in-Publication Data

ISBN 0-415-00373-3

Contents

Abbreviations	vii
Preface	ix
Introduction	1
1. Traditional Birth Control in Modern Society	7
2. The Advent of Modern Contraception	36
3. The Abortion Epidemic	68
4. The Abortion Underworld	89
5. The Mass Acceptance of Modern Contraception	112
6. The Politics of Birth Control	133
Conclusion	163
Suggestions for Further Reading	174
Index	177

Abbreviations

AFk	*Archiv für Frauenkunde*
AGyn	*Archiv für Gynäkologie*
AKAK	*Archiv für Kriminal-Anthropologie und Kriminologie*
ARGB	*Archiv für Rassen- und Gesellschaftsbiologie*
ASA	*Allgemeine Statistisches Archiv*
ASG	*Archiv für Sozialgeschichte*
ASHD	*Archiv für soziale Hygiene und Demographie*
BKW	*Berliner klinische Wochenschrift*
CEH	*Central European History*
CSSH	*Comparative Studies in Society and History*
DMW	*Deutsche Medizinische Wochenschrift*
DZGGM	*Deutsche Zeitschrift für die gesamte gerichtliche Medizin*
JSH	*Journal of Social History*
KW	*Klinische Wochenschrift*
MGG	*Monatsschrift für Geburtshilfe und Gynäkologie*
MK	*Medizinische Klinik*
MKP	*Monatsschrift für Kriminal-Psychologie*
MMW	*Münchener Medizinische Wochenschrift*
MW	*Medizinische Welt*
NG	*Neue Generation*
PS	*Population Studies*
SP	*Sexual-Probleme*
TG	*Therapie der Gegenwart*
TH	*Therapeutische Halbmonatsschrift*
VGMOS	*Vierteljahrsschrift für gerichtliche Medizin und öffentliche Sanitätswesen*
VGMV	*Veröffentlichungen aus dem Gebiete der Medizinal-Verwaltung*

ABBREVIATIONS

WKW	*Wiener klinische Wochenschrift*
WMW	*Wiener Mediziinische Wochenschrift*
ZAF	*Zeitschrift für ärztliche Fortbildung*
ZBGK	*Zeitschrift für Bekämpfung der Geschlechtskrankheiten*
ZGG	*Zeitschrift für Geburtshilfe und Gynäkologie*
ZGSW	*Zeitschrift für die gesamte Strafrechts-Wissenschaft*
ZGVGF	*Zeitschrift für Gesundheitsverwaltung und Gesundheitsfürsorge*
ZGyn	*Zentralblatt für Gynäkologie*
ZMB	*Zeitschrift für Medizinal-Beamte*
ZSWSP	*Zeitschrift für Sexualwissenschaft und Sexualpolitik*

Preface

The two-child family is a hallmark of modern western society. Things were not always so, however, and the process by which German society reduced its fertility is the subject of this book. Oscillations in birth rates have occurred before, but demographers differ in their explanations for these changes. Some argue that fluctuating birth rates reflect the ongoing efforts of society to match population and economy, while others argue that the modern fertility decline, which is distinctive for its irreversible reduction of birth rates to unusually low levels, can only be the result of a radical innovation in popular behaviour sparked by the introduction of new methods of birth control that made effective fertility control on a national scale possible. This book argues for the innovation approach.

The following study is based primarily on medical sources — books, articles and dissertations — which describe the new birth control techniques as they became available in the years after 1871, and which record the steady diffusion of these techniques throughout Germany during the late nineteenth and early twentieth centuries. Research for the book was conducted in medical libraries at the University of Toronto, McGill University, Northwestern University, the University of Chicago, the John Crerar Library and the Center for Research Libraries. In Germany research centered on the Berliner Medizinische Zentralbibliothek, the Preussische Staatsbibliothek, the Bayerische Staatsbibliothek, the Senckenburg Bibliothek at the University of Frankfurt, the Frankfurt Stadtarchiv, the Medizinische Zentralbibliothek at the University of Köln, the Institut für Geschichte der Medizin at the University of Düsseldorf, the Institut für Geschichte der Medizin at the University of Erlangen and the University of Mainz. I consulted abortion records at the Frauenkliniken affiliated with the University of Munich, the University of Düsseldorf, and the Free University of Berlin, with the permission of Professor J. Zander, Professor Schadewaldt and Professor Lax, respectively.

I want to thank the following individuals for their assistance and support: Dr Manfred Stürzbecher, Dr Hans Simmer, Dr Hans Schadewaldt, the Interlibrary Loan staff at Robarts Library, University of Toronto, Dr and Frau Lacher, and particularly Frau Ropers at the Institut für Europäische Geschichte in Mainz for her indefatigable interlibrary loan efforts. Professor Karl Freiherr von Aretin generously provided the opportunity to conduct research at the

PREFACE

Institut für Europäische Geschichte. The School of Graduate Studies at the University of Toronto also provided essential support. The manuscript in its present incarnation owes much to the criticism of Edward Shorter, John Gillis, John Ingham, David Levine and John Beattie. Translations represent my improvisation unless otherwise indicated.

Introduction

Fertility rates across Europe fell by half during the past century. In western countries the fertility decline began in the late nineteenth century and ended before the Second World War, while in eastern Europe the decline usually began after the turn of the century and ended only recently. Around 1900 half of all provinces in Europe had demonstrated the onset of the decline, while by 1950 virtually all provinces showed a drop of 50 per cent or more in marital fertility. There were exceptions, of course: France began the decline long before other countries, while Ireland, Albania, and parts of Spain, Portugal, and Yugoslavia had not completed the decline by mid-century. Nonetheless the overwhelming impact of a continent-wide drop in fertility within the span of three generations cannot be gainsaid.[1]

At first glance the German fertility decline appears to fit the standard pattern of demographic transition.[2] The German decline began on a national scale in 1895 and ended in 1935. Marital fertility declined by nearly two-thirds during this period, while non-marital birth rates dropped by half. The earliest regional decline occurred in 1879, the latest in 1914. Levels of fertility varied considerably from one area to another before and during the decline, with central Germany starting the decline at lower levels of fertility than western, southern, or eastern Germany. It is not clear whether some or all social groups in areas of low fertility were practising some form of birth control, or whether variations in natural fertility are responsible. Whatever the reason for these existing and long-standing differentials, there is no evidence of a sustained fertility decline beginning anywhere in Germany much before the 1880s.[3]

Once fertility began to decline all regions of the country became involved, though again regional differentials characterised the process. Fertility was more likely to start declining in urban centres within a given administrative area, but spread quickly to the surrounding countryside. Once the decline began, it continued apace for all sectors within each area, whether urban or rural. Protestant regions displayed lower pre-decline levels of fertility and an earlier onset of the decline than did Catholic areas, which declined later and less rapidly. In Prussia Protestant regions commenced the decline around 1890, while Catholic regions began in 1910. But differences are less pronounced in Bavaria, and non-existent in other states.[4]

INTRODUCTION

Table 1: Marital fertility in Germany, 1900–1925 (live births per 1000 married women under age 45)

Region	1900	1910	1925
Germany	279.7	224.5	146.3
Prussia	283.1	230.4	145.4
Bavaria	307.8	252.7	169.0
Wurttemburg	308.5	248.2	159.2
Baden	292.7	234.7	161.5
Thuringia	252.3	202.3	134.1
Hesse	260.6	202.2	141.8
Hamburg	202.0	146.4	87.7
Mecklenburg-Schwerin	216.7	184.5	138.5
Oldenburg	293.4	258.5	186.2
Braunschweig	234.0	178.0	120.2
Anhalt	237.2	174.8	126.0
Bremen	237.6	178.2	105.3
Lippe	290.8	250.9	179.2
Lubeck	230.7	175.8	108.7
Mecklenburg-Strelitz	233.1	198.6	152.2
Waldeck	265.7	222.4	169.8
Schaumburg-Lippe	232.4	196.6	125.7

Source: Germany, Statistisches Reichsamt, 'Beiträge zum deutschen Bevölkerungsproblem', *Wirtschaft und Statistik*, Sonderheft 5 (1929), pp. 8, 14–15

The drop in birth rates among married women is especially important because they constitute the bulk of the childbearing population. Fertility declined among married women of all ages, while the age at last birth fell steadily as older women halted childbearing at ever lower numbers of children; completed family size fell to one-third of former levels. Average parity (total deliveries per woman) declined systematically from the 1880s as the percentage of women having five or more births virtually disappeared, while the percentage of first-borns among all births rose dramatically, reaching one-half in Berlin in 1926, one-third for all Prussian urban areas, and one-fourth for rural areas. In Saxony first-borns accounted for 25 per cent of all births in 1913 and nearly 40 per cent in 1924. Women also increasingly delayed having their first child, especially after the First World War. And the pauses between children lengthened as well, from 28 months in 1901–2 to 33 months in 1911–12.[5]

Fertility declined among all socio-economic groups in Germany, but again with significant differentials. Even before 1880 birth rates among civil servants and professionals were suspiciously lower than those for other classes, and these occupations, along with persons in trade and commerce, demonstrated a further decline in fertility by 1895. Between 1895 and 1907 fertility began to decline for all other occupational sectors except agriculture and mining. Within the primary, secondary and tertiary sectors of the economy owners and white-collar workers demonstrated an earlier and more substantial decline than did workers, but by the 1920s fertility had declined substantially in all occupational groups. The 1939 census of completed family size shows that total children per family declined steadily in all classes and in all regions from the turn of the century onwards. While at any given time workers had higher numbers of children than other groups, the differences lessened over time.[6] In short, the fertility decline did not affect everyone in Germany at the same time. But it did start throughout Germany within one generation, and was essentially completed within two generations.

Table 2: Children ever born, current marriages (1939)

Married	By place of residence			
	Germany	Metropolitan	Urban	Rural
Pre-1905	4.67	3.86	4.76	5.29
1905-9	3.58	2.74	3.65	4.42
1910-14	3.07	2.28	3.12	3.91
1915-19	2.58	1.90	2.62	3.37

Married	By occupation				
	Professions	White collar	Farmer	Farm workers	Other workers
Pre-1905	3.21	3.39	5.56	6.05	4.67
1905-9	2.47	2.66	4.69	5.20	3.82
1910-14	2.17	2.26	4.12	4.68	3.27
1915-19	1.84	1.91	3.48	4.08	2.76

Source: Adapted from John Knodel, *The decline of fertility in Germany, 1871-1939* (Princeton University Press, Princeton, 1974), pp. 107, 124; Reinhard Spree, *Soziale Ungleichheit vor Krankheit und Tod* (Vandenhoek and Rupprecht, Göttingen, 1981), p. 180.

Although there is no agreement on the ultimate cause of the fertility decline — the 'why' of the demographic transition — there is consensus on the 'how': birth control is universally credited for the drop in birth rates. But it is not clear whether the widespread practice of birth control is due to a popular response to massive structural changes in economy and society which rendered traditional fertility levels disadvantageous, or to the development and diffusion of new techniques for controlling fertility which had been unknown or unaccepted but which fundamentally and irreversibly altered western fertility behaviour.

There are three main reasons for supposing that modern birth control techniques lay behind the fertility decline of the late nineteenth century. Traditional methods — principally coitus interruptus — are notoriously unreliable in the absence of strong motivation; the complicated mechanics and the constraint on sexual spontaneity conspire against consistent and successful implementation. Although traditional birth control was employed at different times in different places by different classes anxious to maintain property and status, it had less appeal for the lower classes; sinking from abject to grinding poverty has less psychological impact than falling from bourgeois comfort to proletarian squalor. The simultaneous decline in marital and non-marital fertility rates reinforces this argument. Unmarried people surely had strong motivation for avoiding conception and would probably have utilised contraception for that purpose if the methods available had not interfered with the sexual passion that was, presumably, the *raison d'être* of their liaison in the first place. Since illegitimate fertility rates fell throughout Europe in the decades after 1871 we can assume that new and more satisfactory methods were responsible. And the further decline in fertility rates that has occurred since the proliferation of oral contraceptives in the 1960s demonstrates once again the importance of technology for effective birth control.[7]

Modern birth control began in the 1880s as entrepreneurs inspired by the public discussion of Neo-Malthusianism recognised a potential market and quickly adapted technical advances to produce a variety of rubber and chemical products 'for the Malthusian'. At the same time both professional and popular health-care practitioners — doctors, midwives, naturopaths, masseurs, and 'wise women' — exploited advances in medical science to make reliable methods of abortion and sterilisation readily available. The marketing of these products and services utilised new techniques of mass advertising and nation-wide distribution networks to ensure their rapid diffusion. Prior experience with a tradition of medical self-help, centring on patent medicines and naturopathy, facilitated popular acceptance of modern birth control. And in Germany the national Health Insurance Programme supplemented commercial efforts by making birth control available to those who could not otherwise afford it.

Nonetheless, birth control did not spread through Germany overnight. When Mensinga publicised the diaphragm in 1882, sixty million Germans did not line up in Flensburg. Logistics alone dictated a prolonged process of diffusion, and cultural factors compounded this. For a variety of reasons many people remained ignorant of modern contraceptives well after the turn of the century, while religious or psychological reasons delayed their use by others. But market forces, public discussion, and concerted efforts by governmental and voluntary organisations gradually overcame this resistance, so that by 1930 virtually everyone had access to modern methods of birth control. And by 1930 the German fertility decline was essentially complete.

NOTES

1. Ansley Coale, 'The Decline of Fertility in Europe, 1789-1940' in S.J. Behrman, Leslie Gorba, Jr, and Ronald Freeman (eds), *Fertility and family planning: a world view* (University of Michigan Press, Ann Arbor, 1969), pp. 3-19; Patrick Festy, *La Fécondité des Pays Occidentaux de 1870 à 1970* (Presses Universitaires de France, Paris 1979), pp. 51-2; Massimo Livi-Bacci, *A history of Italian fertility during the last two centuries* (Princeton University Press, Princeton, 1977), p. 108; Michael Teitelbaum, *The British fertility decline: demographic transition in the crucible of the industrial revolution* (Princeton University Press, Princeton, 1984), pp. 76-7, 117-19; Ansley Coale, Barbara Anderson, and Erna Härm, *Human fertility in Russia since the nineteenth century* (Princeton University Press, Princeton, 1979), pp. 41-3. All dates are approximate.

2. Also at second glance. Using multiple correlation analysis Toni Richards found that once regional differences are taken into account modernisation (i.e. urban industrialisation) does explain the German fertility decline, which occurred in response to changes in the costs and economic returns of children, changes in consumer tastes, and intensification of the transportation and communication networks. See T. Richards, 'Fertility decline in Germany: an econometric appraisal', *PS*, 31 (1977), pp. 537-53.

3. John Knodel, *The decline of fertility in Germany, 1871-1939* (Princeton University Press, Princeton, 1974), pp. 41-2, 44, 46-7, 49-50, 52, 54, 61, 64, 246, 248.

4. Knodel, *Decline*, pp. 98, 100, 103, 105-6, 108, 133-4, 139, 251-3.

5. Knodel, *Decline*, p. 252; Statistisches Reichsamt, 'Beiträge zum deutschen Bevölkerungsproblem', *Wirtschaft und Statistik*, Sonderheft 5 (1929), pp. 8, 17-19, 21; Friedrich Burgdörfer, *Der Geburtenrückgang und seine Bekämpfung* (Schoetz, Berlin 1929), pp. 78-80.

6. Knodel, *Decline*, pp. 116-20, 122, 127, 130, 251-2, 260; Christoph Tietze, 'Ein Beitrag zur Dynamik des Geburtenrückgangs', *ARGB*, 25 (1931), pp. 222-5; R. Spree, *Soziale Ungleichheit vor Krankheit und Tod: Zur Sozialgeschichte des Gesundheitsbereichs im Deutschen Kaiserreich* (Vandenhoek und Rupprecht, Göttingen, 1981), pp. 62-3, 76, 80, 82, 90, 92.

7. John Knodel, 'Family limitation and fertility transition: evidence from age patterns of fertility in Europe and Asia', *PS*, 31 (1977), p. 244; Ansley Coale, 'The Demographic Transition', International Union for the Scientific

INTRODUCTION

Study of Population, *International Population Conference* (IUSSP, Liege, 1973), pp. 54, 62; Etienne van de Walle and John Knodel, 'Europe's fertility transition: new evidence and lessons for today's developing world', *Population Bulletin*, 34 (1980), pp. 23–4; Edward Shorter, John Knodel and Etienne van de Walle, 'The decline of non-marital fertility in Europe, 1880–1940', *PS*, 25 (1971), pp. 375–93; Festy, *Fécondité*, p. 67; Teitelbaum, *British Fertility Decline*, p. 219; Ronald Lesthaeghe, *The decline of Belgian fertility, 1800–1970* (Princeton University Press, Princeton, 1977), p. 140; David Weir, 'Fertility transition in rural France, 1740–1829', *Journal of Economic History*, 44 (1984), pp. 612–14.

1

Traditional Birth Control in Modern Society

The desire to control fertility is almost as old as the desire to have children.[1] Human societies have demonstrated a broad range of efforts to achieve birth control, although historically most emphasis was on post-conceptive and even post-natal techniques.[2] Such methods seldom made a statistical dent in western fertility rates. But some traditional techniques do work when properly implemented, and others can be made to work with the addition of technical refinements. Moreover, these older practices remained culturally acceptable to people who rejected the newfangled products and practices of the late nineteenth century as immoral and unnatural. For these reasons, then, traditional birth control constitutes an integral chapter in the history of modern fertility.

The simplest approach to contraception is to avoid intercourse. Abstinence has always been promoted by the Roman church as the ideal sexual behaviour, especially for unmarried people, but in the late nineteenth century the medical profession, becoming involved with the physiology and psychology of sex, expressed concern over possible adverse consequences of prolonged abstinence, particularly for individuals with strong libidos. Abstinence was recommended for the young as a way of avoiding venereal disease and to keep themselves pure for their one true love, but was not considered practical for married people, surrounded as they were by constant temptation.[3]

The cause of celibacy was promoted by the *Weisse Kreuz*, a German affiliate of the White Cross Society. This organisation had been established by the Church of England in 1883 to foster social purity among young men by combatting masturbation and prostitution, by opposing the double standard of morality, and by promoting respect for womanhood. The English Society achieved its greatest success in cooperation with the Boy Scout movement of Baden-Powell, while American chapters worked with several organisations involved in the Social Purity movement, including the Women's Christian Temperance Union and the Young Men's Christian Association.[4]

In Germany the principal supporting institution affiliated with the *Weisse Kreuz* was the *Innere Mission*, the domestic social arm of the Evangelical Church. In 1911 at the International Hygiene Exhibition in Dresden the *Weisse Kreuz* and the German Society for Combatting Venereal Diseases jointly sponsored a popular and controversial display on the dangers of infection from prostitutes and the advantages of abstinence. Abstinence sentiment persisted into the First World War, when several medical students and professors at the University of Leipzig formed the German Medical League for Sexual Ethics, pledging to stay pure until age twenty-four.[5]

As might be expected, abstinence seldom proved popular among married people. Studies in the United States found that only 2 to 8 per cent of couples relied on abstinence for birth control. In contrast, Paul Thompson ranked abstinence second only to coitus interruptus among British methods at the turn of the century.[6] In Imperial Germany abstinence found acceptance primarily among farmers and civil servants. Couples who worried about holding on to the family farm slept separately, or had relatives move in to act as a sexual deterrent, especially the 'utterly tyrannical grandmas'.[7]

Civil servants were compelled to observe abstinence because of the expectation that their lifestyle should reflect their status as representatives of the state. The effort to maintain a good image on a fixed income during periods of inflation led to an increase in the number of civil servants remaining single, a rising age at first marriage, and unusually high rates of childless marriages (one in five couples in some areas).[8] Regulations sometimes required that officials demonstrate a level of income adequate to support a family properly before marrying; in Bavaria the state reserved the right to veto the intended spouse. Single and childless candidates were favoured for promotions. Not surprisingly, the children of civil servants frequently sought other careers.[9]

For most couples, however, abstinence represented a last resort. Dr Max Marcuse, in a wartime study of two hundred couples practising birth control, found none using abstinence. But in the uncertain times of the 1920s some people unable to afford other methods relied on abstinence for short periods.[10]

Rhythm provided an alternative for those who wanted a temporary form of abstinence. Ovulation occurs at mid-cycle; conception is most likely to take place at this time, with the probability diminishing steadily until the middle of the next cycle. The probability of conception also depends on the frequency of intercourse: one random coitus during the menstrual cycle has a 2 to 4 per cent chance of impregnation, but if coitus takes place two or three times per week the probability jumps to 20 to 40 per cent.[11]

The risk associated with rhythm stems from the fact that not every woman has a textbook-perfect 28 day cycle. Variation occurs within the life cycle of each woman and among the entire female population. Furthermore, the time required for the ovum to migrate through the tube, together with the life-span of spermatozoa (two or three days after intercourse) introduce additional elements of uncertainty, which were compounded in the nineteenth century by the common assumption that mid-cycle was the safe period. Under these circumstances it is not surprising that rhythm acquired the epithet, 'Vatican roulette', which also reflected its greater popularity among Catholics.[12]

In 1930 Knaus in Austria and Ogino in Japan concurrently developed the modern rhythm method, which is based on the observation of the individual woman's cycle over a six to twelve month period. Knaus determined that conception can occur during a period of eleven to seventeen days before the onset of the next menses, while Ogino reckoned the period of risk at twelve to sixteen days before the next period. For people willing to wait several months before commencing birth control, the rhythm method had finally become practical.[13]

A third 'natural' form of contraception is lactational amenorrhea — the suppression of ovulation during breast feeding. Post-partum amenorrhea normally last two months, and is followed by another two months of anovular cycles. This period of infertility can be prolonged by breastfeeding for several months.[14] The practice was widespread in Germany, both for infant nutrition and because folklore ascribed a contraceptive effect to it.[15] A recent study found no physiological correlation between breastfeeding and fertility in Germany, but cultural factors such as a taboo on intercourse during lactation might have the same result. In actuality breastfeeding was losing out to bottle feeding by the turn of the century, especially in the cities.[16]

Around the turn of the century Carl Buttenstedt advocated a variation on lactational amenorrhea as part of a more ambitious programme of rejuvenation through the mutual sharing of vital bodily fluids. Buttenstedt believed he had found the fountain of youth in the breasts of young virgins. Their milk contained pure essence of life-force. He proposed that married women draw milk from young virgins to revitalise themselves, then permit their husbands to draw milk from them for their rejuvenation (apparently men were not to be trusted with the breasts of young virgins). During intercourse the vital life-force would return to the woman, and the pattern could be repeated. Although he stressed the rejuvenating effect of the practice, Buttenstedt also acknowleded its contraceptive significance. Whether for this reason or for his interest in virgin breasts, Buttenstedt was charged with production of an obscene book, but won acquittal after testimony from a number of physicians, including the sexologist Magnus Hirschfeld, and the book went through several editions.[17]

A variety of sexual practices were available to people who wanted to indulge in recreational rather than procreational sex. Mutual masturbation, oral sex, anal intercourse, and 'careful' variants of coitus were all utilised by married and unmarried couples eager for the joy of sex without a little bundle of joy to show for it. Physicians reported an increase in polymorphous practices during the early twentieth century that was attributed in part to the desire for contraceptive sex.[18]

Oral sex was common in all classes of society. Dr Horch, a divorce lawyer in Mainz, considered oral sex to be 'shockingly frequent — as much as coitus interruptus'. Horch based his estimate on the observation that virtually all women who sought divorce mentioned oral sex as one of their 'irreconcilable differences'. A farmer's wife complained that her husband satisfied his sex drive almost exclusively through cunnilingus, which he performed even during work, causing her 'mental anguish'. On the other side of the coin, a day labourer complained that his wife demanded cunnilingus and refused coitus. There were apparently no complaints over fellatio.[19]

Anal sex likewise appeared to be a widespread form of birth control. Starting in the 1890s doctors noticed an increasing incidence of anal gonorrhea among women. One clinical survey of 770 female VD patients found 163 with anal gonorrhea. Prostitutes were especially likely to have these symptoms, and this was credited directly to the new popularity of anal intercourse.[20] But other doctors reported that the practice was common among farmers and workers as well. Dr Paul Näcke reported in the *Archiv für Kriminal-Anthropologie* that several general practitioners relayed to him accounts of working-class women who relied on anal sex as a contraceptive practice that resembled coitus, but without the risk of pregnancy. Näcke's correspondents claimed that upper-class women were equally involved but were less willing to discuss the subject. Some of the women who did indulge found the practice pleasurable, and tried it in various positions. Näcke himself denounced anal intercourse as aberrant and argued that people who wanted 'pseudo-intercourse' should rely on coitus interruptus.[21] But, as we shall see, coitus interruptus does not provide the same contraceptive security as anal intercourse. If anything, the practice increased during the 1920s, although this may partly reflect improved methods for detecting anal gonorrhea. Anal intercourse continues to be popular today, whether for contraception or for polymorphous indulgence.[22]

There were other sexual practices used for contraception. Coitus reservatus involved intercourse culminating in intra-vaginal detumescence without ejaculation. This technique is probably best known as the favoured practice of the Oneida community in nineteenth-century America, where John Noyes made 'male continence' the cornerstone of 'communal love'. Variations included 'Alpha-ism', advocated by Elmira Slenker, and 'Karezza', promoted by Alice Stockham.[23] Coitus obstructus — induced retrogressive ejaculation — was also called coitus saxonicus after the German settlers of Rumania, where it was thought to have originated. The procedure involved applying pressure to the base of the penis at the moment of ejaculation in order to force the semen into the bladder. The same technique intensifies male stimulation, and this may account for its increasing popularity.[24] Other practices aimed at depositing the semen in the lower portion of the vagina or between the legs or breasts of the woman. 'Usus equae', reported in the Breslau region, consisted of huffing and puffing in order to 'cough out' the semen after intercourse. And some women tried to remain cold during sex on the popular but erroneous assumption that their lack of excitement hindered the movement of sperm into the uterus.[25]

But it was coitus interruptus that remained the single most common contraceptive practice.[26] It is simple, spontaneous, and cheap: the male simply has to withdraw in time. Unfortunately, this is easier said than done. The man has to recognise the proper moment to withdraw, have the resolve to do so, and ensure that no ejaculate enters the vagina. But because coitus interruptus proceeds as regular coitus it was readily accepted by people as a 'natural' practice. Marcuse found that 173 of 225 couples relied on withdrawal; Dr Polano of Wurzburg reportred 280 out of 339 couples used the practice; and several other studies confirm its popularity.[27]

All of these coital practices erred in assuming that so long as sperm was not deposited directly on the cervix, conception could be avoided. This ignored both the physiology of male arousal — with the possible presence of spermatozoa in the secretions — and the motility of sperm, which could find their way into the vagina if they landed anywhere in the vicinity.[28] The disruption of intercourse presented yet another difficulty. Physical and nervous disorders might arise if sexual resolution did not otherwise occur. This was especially true for women, though even as late as 1928 Dr Mager of Arnstadt could express the opinion that 'women usually have no orgasm during intercourse and won't notice any difference with coitus interruptus'.[29]

The problematic character of these practices, and the ensuing anxiety which they were thought to provoke, led many physicians, including some who were sympathetic to birth control, to condemn preventive intercourse. Opponents argued that the organs of the body have specified functions to perform in a foreordained manner. Some are automatic, like the heart and lungs, while others are subject to conscious volition. But the conscious use of these organs must be harmonious with their natural function or illness would result. Any 'abnormal' use of the sex organs must lead to physical and mental disorders, including impotence, cramps, backache, stomach ache, loss of appetite, bowel irregularity, hemorrhoids, tired blood, pallid skin, baldness, prostatitis, colds, diminished clarity of thought, changes in personality, insomnia, fatigue and the ubiquitous neurasthenia.[30]

Although these attitudes persisted into the twentieth century, most doctors questioned the alleged harmfulness of coitus interruptus. As early as 1879 two French physicians, Doctors Leblond and Lutaud of the Saint-Lazare Hospital in Paris, stated at a Neo-Malthusian meeting held in conjunction with the International Medical Congress in Amsterdam that 'conjugal prudence' produced no ill-effects among French couples. This view entered the medical consensus by the turn of the century. People who practised coitus interruptus generally dismissed the scare stories: 'If they were true then everyone would be sick'; 'It's safer than having a lot of kids'. Henceforth the only real concern over coitus interruptus was the high failure rate, which clinical experience placed at 60 to 80 per cent.[31]

These sexual gymnastics were supplemented by a variety of concoctions alleged by folklore to ward off conception. Custom held that the forces of nature could be influenced for good or ill by magic, and common folk employed a variety of amulets, potions, and practices to secure favours from Mother Nature. Several plants containing volatile oils — parsely, marjoram, thyme and lavender — were brewed in teas, while purgatives such as aloes were taken with brandy. Savin and juniper were taken orally or inserted vaginally, while other substances — salt, soda, or magnesia — were used in hot baths. In some parts of Germany superstitious rituals to ensure sterility included drinking ram's urine or carrying the severed finger of a stillborn child. Religious girls said a rosary after sex to prevent conception. Somewhat greater certainty was provided by the practice of wadding linen rags in the vagina prior to intercourse as a crude tampon.[32]

Tampons or vaginal sponges were a popular contraceptive in the nineteenth century. As early as 1822 Francis Place recommended the use of sponge for working-class couples, and similar ideas were expressed in Germany. Tampons were small sponge or cotton balls moistened with an antiseptic solution and inserted in the vagina before intercourse. They worked by blocking the cervical opening and absorbing the sperm. For added protection women usually douched before removing the tampon.[33]

In order to work properly the sponge had to remain in front of the cervix, but small tampons frequently became dislodged during intercourse, while large tampons were uncomfortable for both partners. Because of these practical difficulties and the availability of better methods tampons went out of style by the First World War. Marcuse found that only seven out of two hundred couples used tampons, and they were usually from rural areas. Dr Hanssen reported the use of tampons 'here and there' in Schleswig-Holstein.[34] After the war Dr Levy-Lenz, in an effort to provide poor women with a cheap and effective contraceptive, developed a variant of the older 'un-safety sponges'. He used natural sea sponge rather than cotton. The sponge was placed in the vagina dry, and the woman then douched with a vinegar or lemon juice solution. With this technique the tampon could be left in place overnight and removed the next morning without another douche. These tampons proved reliable and were acceptable to women who could not afford other methods.[35]

Douching for contraception was recommended by Charles Knowlton in 1832. Vaginal syringes consisting of a rubber balloon filled with water that was injected into the vagina through a rubber tube were popular in Germany by the 1870s. But the standard device was the 'Irrigator', an apparatus consisting of a one-litre container to hold the douching solution (water, possibly mixed with vinegar, carbolic acid, or lysol), and a thin nozzle for insertion. The woman sat over a basin or in a bathtub and turned a valve to regulate the flow of the douche.[36]

A second type of douche, the Ebell Irrigator, consisted of a rubber bulb which fitted snugly over the vagina to collect the solution after injection. This permitted douching in bed, which was both congenial and practical: the woman no longer had to bound out of bed immediately after intercourse to perform her ablutions, and by remaining in a reclining position she had a better chance of contraceptive success.[37]

A third model, the Klyso-pump, was used while standing. Because it circulated the antiseptic solution more vigorously than the others it was especially recommended for contraception. Both the Klyso-pump and the Ebell Irrigator were portable. Women, mainly working-class women, were no longer dependent on access to running water — much less a bathtub — and there was no need to explain to inquisitive neighbours the purpose of the odd gadget mounted on the wall (where the irrigator was often placed to provide better pressure).[38]

Douching was widespread in the nineteenth century because of its simplicity and low cost. It was also one of the few contraceptive practices that could 'pass' as a legitimate hygienic function, a matter of special importance to Catholics. The best-selling 'Bilz' handbook of medical self-help recommended douching as the safest contraceptive.[39] The Irrigator was promoted by the Health Insurance Programme for feminine hygiene, and members of local Funds received douches free on prescription. But any woman could buy inexpensive douches in pharmacies and drug stores without prescription. The sale of douches mushroomed after 1900 once they were marketed for contraception as well as hygiene. Mass production lowered the price from 4.50 Marks in 1895 to 1.50 in 1914. Popular brand names included the Comfort Douche 'Gloria', the Fountain Douche, Lady's Doctor, Lady's Friend, Leda, Niagara, Rational and the Wonder Douche.[40]

Women readily assumed that all douching, whether hygienic or contraceptive, was legitimised by the support of the Health Insurance Programme. With each extension of medical coverage more and more women became acquainted with the practice. After 1911 coverage was extended to domestic servants, farm workers, and day labourers; together with industrial workers and their wives the vast majority of working-class women now had access to douching. Marcuse found 62 of 200 couples used douching for contraception.[41]

In principle, douching combined the spermicidal effect of water and chemical additives with mechanical rinsing to immobilise and flush out spermatozoa. To be effective, douching had to be performed immediately after intercourse, preferably without moving. Many women felt condemned to 'restraint' during and after coitus. Douches that required the woman to arise gave sperm opportunity to enter the uterus.[42]

To obviate these disadvantages Dr Hinz devised an 'instant orgasmic douche', the Venus-Apparatus. This device consisted of a small, walnut-size rubber balloon perforated with tiny air-holes that was connected by a thin rubber tube to a larger balloon filled with a lukewarm solution. Before intercourse the smaller balloon was placed inside the vagina against the cervix. Neither it nor the tube caused irritation during coitus; indeed, if coated with vaseline the tube accentuated male stimulation. The larger balloon was held in hand or foot by either partner. At orgasm autonomic reflexes contracting the extremities squeezed the larger balloon, forcing the solution through the tube and out into the vagina, thereby flushing the spermatozoa. Although this procedure required some preliminary preparation — in contrast to regular douching which was entirely post-coital and did not interfere with spontaneity — it permitted both partners to fully enjoy sex; it presented no barrier to stimulation; and it did not disrupt post-orgasmic resolution.[43]

When traditional contraceptive practices failed, women opposed to maternity faced the alternative of abortion. Women seeking to induce abortion relied on a wide range of household articles and homemade preparations to which folklore ascribed an abortifacient quality. The problem confronting the woman was to find some means with which to terminate the pregnancy without terminating her own life. Given the symbiosis between foetus and mother, abortion could be attempted either by poisoning the woman enough to kill the foetus but not quite enough to kill the mother, or by inducing contractions which would lead to expulsion of the foetus. This could be accomplished by ingesting substances which irritated the gasto-intestinal tract, or by taking products which caused uterine bleeding, separation of the foetus from the wall of the uterus, and subsequent expulsion. The success of these products depended on the dosage taken, the skill with which they were employed, the stage of pregnancy, the overall constitution of the woman, and not a little luck.[44]

The range of popular traditional techniques was extensive but ineffective. External methods were employed in efforts to promote venous congestion, or to forcibly dislodge the foetus. The most common of these techniques was the warm bath or steam bath, possibly combined with massage.[45] Physical shocks to the body were also attempted: heavy lifting, jumping off stairs, tables, or streetcars, and carnival rides — 'every day the horsie' — were all tried in efforts to shake the foetus loose. One 'wise woman' recommended vigorous coitus for this purpose, and provided stud service to supplement the flagging efforts of the husband. At least one abortion was traced to a motorbike ride over rough terrain, and in another case a husband beat his wife on the abdomen, then threw her over his shoulder to the ground — to no avail; but abortion did follow a hot bath taken after this workout.[46]

Those distrustful of these indirect methods attempted abortion by inserting household objects — crochet needles, hat pins, pencils, goose feathers — into the uterus in an effort to rupture the amniotic sac or to pierce the foetus, causing bleeding or dislodging and thereby provoking contractions. Not surprisingly these methods, which required some awareness of female anatomy, were usually performed by abortionists, though in some cases experienced women could insert objects themselves.[47]

Minerals and metals were popular substances for abortion. The most commonly used items were lead, arsenic and phosphorus. Their reputation sometimes depended as much on local availability as on their actual effectiveness, as regional preferences demonstrate: nitrobenzine in Magdeburg, for instance, or arsenic in Styria. When they were successful these products worked by way of toxic impact on the blood, kidneys and intestinal tract. Mercury compounds, which had been used in the late nineteenth century after people noticed that women treated for syphilis with mercury aborted frequently, were discontinued once the dangers of mercury poisoning became known.[48]

Two substances had special importance for the history of abortion in Europe. Lead pills marketed under the trade name Diachylon were very popular in England around the turn of the century. And in Sweden a study of 1500 cases of criminal abortion from the late nineteenth century showed that 90 per cent involved phosphorus. In Germany as in Sweden phosphorus was widely available on matches, and women would swallow dozens or hundreds of match-heads, or scrape off the phosphorus and insert it vaginally, in attempts to provoke abortion. In 1903 an international conference recommended a ban on phosphorus matches for general health reasons, and this ban was introduced in Germany in 1907. Although phosphorus continued to be available in other products (e.g. rat poison), its use for abortion ended.[49]

Plant decoctions were the most common means of abortion available to the general public. It was all too easy for a woman fearing pregnancy to rush out into the woods, collect some herbs, and brew up a potion according to a time-honoured recipe.[50] The problem lay in knowing which among the hundreds of plants, shrubs and trees would prove effective. The list of possible candidates reads like a 'What's what' of European flora:[51]

aloes	bryony	celeriac
angelica	camomile	cinnamon
asafoetida	cantharide	cloves
balm	caraway	fennel

garlic	mustard	rue
ginger	myrrh	sabina
hazel	myrtle	saffron
hellebore	nutmeg	sage
juniper	paprika	savin
laurel	pennyroyal	senna
lavender	pepper	thuja
lovage	peppermint	valerian
mint	rosemary	wormwood

Naturally, not every weed growing in the cemeteries of Germany could be effective. Tradition gradually filtered out the unsatisfactory concoctions, leaving a hard core of tried-and-proven abortifacients based on a few widely available plants.[52]

One of the most popular and effective products was ergot of rye. Rye bread was a staple of the German diet. Over time, people noticed that pregnant women who ate bread made from unpurified rye aborted more frequently than other women. In fact it was not the rye itself but a fungus (*claviceps purpurea*) growing on the grain which produced uterine contractions. Ergot was genuinely effective and formed part of clinical procedures for inducing miscarriage and for controlling post-partum bleeding (contractions tightened up the blood vessels). Because of this well-known property of ergot preparations containing it were not available to the general public. But no law in Junker Germany could resist the growing of rye and, for people living in northern and eastern Germany, ergot was readily — albeit seasonally — available. It was in many respects the ideal abortifacient: relatively safe, effective, and easy to prepare. Because it is effective only in the later stages of pregnancy, it does not crop up in abortion records as often as one might expect. Even in East Prussia a survey of 124 criminal abortions in the early twentieth century showed only two involving ergot.[53]

Quinine, like ergot, was used by doctors and midwives to strengthen contractions; also like ergot, it was less effective in the earlier stages of pregnancy. Aloes, a strong laxative, was taken mixed with brandy in an effort to induce gastroenteritis leading to contractions.[54]

Several common plants contain volatile oils which, in sufficient concentration, can have an abortive effect through inflammation of the gastrointestinal tract and subsequent uterine bleeding. In Germany the most popular abortifacients were saffron, savin, ginger and thuja. Distillations of the volatile oils formed the essence of preparations (drops, powders and teas) marketed for 'menstrual irregularity'. Other herbs and spices used alone or in solution with water, rum, coffee or red wine, included camphor, camomile, sassafras, hops, cloves, hellebore and — of course — parsley, sage, rosemary and thyme. Thuja was probably the most widespread of these at the end of the nineteenth century; its use was reported in East Prussia, Silesia, Brandenburg, Thuringia, Hannover, Hesse and Baden.[55]

Apiol, a relative late-comer to the abortion inventory, was a substance derived from parsley and marketed in various formats, including capsules filled with an oily green fluid. Apiol was freely available in pharmacies or by mail-order. In 1931 a series of apiol poisonings from contaminated capsules in Europe and the United States led to a decree from the Prussian Minister of Welfare restricting the sale of apiol products to pharmacies and requiring a valid prescription; similar legislation followed in other jurisdictions.[56]

Folklore remedies suited people living in the countryside with ready access to the appropriate flora, but as millions of people moved to the cities after 1871 the traditional practices became hard to follow. Fortunately Adam Smith's Invisible Hand found a way to pick the plants and deliver them to the urban market. Drawing on popular experience with patent medicines, entrepreneurs marketed packaged drugs for the treatment of 'female complaints'.

Geheimmittel — 'secret remedies' — were products with alleged therapeutic effect whose ingredients or formula were kept confidential by the manufacturer; they compare with the 'patent medicines' of Anglo-Saxon countries. German patent medicines descended from medieval potions connected with alchemy. They took on new life after the Thirty Years' War as entrepreneurs sought to provide medications to a war-ravaged populace and governments inspired by mercantilism sought to promote economic development. The production of drugs centred in Saxony, Thuringia, and Silesia — regions rich in aromatic plants and accessible to major trade routes. The medicines were sold by pedlars throughout Germany.[57]

The demand for patent medicines waned in the early nineteenth century as science produced synthesised drugs of genuine effectiveness (quinine, morphine), and as governments in the era of post-Napoleonic repression curbed the activities of pedlars. But the unification of Germany revived the fortunes of manufacturers. The new Occupational Code for the German Empire enshrined free choice of trade, thereby cancelling governmental restrictions on the production of drugs. A host of new entrepreneurs rushed in to provide local versions of the increasingly popular English, French and American patent medicines that flooded the German market during the 1860s. The sales of German products soared after 1871, accounting for 10 per cent of all medicinal sales in the late nineteenth century.[58]

The success of patent medicines was due to several factors. Rapid urbanisation aggregated millions of people in new cities where the supply of doctors and pharmacies was low. Improvements in transportation and communication permitted newspaper advertising and mail-order merchandising. And, perhaps most important, medical science remained incapable of explaining or curing many of the most common diseases.[59] Into this breach stepped the purveyors of patent medicines. Relying on the popular belief that all illnesses were symptoms of one basic malady, they offered a product that would allegedly strike at the heart of the problem, that was 'all natural', and that promised an immediate and complete cure. From the public's point of view, patent medicines seemed safe and reliable: they were easy to obtain, easy to take, and economical in the long run; although the price was high in relation to the actual cost of the ingredients, no expensive visits to doctors or pharmacists were necessary, and no time was lost from work.[60]

By the end of the century, though, scientific progress had by-passed patent medicines. The development of synthetic drugs like Kairin (1882), Antipyrin (1887), and Aspirin (1897) sounded the death-knell for patent medicines. The new drugs were based on scientific research and development; they were geared to a specific illness; and they really worked. The Health Insurance Programme made them available to broad sections of the populace, and compulsory education ensured that fewer people would go through life with a belief in humoral pathology. The days of the patent medicines were numbered.[61]

Sales of patent medicines persisted in several 'sensitive' areas, however: impotence, sterility, venereal disease and menstrual irregularity. Disruptions of the period were easily linked to traditional beliefs in blood as the vital bodily fluid: restore its essential purity and all would be well. Promoters played upon public uncertainty over menstrual physiology, both to exploit popular gullibility and to stay within the letter of the law. Customers of the natural therapist B. Wagner were required to sign this declaration:

> I hereby declare that I will not take this cure to terminate pregnancy but only to restore my regular monthly cycle, since period disruptions can indeed have several causes.[62]

This 'restoration of regularity' was in fact nothing less than abortion, and purveyors of patent medicines made this clear in the utilisation of plants which folklore considered abortifacient — especially camomile, which appeared in half of all these products — and in the choice of brand names, which were invariably suggestive, sexual, or exotic:[63]

Apiolin	Mensol
Elektra	Menstrolina
Erpiol	Menstruatin
Favorit	Mikado
Felicitas	Minerva
Fortuna	Periodin
Frauenglück	Puella
Frauenhilfe	Regula Mensis
Frauenlob	Reguliertropfen
Frauenpillen	Sabina
Frauenwohl	Salome
Geisha	Sorgenlos
Gloria	Sphinx
Japol	Superol
Kamillol	Sur sécours
Mensistee	Venus
Mensistropfen	Victoria

These products were sold by mail-order. Advertisements were placed in newspapers read by the target audience (local and family papers), especially on weekends when people had more time for reading. The advertisements invariably included statements by 'experts' and testimonials from satisfied customers who happened to be from key social groups: teachers, artisans, farmers and workers.[64]

Ladies!
The most successful product for disruptions of the period is my genuine Japanese menstrual powder, 'Geisha'. Legally available. Better than expensive herbal baths. Packets 3 Marks. Discretion assured. Frau B. writes: Sincere thanks for your powder, the result was excellent. Frau H.: Since it worked in only two days I recommend the powder to all women.[65]

Take Note!   Keep This!
Very important for the Ladies! Intimate Female Complaints, Discharge, Period Disruptions, etc. Sure Relief with my

absolutely harmless special product. My treatment for blood disruptions using my special product is safe and has no side-effects. It consists of taking my blood stimulant Elixir and my Powder in local applications with the patented apparatus 'Lady's Friend', comfortably, privately, and safely. You get everything, with complete instructions, for 12.90 Marks.[66]

Ladies!
Throw away those phony products for menstrual irregularity offered 'in confidence'. Don't be misled by exaggerated and long-winded claims. Only my new, strong, fast-acting product provides relief even in hopeless cases! Amazingly effective! No time lost from work. Guaranteed safe or your money back. (Not for use during pregnancy.)[67]

The most notorious case of mail-order distribution of abortifacients was uncovered in 1908 after a police raid in Zürich. An abortionist there had placed advertisements in German newspapers which netted replies from across the country, though the largest response was from Thuringia.

Women turn with confidence to Frau Musczynski for treatment of menstrual irregularity. Löwenstrasse 55, Zürich. Many testimonials![68]

Upon receiving a letter from a woman complaining of missed period or fear of pregnancy, Musczynski offered to provide assistance for 15 Marks. Her product contained camomile worth 50 pfennigs. With the tea she enclosed a form letter which recommended an array of traditional abortion techniques:

I gratefully acknowledge your letter with payment. Enclosed please find the product which you have requested for treatment of menstrual irregularity. The product is guaranteed safe; it works by regulating blood circulation into a normal pattern, and is in no sense an abortifacient.
Mix one teaspoonful of the powder three to four times daily in coffee, milk, or cocoa, and drink as much as desired. If the irregularity is long-standing and you want stronger measures, you may also mix the powder with warm red wine. I also recommend one or two hot baths daily, together with vaginal douching, and warm foot-baths in the morning and evening during the treatment.

Follow this procedure and your illness will soon disappear as circulation returns to normal.
I look forward with confidence to hearing of your satisfaction, and remain at your service.[69]

Musczynski and her husband, a masseur, had practised abortion in Augsburg until charged with criminal abortion in a case that ended fatally for both the young woman and Bruno Musczynski, who shot himself. Frau Musczynski moved to Zürich to continue her mail-order business. She enclosed a catalogue of syringes with the camomile powder as an indicator of her 'further service'. Along with other abortionists, Musczynski used this ploy to attract women interested in more effective — and more expensive — measures.[70]

The experience with patent medicines demonstrates a curious anomaly in the German legal system: although abortion was illegal, the sale of products and services for abortion occurred openly. One would expect that abortifacients would be strictly controlled, but this was not always true. The Imperial Ordinance on Trade with Medications (1872, revised in 1875, 1890 and 1901; withdrawn in 1969) specified that certain preparations labelled as medications — whether they actually contained pharmaceutical substances or not — should be restricted to sale in pharmacies. In addition, certain substances and preparations containing them were also restricted to sale in pharmacies. Among the abortifacients affected by this Ordinance were ergot, quinine, savin, and valerian oil; saffron was notably omitted. Other products used for abortion that fell under this law were lead, arsenic, nitrobenzine, creosol, and mercury compounds. The law required only that sales of these substances occur in a pharmacy; it did not require a prescription for the sale.[71] Commercial preparations for the restoration of menstrual regularity were not covered by the Imperial Ordinance at first, but the extensive sale of such products and their increasing effectiveness — especially those containing apiol — led the government to amend the law in 1924 to apply to 'products for blood stasis, including those promoted as remedies for cycle, period, or menstrual disruptions'.[72]

The second law affecting abortion products was the Prussian Police Ordinance on Trade with Poisonous Substances (1894; revised in 1901 and 1906), which specified that such substances could only be dispensed by duly authorised persons, and could only be given out to persons intending to use the product for a legitimate commercial, industrial, scientific, or artistic purpose; otherwise only to persons possessing an appropriate permit issued by the police for a specific purchase at a specific time. These provisions did not apply to wholesale trade or to the dispensing of such substances in bulk to technical workshops or state institutions, nor did they apply to the dispensing of poisonous substances for therapeutic use, since this was covered by the Imperial Ordinance. Among the substances affected by the Police Ordinance were arsenic and mercury and their compounds, lead, phosphorus, nitrobenzine, iodine, creosol, carbolic acid, calcium lye, and the extracts of hellebore, savin and ergot.[73]

A third law, the Regulations on the Dispensing of Strong-working Medications (1896), limited the sale of certain substances and products containing them to pharmacies, where they could only be issued to persons with a valid prescription. The purpose of this law was to remove such items from over-the-counter sales.[74]

But legality was less important than technology in determining the usefulness of traditional methods of birth control. Many varieties were available; few were intrinsically reliable, and these required careful implementation if they were to have any chance of working. Ordinarily, only persons with a high degree of motivation were able to control fertility with traditional techniques: civil servants and free professionals concerned about maintaining social status, or farmers, merchants and businessmen anxious to conserve family property by limiting the number of heirs. Demographic statistics indicate that many of these people succeeded in their efforts during the eighteenth and nineteenth centuries, and traditional techniques must take credit for that success.[75]

For most people, however, 'conjugal prudence' was too difficult to maintain on a regular basis. Even today modern contraceptives are sometimes used incorrectly or inconsistently; the situation is worsened when the techniques themselves are faulty.[76] In the heat of passion not every man remembered to pull out in time, not every woman got to the douche in time. When 'accidents' happened, abortion procedures proved equally unreliable. Physical methods were tricky for lay people, while potions required the right dosage of the right substance: too little and nothing would happen, too much and the woman might die along with the foetus. This unpredictability accounts for the infrequency of successful abortions before the turn of the century.[77]

Psychology compounded the problem. Conception affected women primarily, but traditional birth control required male cooperation in many cases — notably in coitus interruptus, the single most common technique — and men were not always willing to cooperate. Tradition-minded men regarded anything that happened after coitus as 'women stuff'. Unfortunately, the things that women could do on their own —

tampons, douching and abortifacients — were among the least reliable methods.[78]

Despite these disadvantages, the experience with traditional birth control was significant for the history of fertility control in Germany. First, the early experience with douches and patent medicines predisposed consumers to buy more effective products once these became available. Second, it demonstrated the cultural acceptability of the principle of birth control. People who initially lacked the desire to limit family size became aware of the fact that others were controlling fertility and living better because of it. And thirdly, traditional methods stood people in good stead when they were unable or unwilling to use modern techniques. Some people remained ignorant of the new products well into the twentieth century, but often the preference for traditional birth control was economical — 'too poor to have kids and too poor to buy other contraceptives'; 'the other products are for the rich people' — or moral: 'I didn't know of such things until I moved to the city, but I don't approve of them.'[79] This latter attitude stemmed from a lingering belief that 'artificial' practices were 'unnatural' and therefore 'immoral' or 'sinful'. Some people even felt compelled to apologise for using traditional methods: 'The things they do in the cities are worse.' But whatever the reason, traditional birth control remained important for many people and played an important part in the German fertility decline.[80]

NOTES

1. Norman Himes, *Medical history of contraception* (Gamut Press, New York, 1936; reprinted 1963), p. xxxiv.
2. Himes, *Medical history, passim*; Keith Hopkins, 'Contraception in the Roman Empire', *CSSH*, 8 (1965-6), pp. 124-51; Edward Shorter, 'Infanticide in the past', *History of Childhood Quarterly*, 1 (1973), pp. 78-80; K. Wrightson, 'Infanticide in European history', *Criminal Justice History*, 3 (1982), pp. 1-20; P. Hoffer and N.E.H. Hull, *Murdering mothers: infanticide in England and New England, 1558-1803* (New York University Press, New York, 1981).
3. Wilhelm Hammer, 'Geschlechtliche Enthaltsamkeit und Gesundheitsstörung', *Monatsschrift für Harnkrankheiten und sexuelle Hygiene*, 1 (1904), pp. 214-17; W. Erb, 'Bemerkungen über die Folgen der sexuellen Abstinenz, *ZBGK*, 2 (1903-4), pp. 1-18; Anton Nyström, 'Die Beziehungen der sexuellen Abstinenz zur Gesundheit und die sich darausgegebenen Folgerungen', *ZBGK*, 13 (1911), pp. 82-91.
4. Edward Bristow, *Purity movements in Britain since 1700* (Gill and MacMillan, London, 1977), pp. 100-4, 136-40; David Pivar, *Purity crusade:*

sexual morality and social control, 1868-1900 (Greenwood, Westport, 1973), pp. 111-14. For contemporary accounts see E. Seidel, *Der Bund des Weissen Kreuzes* (n.p., Dresden, 1908), and Benjamin DeCosta, *The White Cross: its origin and progress* (Sanitary Publishing Co., Chicago, 1887). On the 'sexual economy' theory that lay behind this concern for purity see Peter Cominos, 'Late Victorian sexual respectability and the social system', *International Review of Social History*, 8 (1963), pp. 18-48, 216-50; Ben Barker-Benfield, 'The spermatic economy: the nineteenth century view of sexuality', *Feminist Studies*, 1 (1972), pp. 45-74; Michael Bliss, 'Pure books on avoided subjects: pre-Freudian sexual ideas in Canada'. Canadian Historical Association, *Historical Papers* (1970), pp. 89-108.

5. Georg Meyer, 'Internationale Hygiene-Ausstellung in Dresden', *BKW*, 48 (1911), pp. 2141-3; Dr Woitke, 'Die wissenschaftliche Abteilung der internationalen Hygiene-Ausstellung in Dresden', *DMW*, 37 (1911), pp. 1227-8, 1316-17, 1357-8, 1400-1; Julian Marcuse, 'Die internationale Hygieneausstellung in Dresden', *MMW*, 58 (1911), pp. 1459-60; 'International Hygiene Exhibition', *Journal of the American Medical Association*, 57 (1911), pp. 751-2. For the abstinent young doctors see J. Büsching, 'Die deutsche Aerztebund für Sexualethik', in Anna Pappritz (ed.), *Einführung in das Studium der Prostitutionsfrage* (J.A. Barth, Leipzig, 1919), pp. 272-81.

6. Robert L. Dickinson and L.S. Bryant, *The control of conception*, 2nd edn. (Williams and Wilkins, Baltimore, 1938), p. 1; Carl Degler, *At odds: women and the family in America from the Revolution to the present* (Oxford University Press, New York, 1980), p. 213; Paul Thompson, *The Edwardians: the remaking of British society* (Weidenfeld and Nicolson, London, 1975), pp. 71-2; Malcolm Potts and Peter Selman, *Society and fertility* (Macdonald and Evans, Estover, 1979), p. 172.

7. Allgemeine Konferenz der Deutschen Sittlichkeitsvereine, *Die geschlechtlich-sittlichen Verhältnisse der evangelischen Landbewohner im Deutschen Reiche*, ed. C. Wagner, (2 vols, Reinhold Werther, Leipzig, 1895-6), vol. II, pp. 139, 368, 445; Hermann Gebhardt, *Zur Bäuerlichen Glaubens- und Sittenlehre*, 3rd edn (Gustav Schlossmann, Gotha, 1895), p. 124.

8. John Gillis, *The Prussian bureaucracy in crisis, 1840-1860* (Stanford University Press, Stanford, 1971), pp. 202-3; Otto Most, 'Zur Wirtschafts- und Sozialstatistik der höheren Beamten in Preussen', *Schmollers Jahrbuch*, 39 (1915), pp. 181-218; H.L. Eisenstadt, 'Über die Kinderarmut der mittleren Postbeamten', quoted in Max von Gruber, *Ursachen und Bekämpfung des Geburtenrückganges im Deutschen Reich* (Viewig, Braunschweig, 1914), p. 15; Allgemeine Konferenz, *Verhältnisse*, vol. I, pp. 75, 107. On similar pressures in England see Joseph Banks and Olive Banks, *Feminism and family planning in Victorian England* (Schocken, New York, 1964).

9. Most, 'Wirtschafts- und Sozialstatistik', pp. 212-13; Felix Theilhaber, *Das sterile Berlin* (Marquardt, Berlin, 1913), pp. 94-5; Max Marcuse, *Der eheliche Präventivverkehr: seine Verbreitung, Verursachung und Methodik* (Enke, Stuttgart, 1917), case no. 277. Marriage restrictions were dropped in 1920-1: Erich Brauer, *Die abnehmende Fruchtbarkeit der berufstätigen Frau: Ein Beitrag zur Untersuchung der sozialpsychologische Seite der Unfruchtbarkeit. Sexus* (Ernst Bircher, Leipzig, 1921), vol. 3, p. 48.

10. Marcuse, *Eheliche Präventivverkehr, passim*; Helene Stöcker, 'Zur Geschichte der Geburtenregelung', in Komittee für Geburtenregelung, *Geburtenregelung: Vorträge und Verhandlungen*, (Selbstverlag, Berlin, 1929), p. 16.

11. Robert Potter Jr, Philip Sagi and Charles Westoff, 'Knowledge of the ovulatory cycle and coital frequency as factors affecting conception and contraception', *Millbank Memorial Fund Quarterly*, 40 (1962), pp. 46–58; Robert Potter Jr, 'Birth intervals: structure and change', *PS*, 17 (1963), pp. 155–66; P.A. Lachenbruch, 'Frequency and timing of intercourse: its relation to probability of conception', *PS*, 21 (1967), pp. 23–32; J. Barrett and J. Marshall, 'The risk of conception on different days of the menstrual cycle', *PS*, 23 (1969), pp. 455–61; Christopher Tietze, 'Introduction: regulation of procreation', in John Money and Herman Musaph (eds), *Handbook of sexology*, (Excerpta Medica, New York, 1977), p. 579.

12. Ludwig Nürnberger, 'Sterilität', in Josef Halban and Ludwig Seitz (eds), *Biologie und Pathologie des Weibes* (Urban and Schwarzenberg, Berlin, 1929), p. 698; John Peel, *Textbook of gynaecology*, 6th edn (Cambridge University Press, London, 1969), p. 300; Enoch Kisch, *The sexual life of woman in its physiological, pathological and hygienic aspects*, trans. Eden Paul (Rebman, New York, 1910), p. 400; Ludwig Fraenkel, *Die Empfängnisverhütung* (Enke, Stuttgart, 1932), p. 32; Marcuse, *Eheliche Präventivverkehr*, case nos 1, 189, 208, 278. Compare Degler, *At odds*, pp. 213–5, and Angus McLaren, 'Birth control and abortion in Canada, 1870–1920', *Canadian Historical Review*, 59 (1978), pp. 319–40.

13. H. Knaus, 'Über die Zeitpunkt der Empfängnisfähigkeit des Weibes', *Allgemeine Deutsche Hebammen-Zeitung*, 45 (1930), p. 291; Dr Ogino, 'Ovulationstermin und Konzeptionstermin', *ZGyn*, 54 (1930), pp. 464–79; Tassilo Antoine, 'Über Konzeptionsverhütung und Sterilisation', *WMW*, 81 (1931), pp. 1370–6; Anton Stecher, *Zeitwahl in der Ehe: Umfassende, lehrkrafte und angewandte Einführung in die Entdeckung Knaus-Ogino auf Grund des neuesten ärztlichen Schriftums*, 4th edn (Hatje, Stuttgart, 1948); Carl Gottfried Hartman, *Science and the safe period* (Williams and Wilkins, Baltimore, 1962).

14. Dickinson and Bryant, *Control of conception*, p. 91; Potter, 'Birth intervals', p. 156; John Knodel and Etienne van de Walle, 'Breast feeding, fertility and infant mortality: an analysis of some early German data', *PS*, 21 (1967), p. 112; Thomas McKeown and J. Gibson, 'Note on menstruation and conception during lactation', *Journal of Obstetrics and Gynaecology of the British Empire*, 61 (1954), p. 824; E. Salber, M. Feinlieb and B. MacMahon, 'Duration of post-partum amenorrhea', *American Journal of Epidemiology*, 82 (1965), pp. 347–58; Jeroen Van Ginneken, 'Prolonged breastfeeding as a birth-spacing method', *Studies in Family Planning*, 5 (1974), pp. 201–6; Ulla-Britt Lithell, 'Breastfeeding habits and their relation to infant mortality and marital fertility', *Journal of Family History*, 6 (1981), pp. 182–204.

15. Kisch, *Sexual life*, p. 403; Fraenkel, *Empfängnisverhütung*, p. 105; Knodel and van de Walle, 'Breast feeding', pp. 110, 123; Alfred Grotjahn, *Geburtenrückgang und Geburtenregelung im Lichte der individuellen und der sozialen Hygiene* (Marcus, Berlin, 1914), pp. 35, 39; Louis Mayer, 'Statistische Beiträge zur Häufigkeit der Menstruation während des Stillens',

Beiträge zur Geburtshülfe und Gynäkologie, 2 (1872), pp. 136–42; J. Grassl, 'Der Erfolg alter und neuer ehelicher Geschlechtssitten in Bayern', *ARGB*, 10 (1913), pp. 597–602. For examples of the use of breastfeeding for contraception see Marcuse, *Eheliche Präventivverkehr*, case nos 35 and 36 (two villages in Hesse-Nassau), and Heidi Rosenbaum, *Formen der Familie: Untersuchungen zum Zusammenhang von Familienverhältnissen, Sozialstruktur und sozialem Wandel in der deutschen Gesellschaft des 19. Jahrhunderts* (Suhrkamp, Frankfurt, 1982), p. 89 and p. 513 n5, citing E. Küch, *Das alte Bauernleben in der Lüneburger Heide* (n.p., Leipzig, 1906). On the use of the technique elsewhere in Europe see Michael Drake, 'Fertility controls in pre-industrial Norway', in David Glass and R. Revelle (eds), *Population and social change* (Edward Arnold, London, 1972), p. 188.

16. Knodel and van de Walle, 'Breast Feeding', pp. 120n, 123; Hans Ferdy, *Sittliche Selbstbeschränkung* (Verfasser, Hildesheim, 1904), pp. 119, 121. On the waning of breastfeeding see W. Thorn, 'Über die Ursachen des Geburtenrückganges und die Mittel zu seiner Bekämpfung', *Praktische Ergebnisse der Geburtshilfe und Gynäkologie*, 5 (1912), p. 54.

17. Carl Buttenstedt, *Die Glücks-Ehe*, 8th edn (Giesecke, Dresden, 1926), pp. 27, 31, 44–50, 57, 60; Carl Buttenstedt, 'Zur Kritik der Glücks-Ehe', *Geschlecht und Gesellschaft*, 2 (1907), p. 268; Magnus Hirschfeld, *Geschlechtskunde*, (2 vols Püttmann, Stuttgart, 1926–7), vol. II, p. 433.

18. Hirschfeld, *Geschlechtskunde*, vol. II, pp. 430–50 *passim*; Dr Laker, 'Über ein besondere Form von Perversion des weiblichen Geschlechtstreibes', *AGyn*, 34 (1889), p. 293; Max Marcuse, *Der Präventivverkehr in der medizinischen Lehre und ärztlichen Praxis* (Marcus and Weber, Stuttgart, 1931), p. 91; Anne-Marie Durand-Wever, *Die Verhütung der Schwangerschaft* (Antäus, Hamburg, 1931), p. 139; R. Fetscher, 'Ehe- und Sexualberatung als Weg der psychischen Hygiene', *ZGVGF*, 1 (1930), p. 521; Potts and Selman, *Society and fertility*, p. 172; Lawrence Stone, *The family, sex and marriage in England, 1500–1800* (Weidenfeld and Nicolson, London, 1977), p. 422.

19. Dr Horch, 'Sexualität und Ehescheidung', *Archiv für Sexualforschung*, 1 (1915–16), pp. 42–50; Fetscher, 'Ehe- und Sexualberatung', p. 521. Statistics on venereal disease provide one source of information on oral sex. See e.g. K.F. Hoffmann, 'Erscheinungen der Geschlechtskrankheiten in die Mundhöhle', *Telos*, 2 (1926), p. 452.

20. Franz Frisch, *Über Gonorrhoea rectalis: Mittheilungen aus der Syphilidoklinik zu Würzburg* (Stakel, Würzburg, 1891); Victor Bandler, 'Über die venerischen Affectionen der Analgegend bei Prostituirten', *Archiv für Klinische und Experimentelle Dermatologie*, 43 (1898), pp. 19–30; T. Baer, 'Weiterer Beitrag zur Lehre von weiblichen Rectal-Gonorrhoe', *Archiv für Klinische und Experimentelle Dermatologie*, 48 (1899), p. 303; Dr Jesionek, "Analgonorrhoe", *Archiv für Klininsche und Experimentelle Dermatologie*, 51 (1907), p. 153.

21. Dr Hanssen, 'Die Abnahme der Geburtenzahlen in den verschiedenen Bevölkerungsklassen und ihre Ursachen', *ASHD*, 7 (1912), p. 394; Max Marcuse, 'Zur Frage der Verbreitung und Methodik der willkürlichen Geburtenbeschränkung in Berliner Proletarierkreisen', *SP*, 9 (1913), case no. 85; Paul Näcke, 'Mitteilung über sexuelle Perversionen in eheliche Verkehre', *AKAK*, 30 (1908), p. 365.

22. Wilhelm Frank, 'Ergebnisse einer Statistik über 985 klinisch behandelte Fälle von Frauengonorrhoe', *AFk*, 13 (1927), pp. 26-34; Eustace Chesser, *Live and let live: the moral of the Wolfenden Report* (Heineman, London, 1958), p. 50; Morton Hunt, *Sexual behavior in the 1970s* (Playboy Press, New York, 1974), p. 204.

23. Fraenkel, *Empfängnisverhütung*, p. 133; Marcuse, *Präventivverkehr*, p. 92; Heinrich Gesenius, *Empfängnisverhütung*, 3rd edn (Urban and Schwarzenberg, Berlin, 1970), pp. 76-7; John Noyes, *Male continence: or, self-control in sexual intercourse* (Office of *The Circular*, Oneida, 1866), published in Germany as *Die Manneskraft und ihre Beherrschung und Erhaltung*, trans. H.B. Fischer (Max Spohr, Leipzig, 1896); Alice Stockham, *Karezza: the ethics of marriage* (R.F. Fenno, New York City, 1896), published in Germany as *Die Reform-Ehe*, trans. H.B. Fischer (Risel, Hagen, 1897). On the American context of these practices see Degler, *At odds*, pp. 203-5; Richard DeMaria, *Communal love at Oneida* (Edwin Mellen, New York, 1978); Lawrence Foster, *Religion and sexuality: three American communal experiments of the nineteenth century* (Oxford University Press, New York, 1981); Louis Kern, *An ordered love: sex roles and sexuality in Victorian utopias* (University of North Carolina Press, Chapel Hill, 1981); Stephen Nissenbaum, *Sex, diet, and debility in Jacksonian America: Sylvester Graham and health reform* (Greenwood, Westport, 1980); Hal Sears, *The sex radicals: free love in high Victorian America* (Regents Press of Kansas, Lawrence, 1977); Linda Gordon, *Woman's body, woman's right: a social history of birth control in America* (Grossman, New York, 1976), pp. 62, 101, 106.

24. Ferdy, *Sittliche Selbstbeschränkung*, p. 64; Kisch, *Sexual Life*, p. 407; Hans Ferdy, *Die Mittel zur Verhütung der Conception*, 8th edn (Max Spohr, Leipzig, 1907), p. 27; H. Gerlach, *Die Einschränkung der Kinderzahl durch verhütung der Empfängnis* (Cassirer and Danziger, Berlin, 1893), p. 16; Marcuse, *Präventivverkehr*, p. 92; Himes, *Medical history*, p. 118.

25. Fraenkel, *Empfängnisverhütung*, p. 133; Kisch, *Sexual life*, p. 403; Hirschfeld, *Geschlechtskunde*, vol. II, pp. 433-50; Marcuse, *Eheliche Präventivverkehr*, p. 171 and case no. 286; Gesenius, *Empfängnisverhütung*, pp. 76-7; Willi Steinhäuser, 'Über das biologische Verhalten von Spermatozoen in chemischen Reagentien', (PhD dissertation, University of Breslau, 1922), p. 5.

26. Gerlach, *Einschränkung*, p. 18; Kisch, *Sexual life*, p. 404; Hanssen, 'Abnahme', p. 393; Grotjahn, *Geburtenrückgang*, p. 242; Marcuse, *Eheliche Präventivverkehr*, p. 171 and *passim*; O. Polano, 'Beitrag zur Frage der Geburtenbeschränkung', *ZGG*, 79 (1917), p. 571. Elsewhere and more recently see Degler, *At odds*, pp. 211-12; Gordon, *Woman's body*, pp. 62-3; E. Lewis-Fanning, *Report on an enquiry into family limitation and its influence on human fertility during the past fifty years* (Papers on the Royal Commission on Population, London, 1949), pp. 7-10; David Glass, 'Family limitation in Europe: survey of recent studies', in C.V. Kiser (ed.), *Research in family planning*, (Princeton University Press, Princeton, 1962), pp. 231-61; Ronald Lesthaeghe, *The decline of Belgian Fertility, 1800-1970* (Princeton University Press, Princeton, 1977), p. 137; Peter Schwaner, 'Der Einfluss sozialer Faktoren auf die Art der Konzeptionsverhütung', PhD dissertation, 1970, University of Erlangen, p. 101.

27. Marcuse, *Eheliche Präventivverkehr*, case nos 6, 53, 77, 92, 154,

204, 295; Fraenkel, *Empfängnisverhütung*, p. 134; Polano, 'Beitrag', p. 567; Fetscher, 'Ehe- und Sexualberatung', p. 521; F. Lehmann, 'Über antikonzeptionelle Mittel', *BKW*, 46 (1909), p. 877; A.W. Bauer, 'Kritik der Konzeptionsverhütungsmittel', *MK*, 26 (1930), p. 962; Ulrich Linse, 'Arbeiterschaft und Geburtenentwicklung im deutschen Kaiserreich von 1871', *ASG*, 12 (1972), p. 227.

28. Bauer, 'Kritik', p. 962; Fraenkel, *Empfängnisverhütung*, pp. 133-5.

29. Dr Mager, 'Besprechung', in Komittee für Geburtenregelung, *Geburtenregelung*, p. 109; see also Gerlach, *Einschränkung*, pp. 18-20.

30. Alfred Damm, *Die gesundheitsschädliche Wirkung der Mittel zur Vermeidung der Conception, contra Hans Ferdy und Andere* (Stagmeyersche Verlagshandlung, Munich, 1887), pp. 7-8, 19, 33-4; Hans Ferdy, *Der Congressus interruptus als ätiologisches Basis nervöser Störungen der Genitalsphäre* (Heuser, Berlin, 1891); A. Eulenburg, 'Über Coitus reservatus als Ursache sexualer Neurasthenie bei Männern', *Internationales Centralblatt für die Physiologie und Pathologie der Harn- und Sexualorgane*, 4 (1893), pp. 3-7; Gustav Aschaffenburg, 'Die Beziehung des sexuellen Lebens zur Entstehung von Nerven- und Geisteskrankheiten', *MMW*, 53 (1906), p. 37; Gerlach, *Einschränkung*, p. 30; Lehmann, 'Antikonzeptionelle Mittel', p. 877; Friedrich Hinz, *Der Wert der antikonzeptionellen Mittel* (Konegen, Leipzig, 1898), p. 357; Wilhelm Mensinga, *Vom Sichinachtnehmen (Heuser, Neuwied, 1905), passim*. On similar concerns elsewhere see Thomas MacArdle, *The physical evils arising from the prevention of conception* (Wood, New York, 1888), and Ilza Veith, *Hysteria: the history of a disease* (University of Chicago Press, Chicago, 1965); Richard Soloway, *Birth control and the population question in England, 1877-1930* (University of North Carolina Press, Chapel Hill, 1982), p. 113; Gail Parsons, 'Equal treatment for all: American medical remedies for male sexual problems, 1850-1900', *Journal of the History of Medicine and Allied Sciences*, 32 (1977), pp. 57-9, 61-2.

31. Marcuse, *Eheliche Präventivverkehr*, case nos 6, 39; Gustav Stille, *Der Neo-Malthusianismus, das Heilmittel der Pauperismus* (Luckhardt, Berlin, 1880), p. 68; Rosanna Ledbetter, *A history of the Malthusian League, 1877-1927* (Ohio State University Press, Columbus, 1976), p. 123; 'Der internationale medicinische Congress in Amsterdam', *BKW*, 16 (1879), pp. 620-1. On medical opinion see Gerlach, *Einschränkung*, p. 34; P. Orlowski, *Die Impotenz des Mannes*, 2nd edn (Kabitzsch, Würzburg, 1910), p. 63; Kisch, *Sexual life*, pp. 406-7; O. Sarwey, 'Über Indikationen und Methoden der fakultativen Sterilisierung der Frau', *DMW*, 31 (1905), p. 295; Fraenkel, *Empfängnisverhütung*, p. 135.

32. Michael Phayer, *Sexual liberation and religion in nineteenth-century Europe* (Rowman and Littlefield, Totowa, 1977), pp. 21-2; Eugen Weber, *Peasants into Frenchmen: the modernization of rural France, 1870-1914* (Stanford University Press, Stanford, 1976), pp. 123-9; Liselotte Hansmann and Lenz Kriss-Rettenbeck, *Amulett und Talisman: Erscheinungsform und Geschichte* (Callwey, Munich, 1966); Oskar Hovorka and A. Kronfeld, *Vergleichende Volksmedizin* (2 vols, Strecker and Schröder, Stuttgart, 1908), vol. I. pp. 522-3; Dr Aigremont, *Volkserotik und Pflanzenwelt* (2 vols, Tensinger, Halle, 1908), vol. I, pp. 49-52, 138-40; Hermann Heinrich Ploss and Max Bartels, *Das Weib in der Natur- und Völkerkunde*, (9th edn, Grieben, Leipzig, 1908), pp. 300-5; Felix Freiherr von Oefele, 'Anticonceptionelle

Arzneistoffen: Ein Beitrag zur Frage der Malthusianismus in alter und neuer Zeit', *Die Heilkunde*, (1898), p. 277; Dr Hirsch, 'Geburtenrückgang und Gesetzgebung nach dem kriege', *ZSWSP*, 6 (1919-20), p. 440.

33. Francis Place, *Illustrations and proofs of the principle of population* (Longman, Hurst, Rees, Orme and Brown, London, 1822); Friedrich Wilde, *Das weibliche Gebär-Unvermögen* (Nicolai'sche Verlag, Berlin, 1838), p. 318; Gerlach, *Einschränkung*, p. 23; Roderick Hellmann, *Über Geschlechtsfreiheit* (Staude, Berlin, 1878), p. 205; Grotjahn, *Geburtenrückgang*, p. 77.

34. Hinz, *Wert*, p. 353; Hanssen, 'Abnahme', p. 394; Marcuse, *Eheliche Präventivverkehr*, case no. 215; Proceedings of the Berlin Gynecological Society, *ZGyn* 38 (1914), p. 729; Fraenkel, *Empfängnisverhütung*, pp. 150-1.

35. Ludwig Levy-Lenz, 'Eine einfache Methode der Schwangerschaftsverhütung', *ZSWSP*, 17 (1931), pp. 501-2; Anne-Marie Durand-Wever, 'Die ärztlichen Erfahrungen über medizinisch indizierte Konzeptionesverhütung', *MW*, 5 (1931), p. 937.

36. Charles Knowlton, *The fruits of philosophy: the private companion of young married people* (1832; reprinted Freethought Publishing Co., London, 1877); Hellmann, *Geschlechtsfreiheit*, pp. 204-5; see also Gerlach, *Einschränkung*, pp. 20-1; Olga Zschommler, *Malthusianismus: Verhütung der Empfängnis und ihre gesundheitlichen Folgen* (Wilhelm Möller, Berlin, 1891), p. 20; Lehmann, 'Antikonzeptionelle Mittel', p. 878; Ferdy, *Mittel*, p. 29; Grotjahn, *Geburtenrückgang*, p. 70.

37. Gerlach, *Einschränkung*, p. 21; Lehmann, 'Antikonzeptionelle Mittel', p. 878; Ferdy, *Mittel*, p. 29.

38. Gerlach, *Einschränkung*, pp. 21-2; Martha Ruben-Wolf, 'Mechanische und chemische Verhütungsmittel', Komittee fur Geburtenregelung, *Geburtenregelung*, p. 34.

39. Friedrich Bilz, *The natural method of healing* (2 vols, F.E. Bilz, London, 1898), vol. II, p. 1591; Linse, 'Arbeiterschaft', p. 227; Marcuse, *Eheliche Präventivverkehr*, case nos 208, 278; Degler, *At odds*, pp. 215-16.

40. Lehmann, 'Antikonzeptionelle Mittel', p. 878; E.R. May, 'Zur Frage des Geburtenrückganges', *Schmollers Jahrbuch*, 40 (1916), p. 61; B. Schlegtendahl, 'Von Kampf gegen Unzucht und Unsittlichkeit', *ZMB*, 27 (1914), p. 126; Dr Kantor, 'Geburtenrückgang und Kurpfuscherei', *TH*, 30 (1916), pp. 563, 567.

41. Grotjahn, *Geburtenrückgang*, p. 242; Marcuse, 'Frage', p. 779; Polano, 'Beitrag', p. 571; Max Hirsch, *Fruchtabtreibung und Präventivverkehr im Zusammenhang mit dem Geburtenrückgang* (Kabitzsch, Würzburg, 1914), p. 10; R. Spree, 'Modernisierung des Konsumverhaltens deutscher Mittel- und Unterschichten während der Zwischenkriegszeit', *Zeitschft für Soziologie*, 14 (1985), p. 408.

42. Lehmann, 'Antikonzeptionelle Mittel', p. 878; Antoine, 'Konzeptionsverhütung', p. 1371; Zschommler, *Malthusianismus*, p. 20; Max Baum, *Die künstliche Beschränkung der Kinderzahl: Ein Mittel zur Verhütung der Conception* (Schmidt, Berlin, 1892), p. 48.

43. Hinz, *Wert*, pp. 349-50, 353-5; Friedrich Hinz, *Kritik der antikonzeptionellen Mittel, für Aerzte und Gebildete aller Stände*, 4th edn (Hugo Bermühler, Berlin, 1907), pp. 12, 38-41.

44. Ploss and Bartels, *Das Weib*, p. 308; Leopold Bürger, 'Häufigkeit

und gebräuchliche Methoden des kriminellen Abortus', *Friedrichs Blätter für gerichtliche Medizin und Sanitätspolizei*, 60 (1909), p. 388; Franz Kisch, *Das Problem der Fruchtabtreibung vom ärztlichen und legislativen Standpunkt* (Urban and Schwarzenberg, Berlin, 1921), p. 9; Louis Lewin, *Die Fruchtabtreibung durch Gifte und andere Mittel*, 4th edn (Stilke, Berlin, 1925), pp. 194, 206; Georg Strassmann, 'Brauchbare und unbrauchbare Abtreibungsmittel', *MGG* 75 (1926), p. 80; H. Heiss, *Die künstliche Schwangerschaftsunterbrechung und der kriminelle Abort* (Enke, Stuttgart, 1967), p. 284.

45. Bürger, 'Häufigkeit', p. 388; Asrican, 'Über Selbstabtreibung', *MK*, 24 (1928), pp. 1551-2; Hellmuth Hahn, 'Gerichtsärztliche Erfahrungen über den kriminellen Abort am Landgericht Göttingen in den Jahren 1910 bis 1919', PhD dissertation, University of Göttingen, 1920, p. 18; Hans Reichling, 'Abortivmittel und Methode des kriminellen Aborts im Landgerichtsbezirk Essen', PhD dissertation, University of Münster, 1940, p. 19; Marcuse, 'Frage', pp. 779-80; Edward Shorter, *A history of women's bodies* (Basic Books, New York, 1982), p. 190.

46. Marcuse, 'Frage', case nos 4, 5, 25, 48, 61, 93; G. Leubuscher, 'Krimineller Abort in Thüringen', *VGMOS* (3rd series), 50 (1915), p. 9; F. Pietrusky, 'Zur Frage der kriminellen Fruchtabtreibung', *DZGGM*, 17 (1930), p. 58; Walther Benthin, 'Über kriminelle Fruchtabtreibung: Mit besonderer Berücksichtigung der Verhältnisse in Ostpreussen', *ZGG*, 17 (1915), p. 595; Ernst Bumm, 'Zur Frage des künstlichen Abortus', *MGG*, 43 (1916), p. 387; J.R. Spinner, *Aerztliches Recht* (Springer, Berlin, 1914), p. 374.

47. Spinner, *Aerztliches Recht*, pp. 370-1; Leubuscher, 'Krimineller Abort', p. 16; Reichling, *Abortivmittel*, pp. 23, 25-7, 31; Raimund Werb, 'Die Wandlung der Abtreibungsmethoden und ihre forensische Bedeutung', PhD dissertation, University of Marburg, 1936, pp. 30-2.

48. Spinner, *Aerztliches Recht*, pp. 371, 372n; Lewin, *Fruchtabtreibung*, pp. 295, 311, 318-24, 346, 387; Werb, 'Wandlung', pp. 8-14; Hubert Braun, 'Ein Beitrag zur kriminellen Fruchtabtreibung mittels Seifenwasserlösung', PhD dissertation, University of Munich, 1927, p. 5; Frederick Taussig, *Abortion, spontaneous and induced* (Mosby, St Louis, 1936), pp. 334, 354; Bürger, 'Häufigkeit', pp. 268-74; Heinrich Fritsch, *Gerichtsärztliche Geburtshülfe* (Enke, Stuttgart, 1901), p. 119; Dr Schild, 'Sechs Fälle von Nitrobenzol-Vergiftung', *BKW*, 32 (1895), p. 187.

49. On the use of lead and iron pills in England see Angus McLaren, *Birth control in nineteenth century England: a social and intellectual history* (Holmes and Meier, New York, 1978), p. 242; R. Sauer, 'Infanticide and abortion in nineteenth century Britain', *PS*, 32 (1978), p. 91; P.S. Brown, 'Female pills and the reputation of iron as an abortifacient', *Medical History*, 21 (1977), p. 301. On phosphorus in Sweden see G. Hedren, 'Zur Statistik und Kasuistik der Fruchtabtreibung', *VGMOS*, 29 (1905), pp. 44-53.

50. Shorter, *Women's bodies*, pp. 78, 180. The classic compendium of recipes was Johann Staricius, *Geheimnisvoller Heldenschatz*, first published in 1616 and reissued in many editions. English folklore also included 'cookbooks' with recipes for teas to 'restore the menses', some of which found their way into package products such as Hooper's Female Pills or Welch's Female Pills. During the eighteenth century their use seems to have been limited to restoring irregular menstruation, but by the late nineteenth century their use was wholly abortifacient. See McLaren, *Birth control*, p. 241;

Angus McLaren, 'Abortion in England, 1890-1914', *Victorian Studies* 20 (1977), p. 390; James Mohr, *Abortion in America: origins and evolution of national policy, 1800-1900* (Oxford University Press, New York, 1978), pp. 6-12, 55-8.

51. Heiss, *Schwangerschaftsunterbrechung*, p. 288; Wolfgang Jöchle, 'Menses-inducing drugs: their role in antique, medieval, and Renaissance gynecology and birth control', *Contraception*, 10 (1974), pp. 428-36.

52. A recent survey came to the conclusion that 'there is no safe, reliable drug available at this time which will cause termination of early pregnancy in human beings'. B. Nathanson, 'Drugs for the production of abortion: a review', *Obstetric and Gynecologic Survey*, 25 (1970), p. 730; cf. Martin Cole and A.F.M. Brierley, 'Abortifacient drugs', *Journal of Sex Research*, 4 (1968), pp. 16-25. Edward Shorter argues that the failure of abortifacients lay in part in the manner of preparation: Shorter, 'Has a desire to limit fertility always existed? The question of drug abortion in traditional Europe', paper presented at the International Union for the Scientific Study of Population Conference in Bad Homburg, 1980.

53. Fritsch, *Gerichtsärztliche Geburtshülfe*, p. 120; Bürger, "Häufigkeit", p. 374; Lewin, *Fruchtabtreibung*, p. 361; Taussig, *Abortion*, p. 353; Benthin, "Kriminelle Fruchtabtreibung", p. 595; Shorter, *Women's bodies*, p. 184.

54. Fritsch, *Gerichtsärztliche Geburtshülfe*, p. 119; Lewin, *Fruchtabtreibung*, p. 389; Ploss and Bartels, *Das Weib*, p. 304.

55. Lewin, *Fruchtabtreibung*, pp. 123, 377; Werb, 'Wandlung', pp. 15-16; Ploss and Bartels, *Das Weib*, p. 305; Taussig, *Abortion*, p. 353; Spinner, *Aerztliches Recht*, p. 371; Anton Joseph Scholz, 'Pharmazeutischgebräuchliche Coniferen-Blattdrogen insbesondere Juniperus Sabina und seine Verfälschungen', PhD dissertation, University of Basle, 1923; Heinrich Lehmann, 'Beiträge zur Geschichte von Sambucus nigra, Juniperus communis, und Juniperus sabina', Phd dissertation, University of Basle, 1935; Braun, 'Beitrag', p. 5; Leubuscher, 'Krimineller Abort', pp. 10-11. On the use of savin and saffron see Allgemeine Konferenz, *Geschlechtlich-sittliche Verhaltnisse*, vol. I, pp. 50, 67, 101, 136; vol. II, 43, 69, 313, 368, 409, 634; Lewin, *Fruchtabtreibung*, pp. 255-6; Heiss, *Schwangerschaftsunterbrechung*, pp. 297-8. Savin was the most commonly used abortifacient in America, followed by rue, tansy, aloes, calomel and seneca; see Mohr, *Abortion in America*, pp. 6-12, 55-8. In England the most popular plants were aloes, savin and pennyroyal; see McLaren, *Birth control*, p. 241; McLaren, 'Abortion in England', p. 390.

56. Strassmann, 'Abtreibungsmittel', p. 82; Ludwig Guttmann, 'Über ein im Abortivum "Apiol" vorkommendes elektives Nervengift (Triorthokresolphosphat)', *MK*, 28 (1932), p. 717; G. Joachimoglu, 'Apiolum viride als Abortivum', *DMW*, 52 (1926), p. 2080; Dr Mantey, 'Apiol, ein gefährliches Abortivum', *ZMB*, 45 (1932), pp. 245-7; Shorter, *Women's bodies*, p. 215. Both Apiolin and Erpiol were listed in *Riedel's Mentor* before 1910: J.R. Spinner, 'Periodenstörungsmittel. Ein Beitrag zur Kenntnis des kriminellen Kurpfuschertums', *AKAK*, 54 (1913), p. 243. The text of the 'Runderlass des Ministers für Volkswohlfahrt betreffend die Abgabe von Apiol in den Apotheken' is reprinted in *ZMB*, 45 (1932), Supplement 6, p. 23. See also Werb, 'Wandlung', p. 19.

57. Heinz Peickert, 'Geheimmittel im deutschen Arzneiverkehr. Ein Beitrag zur Wirtschaftsgeschichte der Pharmazie und zur Arzneispezialitätenfrage', PhD dissertation, University of Leipzig, 1932, pp. 8, 17, 41–5, 54, 59. On patent medicines see James Young, *The toadstool millionaires: a social history of patent medicines in America before federal regulation* (Princeton University Press, Princeton, 1961); Sarah Stage, *Female complaints: the business of women's medicine* (Norton, New York, 1982); Matthew Ramsey, 'Traditional medicine and medical enlightenment: the reputation of secret remedies in the ancien regime', *Historical Reflections*, 9 (1982), pp. 215–32.

58. Peickert, 'Geheimmittel', pp. 64, 79–81, 84; Elmar Ernst, *Das 'industrielle' Geheimmittel und seine Werbung. Arzneifertigwaren in der zweiten Hälfte des neunzehnten Jahrhunderts in Deutschland* (Jal, Würzburg, 1975), p. 67.

59. Ernst, *Geheimmittel*, pp. 22, 25–8, 172, 175–6; Stage, *Female complaints*, pp. 45–50.

60. Ernst, *Geheimmittel*, pp. 26–7, 141–3, 178; Peickert, 'Geheimmittel', p. 25; R. Schenda, 'Stadtmedizin-Landmedizin' in Gerhard Kaufman (ed.), *Stadt-Land Beziehungen* (Schwartz, Göttingen, 1975), pp. 147–9; Young, *Toadstool*, p. 184; James Young, *Medical messiahs: a social history of health quackery in twentieth-century America* (Princeton University Press, Princeton, 1967), pp. 424–5.

61. Ernst, *Geheimmittel*, pp. 40, 52–3, 179; Peickert, 'Geheimmittel', pp. 27, 79–80, 90; Shorter, *Women's bodies*, p. 180; Young, *Toadstool*, p. 5; W. Bernsmann, 'Arzneimittelforschung und Arzneientwicklung in Deutschland in zweiten Hälfte des neunzehnten Jahrhunderts', *Pharmazeutische Industrie*, 29 (1967), pp. 669–70; L.F. Haber, *The chemical industry during the nineteenth century* (Oxford University Press, Oxford, 1958), pp. 113, 118, 133–5.

62. Carl Reissig, 'Geheimmittelschwindel und Geschlechtsleben in der Annonce, *Aerztliche Vereinsblatt Deutschland*, 36–8 (1909), pp. 7–8; Karin Bergmann-Gorski, 'Aerztliche Standes- und Berufspolitik in Deutschland von 1900 bis 1920', PhD dissertation, University of Berlin, 1966, p. 53. For a representative list of 'sensitive' *Geheimmittel* see Eduard Hahn, *Die Wichtigsten der bis jetzt bekannten Geheimmittel und Specialitäten* (Springer, Berlin, 1871; subsequent editions in 1874, 1876, 1879).

63. Spinner, 'Periodenstörungsmittel', pp. 226–7, 236–8, 247–8, and listing of brand names, pp. 242–8; Ernst, *Geheimmittel*, pp. 59, 62; Kantor, 'Geburtenrückgang', pp. 566–7; Paul Cattani, 'Die Medizin in der politischen Presse', Phd dissertation, University of Zurich, 1913, p. 55; Young, *Toadstool*, p. 167.

64. Reissig, 'Geheimmittelschwindel', pp. 25–7; Spinner, 'Periodenstörungsmittel', p. 227; Ernst, *Geheimmittel*, pp. 118–19, 126–7, 164–5; Stage, *Female complaints*, p. 103; Young, *Toadstool*, pp. 39, 100.

65. Reissig, 'Geheimmittelschwindel', p. 6.

66. Spinner, 'Periodenstörungsmittel', p. 232.

67. Mantey, 'Apiol', p. 247.

68. For a list of cities and countries where Musczynski's advertisement appeared see Cattani, 'Medizin', pp. 56–8.

69. Spinner, 'Periodenstörungsmittel', p. 228; see also Cattani, 'Medizin', p. 61; Leubuscher, 'Krimineller Abort', p. 18; Konstantin Inderheggen, *Das Delikt der Abtreibung im Landgerichtsbezirk Mönchen-Gladbach in der Zeit von 1908 bis 1938* (Frommann, Jena, 1940), pp. 22, 34; W. Köhler, *Das Delikt der Abtreibung im Landgerichtsbezirk Gera, 1896–1930* (Fromm, Jena, 1935), p. 43.

70. Spinner, 'Periodenstörungsmittel', pp. 227–31, 241; Kantor, 'Geburtenrückgang', p. 518; Cattani, 'Medizin', p. 54; Leubuscher, 'Krimineller Abort', pp. 17, 19; Hans Schneickert, 'Die gerwerbsmässige Abtreibung und deren Bekämpfung', *MKP*, 2 (1906), pp. 624–5.

71. The Imperial Ordinance underwent several modifications over the years as the government sought to keep up with the rapid proliferation of drugs. The complete text of the ordinance and its revisions can be found in Johannes Thiessen, *Die deutsche Drogisten. Geschichte des Deutschen Drogisten-Verbandes, 1873–1926* (Müller, Berlin, 1926), pp. 290–5 (1872), 295–9 (1875), 300–7 (1890), 309–18 (1901). On the rationale behind the law and the debates over its revision see Ulla Meinecke, 'Apothekenbindung und Freiverkäuflichkeit von Arzneimitteln', PhD dissertation, University of Marburg, 1971, pp. 141–2, 188–91, 195–6, 203–8. See also Hermann Böttger, *Die reichsgesetzlichen Bestimmungen über den Verkehr mit Arzneimitteln ausserhalb der Apotheken*, 4th edn (Springer, Berlin, 1902), pp. 1–14. For a list of products which could not be sold outside of pharmacies see Böttger, *Bestimmungen*, pp. 101–7.

72. 'Verordnung des Reichspräsidenten über den Verkehr mit Arzneimitteln, 9 Dezember 1924', in Thiessen, *Drogisten*, pp. 323–8, and also in Ernst Urban, *Apotheken-Gesetz nach deutschem Reichs- und Preussischem Landesrecht*, 6th edn (Springer, Berlin, 1927), pp. 115–16, 123–5.

73. 'Polizeiverordnung der preussischen Minister der geistlichen, Unterrichts- und Medizinalangelegenheiten, des Innern und für Handel und Gewerbe, über den Handel mit Giften', in Thiessen, *Drogisten*, pp. 336–47; Böttger, *Bestimmungen*, pp. 222–7; H. Böttger and E. Urban, *Die preussische Apothekengesetze*, 5th edn (Springer, Berlin, 1913), pp. 377–88; H. Böttger, *Giftverkaufbuch für Apotheken und Drogisten*, 4th edn (Springer, Berlin, 1906), pp. 7–12.

74. 'Vorschrift betreffend die Abgabe stark wirkender Arzneimittel', in Böttger and Urban, *Apothekengesetze*, pp. 353–61; Urban, *Apotheken-Gesetze*, pp. 199n–200n.

75. W.R. Lee, *Population growth, economic development and social change in Bavaria, 1750–1850* (Arno, New York, 1977), p. 366; Arthur Imhof, 'An approach to historical demography in Germany', *Social History*, 4 (1979), pp. 356–7.

76. Eugene Sandberg and Ralph Jacobs, 'Psychology of the misuse and rejection of contraception', *American Journal of Obstetrics and Gynecology*, 110 (1971), pp. 227–37.

77. Spinner, 'Periodenstörungsmittel', p. 238; Shorter, *Women's bodies*, p. 180.

78. Marcuse, 'Frage', p. 776; Reissig, 'Geheimmittelschwindel', p. 25; Leubuscher, 'Krimineller Abort, pp. 18–21; Shorter, *Women's bodies*, p. 9.

79. Marcuse, *Eheliche Präventivverkehr*, case nos 88, 92, 119; cf. case nos 53, 77, 98, 103, 204, 208, 295.

80. Marcuse, *Eheliche Präventivverkehr*, case no. 215; Polano, 'Beitrag', p. 576. Compare McLaren, *Birth control*, pp. 221–4. Potts and Selman argue that the role of coitus interruptus has usually been underestimated in the fertility decline: *Society and fertility*, p. 172.

2

The Advent of Modern Contraception

In the late nineteenth century the marriage of ideology and technology sparked the birth of modern contraception. Neo-Malthusianism prompted entrepreneurs to utilise advances in science and industry to produce reliable mechanical and chemical contraceptives. The vulcanisation of rubber in the 1840s and the synthesis of drugs in the 1880s laid the basis for the manufacture of products to block, immobilise, and kill spermatozoa. At the same time, progress in medical science led to the perfection of techniques for sterilisation, which provided the greatest degree of contraceptive protection. Market forces ensured the rapid diffusion of these products and services. By the turn of the century the German public had access to virtually the same range of contraceptives that we have today.[1]

Neo-Malthusian sentiment arose early in the nineteenth century in reaction to the dire predictions — and equally dire prescriptions — of Thomas Malthus. Pastor Malthus had argued in his 1798 *Essay on population* that the unrestrained fertility of the lower classes would inevitably outstrip economic productivity and lead to ever-increasing social misery. But the material advances which continuing industrialisation seemed to promise led to a revision of this gloomy forecast by the more optimistic utilitarian philosophers of the early nineteenth century. Political theorists argued that social problems were not the immutable result of the laws of nature but rather the product of specific social institutions and practices which could be changed. 'Self-help' became the watchword among concerned middle-class observers, and they included birth control among the measures which the poor could and should use to improve their situation. Proponents of this argument included John Stuart Mill in his *Principles of political economy* (1848; German edition 1854) and Charles Drysdale, in *Elements of social science* (1854; German edition 1872). The birth control measures which they envisaged were those advocated by Richard Carlile, *Every woman's book* (1826), Robert Dale Owen, *Moral Physiology* (1830), and Charles Knowlton, *Fruits of philosophy* (1832) — namely, tampon with condom (Carlile and Owen) or with douche (Knowlton).[2]

In 1857 Lord Campbell's Obscene Publications Act threatened to stifle public discussion of birth control, although sales of the early pamphlets continued without incident into the 1870s. In 1877 the efforts of secularists like Charles Bradlaugh to promote birth control clashed with the efforts of the Society for the Suppression of Vice to produce the notorious Bradlaugh-Besant trial. When the smoke cleared, sales of Knowlton's pamphlet soared a hundred-fold and the Malthusian League stood firmly established and ready to advocate birth control to the British public.[3]

German unification in 1871 sparked interest in the population question in that country. The massive shift of population from east to west in the decades after 1871; the intensive pace of urbanisation, which shifted another third of the populace into urban areas in less than half a century; and the relaxation of restrictive marriage laws in some constituent states, with the concomitant burst of new marriages and new births all led to reactions like that of the political economist Gustav Rümelin: 'I am convinced that Germany is overpopulated and that this is our most important problem.'[4]

Like their English counterparts, German Neo-Malthusians argued that the imbalance between population and resources was artificial and could be corrected through conscious action. They rejected the respect traditionally accorded large families: children might be a blessing, but the benediction was not cumulative. Reflecting their middle-class bias, Neo-Malthusians urged restraint on fertility for the sake of social mobility: 'Everyone wants to get ahead in life.'[5] But the individual could advance only if unencumbered by swarms of babies; the family could maintain its status only by matching expenses to income; the nation could only maintain its productivity if population growth was regulated sensibly. This was not only desirable, but necessary: 'It is no longer possible to defend the right of every German to produce as many children as he chooses without regard for the cost to society.'[6]

Neo-Malthusians resented social taboos on the public discussion of birth control. Unlike Pastor Malthus, they virtually insisted on contraception within marriage, arguing that if this was 'unnatural' so were clothing, cooking, housing, and other products of civilisation; to become 'natural' people would have to live from fruits and berries.[7]

Birth control was promoted not only as sensible but as moral behaviour that reflected the higher sense of responsibility that should characterise civilised people.

> Precisely because our reason enables us to perceive and to prevent the inevitable consequences of excess reproduction, we mock the goodness and the wisdom of the Creator if we let unrestrained indulgence lead to overpopulation.[8]

But Neo-Malthusian references to 'restraint' stopped short of specifics. Otto Zacharias, writing in the 1880s, deferred discussion of contraceptive details to the privacy of the doctor-patient relationship.

> Certain things shouldn't be discussed in public. I disapprove of lectures on family limitation such as those given in England. Propriety must be respected if we are to preserve the sanctity of conjugal relations and the integrity of marriage.[9]

Neo-Malthusianism spread throughout Europe during the late nineteenth century. As early as 1879 Charles Drysdale was able to convene a Neo-Malthusian conference which met concurrently with the International Medical Congress in Amsterdam. This sparked the emergence of the Dutch organisation, and eventually led to the creation of similar groups in most European countries.[10] But the real significance of Neo-Malthusianism lay in the incentive which the events of the 1870s gave to the emergence of the modern contraceptive industry. In 1882 Dr Wilhelm Mensinga publicised diaphragms, and in 1885 the London pharmacist, Rendell, developed the first chemical suppository. Within a few years these products found scores of imitators, and were joined by a host of other devices; together they made contraception safer and more effective than ever before.

Condoms date back to Fallopius, who recommended the use of a sheath made from lamb intestine as a prophylactic against syphilis. Cecal condoms continue to be in use in the twentieth century, but because of their high cost they remained in the hands of the upper classes until recently. Cheap, mass-produced condoms awaited vulcanisation (1844) and other improvements in manufacture. Rubber condoms appear to have been in use in the United States at the time of the Civil War. In 1872 Dr J.K. Proksch recommended rubber condoms for prophylaxis in place of the usual cecal type, and from then on the cheaper kinds prevailed.[11]

The first generation of rubber condoms were thick enough to

deaden sensation — 'like covering the penis with a layer of dead skin' — but thin enough to develop small air-holes during manufacture, giving rise to the epithet, 'as strong as gossamer, as sensual as armour'. Improved technology made the production of reliable condoms feasible, even if it did not guarantee that manufacturers would produce them.[12]

By the early twentieth century German physicians felt confident in recommending condoms for contraception. Testing for leaks before use and careful withdrawal were advised, but with these precautions doctors considered condoms to be the best contraceptive then available. Early concerns over harmful effects on the nervous system were dismissed as 'fairy tales' once thinner, more sensitive condoms made their appearance. But the general favour for condoms did not extend to the cap variety, which apparently originated in the United States and became available in Germany around the turn of the century. The brief scope of the cap permitted greater penile sensation during intercourse, but the cap was held in place only by an elastic band around the glans and could easily slip off.[13]

Condoms were readily available in drug stores, barber shops, and rubber goods stores. Sales were considerable: German firms produced millions of condoms each year, although many were exported. Brand names were sometimes chosen to encourage consumers (e.g. Panzerette); other types were coated with a chemical spermicide for double protection (e.g. Primeros).[14]

In practice, the advantages of condoms could be outweighed by psychological considerations. Some men resented the 'interference' of the condom during coitus, and some couples objected to the need to break off foreplay long enough to put it on. More importantly, men might delay putting on the condom, and the same problem that plagued coitus interruptus could undermine the use of condoms. The traditional association of condoms with prostitutes and venereal disease also hindered popular acceptance of condoms for contraception.[15]

The most widespread mechanical contraceptive for women, the diaphragm, was first publicised by Mensinga in 1882. Mensinga credited his general practice in Leipzig and later in Flensburg, particularly his experience with poor women afflicted with tuberculosis, for his work in developing a contraceptive that would 'give the defenseless woman a weapon against male brutality'.[16]

The diaphragm was a half-sphere of soft rubber inserted sideways into the vagina, where it covered the cervix and posterior fornix to prevent sperm from entering the uterus. One size did not fit all; there were five graduated models to choose from. A physician selected the appropriate one for a woman and instructed her on the procedure for insertion, which most learned easily. Doctors recommended insertion before intercourse and removal the following morning after a precautionary douche, although the diaphragm could be left in longer. Diaphragms could be washed in soap water and re-used; under normal wear-and-tear they lasted a year or more.[17]

Diaphragms initially cost 2.50 Marks, to which was added the cost for medical consultation and for the douching equipment. These considerations tended to make diaphragms the prerogative of upper and middle-class women until the Health Insurance Programme began providing prophylactic measures to the working class. Nevertheless, the use of diaphragms spread quickly in all classes and all regions. In the 1890s common parlance in Thuringia spoke of contraception as 'going to Flensburg', and a comprehensive survey of rural sexual morality reported the use of diaphragms in Hannover, Saxony and Hesse. Young people learned about them in the cities; domestic servants were especially likely to observe the hygienic accoutrements of their employers.[18]

Once the popularity of the diaphragm became apparent, imitators sprang up by the dozen. Variations in construction were introduced to 'improve' on the original design by strengthening the edge with extra rubber or by inserting a watch-spring (Ramses, Dutch, Haire, and Earlet models), or by incorporating a chemical contraceptive coating for double protection (Timex and Matrisalus models).[19]

Mensinga and the thousands of doctors who accepted the diaphragm for their patients believed that therapeutic contraception was at least as moral as therapeutic abortion, and a lot safer. But there were practical concerns involved with the use of diaphragms. Although the initial fitting was done by a physician, there was no guarantee that women would always insert the device correctly, or that it would stay in place during coitus. Moreover, it was feared that the physical presence of the diaphragm would constrict penile manoeuvring during intercourse, and that women would suffer from the blockage of vaginal secretions to the cervix at orgasm.[20]

There were moral objections to the diaphragm as well — concerns that led Mensinga to publish his first essay under a pseudonym. A Catholic priest, Carl Capellman, denounced the diaphragm and recommended temporary abstinence as the only acceptable form of birth control. Dr Otto was quick to criticise Capellmann. He pointed out that Mensinga had discussed the diaphragm in a publication intended only for doctors. Capellmann had discussed birth control in a public tract, and had discussed a method available to anyone, married or single. Otto argued that moral considerations were irrelevant to medical issues.[21]

The second type of contraceptive available to women was the cervical cap, which offered even more protection than the diaphragm. The Berlin physician Dr Wilde first suggested the use of an elastic cap in 1838. He argued that preventing conception in some cases was preferable to the risks associated with Caesarian section. Wilde advocated use of a cap made of rubber and designed to fit over the cervix.[22] In the early twentieth century Dr Kafka designed a cap made from metal (gold or silver) which would be resistant to corrosion. Later models included rubber caps (Dumas, Mizpah, Guaranto, and Pro-Race models); celluloid caps (popular among prostitutes); and the Prospero gelatine cap, which was attached to the cervix before intercourse and dissolved afterwards with a spermicidal solvent douche. Other varieties included the Orga cap, which featured small holes to permit menstrual outflow without removing the cap (the holes were loosely plugged with tiny spermicidal pellets), and the Koeser or Hygibe cap, which featured a little trap door that could be opened during menstruation. Neither the Orga nor the Koeser caps remained in favour for long.[23]

Cervical caps offered the advantages of certainty and convenience: once properly fitted they remained in place for a month at a time and provided complete security. It was necessary to remove the cap at menstruation, and this as well as the initial fitting necessitated medical consultation. Finding the right size was important because a loose cap could slip off, while one that was too tight would irritate the cervix. The constant need for medical consultation was presented as an argument in favour of the cap:

> and whereas all other commercial aids are self-applied and separate patients from doctors, the Adhesion Cap brings them back, attaches them to the physician, and ensures regular medical control which is so important.[24]

For those who could afford it, though, this 'regular medical control' was a small price to pay for the security which caps provided.

Intra-uterine devices offered security without dependence. Devices of various kinds had been used by gynaecologists during the nineteenth century to correct malposition of the uterus, but reports of injuries led to the abandonment of these items for therapeutic purposes.[25] The medical profession forgot about them until a criminal trial in Magdeburg in 1902 made them realise that intra-uterine devices had found a new lease on life. A Dr Hohlweg (also spelt Hollweg) had moved to Magdeburg in 1896. Two years later he developed an intra-uterine device, the Obturator, which he dispensed for the purpose of birth control. The Obturator or Sterilett was a seven-centimetre stick with spring arms at one end which opened up inside the uterus after insertion to hold the device in place. Hohlweg inserted the Obturator in more than seven hundred patients, and marketed it nationally through a Berlin company. In 1902 he was indicted on five counts of negligence causing bodily harm for inserting the device in women without a preliminary uterine examination, and for failing to provide adequate follow-up care. All five of the women had complained to Hohlweg about vaginal discharge and pain, but he argued that the device was not at fault. Four of the women went to other doctors, who detected uterine inflammation in each case. In the fifth case an autopsy revealed that bleeding and suppuration caused by the device had aggravated the women's tuberculosis and contributed to her death. Hohlweg was convicted and sentenced to five months in prison, but he fled to the Netherlands and set up a network of saleswomen to peddle the device in Germany.[26]

The Sterilett consisted of a flat, button-like disc attached to a curved stick. Once inserted, the disc lay over the cervix to block entry by spermatozoa, while the stem reached through the cervix into the uterus, where the expandable wings held it in place. Similar devices included the Obstavit, the Weltpessar, and the Stempessar. Technically, these items were all inter-cervical devices; a true intra-uterine device (IUD) was first developed by Dr Richter of Waldenburg, Silesia. It consisted of a ring of silk thread inserted into the uterus, anticipating the later metal ring devised by Gräfenberg. Richter identified the *modus operandi* of modern IUDs as a hyperdecidual reaction in which the constant irritation of uterine membrane provoked by the device prevented implantation of an ovum.[27]

In pre-war years, stem models were the most common type of IUD. They were readily available in drug or toy stores, and from pedlars who sold them in rural areas. Midwives, doctors, and naturopaths sold and inserted the devices for fees ranging from 15 to 40 Marks. One distributor asked customers to sign a declaration that 'to the best of my knowledge I am not pregnant, nor suffering from abdominal pain'.[28] A 1913 survey of 250 doctors reported that stem IUDs were widespread in northern and central Germany, and in the Ruhr cities of Essen, Gelsenkirchen, Bochum, Mulheim, Duisburg, and Düsseldorf.[29]

Doctors worried over the increasing reports of injuries associated with intra-uterine devices. Bleeding, perforation, or infection could occur during insertion of the device, especially at the hands of untrained persons. Once in place, the devices could cause abortion if conception occurred. The 1913 survey recorded 78 abortions, of which 61 were febrile; 56 involved uterine bleeding, 37 involved abdominal inflammation and 13 caused death. These considerations led doctors to petition the government to ban the manufacture, sale and distribution of intra-uterine devices.[30]

Chemical products supplemented these mechanical devices. Chemical contraception acts to prevent conception by destroying spermatozoa before they enter the cervical canal. The normal vagina contains an organism, Döderlein's bacillus, which maintains an acidic environment hostile to external organisms, including spermatozoa. During sexual stimulation vaginal secretions become alkaline to provide a conducive environment for spermatozoa. The objective of chemical contraception, therefore, is to restore an acidic state to the vagina in order to kill the sperm before they spread. Contemporary physicians believed ordinary water to be an effective spermicide, but since slogging around in a water-logged vagina dampens coital ardour, the search was on to find some chemical substances which could accomplish the objective more practically.[31]

Suppositories are tablets placed in the vagina before intercourse. Body temperature melts the fat base (initially cocoa butter, later glycerine), releasing the spermicide (quinine or other chemical). Suppositories were first developed by the English pharmacist Rendell in 1885. German versions followed quickly. The most popular brands in the years before 1914 included Amorkugeln, Asperman, Bellmann's Schützkörper, Efem, Gloria Sicherheisbowle, Mimi, Noffke's Hygiea tablets, Patentex, Schaeffer's and Schweitzer's suppositories, Secura and Semori tablets, Sib-torpedoes, and Spermathanaton. Contraceptive creams were sold in tubes which were squeezed to apply a precise amount directly on the cervix. Brand names included Pudi de Paris, Reform, and Patentex. Jellies acted like suppositories by coating the entire vagina. Foam tablets reacted with body moisture to produce a foam barrier that trapped sperm long enough for the spermicide to work.[32] Spermicidal powders were a dry form of chemical contraception. Dr Justus devised Atokos spray powder in the 1890s, which he reissued later under the name, 'For the Malthusian'. The powder consisted of boric, citric and tannic acids in a gum base. The most popular brand of powder was Kroning's; others included Pneumatik, Victoria, Einzig, Omega, Menschenliebe, Sorgenbrecher, and Dr Hüter's Vaginal Powder. The powder was sprayed directly into the vagina to coat the surface.[33]

The effectiveness of chemical contraception depended on both the quality of the product and the accuracy with which it was applied. Quality was impossible for consumers to ascertain. Manufacturers relied on the privilege of corporate secrecy and refused to indicate the composition of their products. But even if the active ingredients were indeed active, their effectiveness could vary from one product lot to another due to differences in the concentration of chemicals or to the presence of air or moisture in the package.[34] Effective application required that suppositories, creams and jellies coat the vagina evenly, but with special concentration on the cervix. Foam tablets require adequate vaginal moisture, but the degree of moisture varies and might prove insufficient on any given occasion. Foam jellies were considered to be best because they did not require vaginal moisture and because the foam barrier combined a blocking action with spermicidal effect.[35]

Convenience was another factor in the use of chemical contraceptives. Most had to be inserted some time before coitus. Men sometimes complained that the jellies made the vagina too slippery for sex, while powders often created a grainy or sticky coating that irritated both partners. Helpful manufacturers responded to these problems with commercial overkill. An array of devices for the 'correct' application of each product became available, often at a price higher than that of the chemical, and other firms proliferated 'new and improved' versions of their products, or sold the same item under several different brand names. Less imaginative manufacturers simply raised the price, preying on the public's assumption that quality was expensive. The result was profit for the companies and confusion for the customers.[36]

Unfortunately, no agency in Germany had responsibility for testing these products, so people had no way of knowing which, if any, were effective, or whether generic equivalents were available at a lower price. A clinical study of spermicides lay buried in a medical journal. In 1906 Dr Gustav Günther of Vienna, using ejaculate from live animals, recorded the time required for motility of sperm to cease after exposure to each agent. Boric acid, a favoured contraceptive ingredient at the time, was least effective, while citric acid, acetic acid, formaldehyde, carbolic acid, sublimat, creosole and lysol were the most effective. Günther noted that the acids only curtailed the motility of the sperm but did not destroy them: if alkalinity was restored they revived. He also showed in a comparison test using human sperm that all chemical agents required more time or stronger concentrations to be effective for contraception. But Günther refrained from applying these results to particular commercial preparations; consumers would have to wait until the 1920s for specific product tests.[37]

Customers also had no way of knowing which brands of contraceptives were safe, and this uncertainty was sometimes compounded by scare stories spread by doctors. For example, Dr Fecht claimed that chemical contraceptives caused 150 cases of primary sterility, 200 cases of secondary sterility, 275 cases of endometritis and 200 cases of tubal inflammation. He also charged that carcinogens in suppositories could cause uterine cancer, and blamed chemicals for five cases of birth defects; responsible observers dismissed these claims as *post-hoc* speculation.[38]

The greatest degree of contraceptive security was provided by sterilisation. Gynaecologists had noted the desirability of sterilisation early in the nineteenth century, but only after the development of modern surgical measures in the second half of the century did operative measures become practical.[39] Female sterilisation involves removing one or more parts of the reproductive system — ovaries, tubes, or uterus — or obstructing the normal passage of the ovum. Oophorectomy is the most serious operation, since it constitutes castration with all its endocrinological consequences. Hysterectomy, by contrast, prevents menstruation and conception but does not affect femininity; it became the favoured approach for women who had already borne children.[40]

The most common procedures for sterilisation attack the fallopian tubes. Simple ligature was introduced by Lungren in 1880, but failure was not infrequent due to slippage in the stitching used to bind the tube and the subsequent ability of the ova to slip through into the uterus. Kehrer modified this procedure by first cutting the tubes and then binding the severed ends. Other variations included excising a portion of the tubes and binding the ends; removing the cornua or sealing them through cauterisation; and removing the entire tube. The simplest and most widespread method was devised by Madlener in 1910: crushing a portion of the tubes, followed by ligature. Vasectomy or male sterilisation was introduced in 1894.[41]

Although operative sterilisation remained the only practical method during the first third of the twentieth century, research continued along other lines as well. Dr Manfred Fraenkel advocated radiation to sterilise the ova, but critics questioned whether the dosage could be accurately controlled so as to prevent genetically malformed ova. Inserting radium into the uterus was rejected because of possible tissue damage.[42]

The legal status of sterilisation was anomalous. According to the Criminal Code any act of wounding which resulted in the loss of reproductive capability was punishable with up to five years in penitentiary, or up to ten years if done intentionally. Most jurists argued that since the Criminal Code had been drafted in 1871, long before the rise of modern surgery, it referred only to castration and not to sterilisation. But since the law had not yet been modified to explicitly recognise therapeutic sterilisation, doctors feared prosecution.[43]

The legal issue involved first of all the question of whether surgical operations constituted 'wounding'. The *Reichsgericht* declared in 1894 that, objectively, they did, but that in practice doctors were not culpable so long as the operation was performed for therapeutic purposes according to strict professional standards. In other words, the medical profession did not stand above the law, and doctors could not carve up people as they saw fit. But proper operations on consenting patients for therapeutic purposes were legal.[44]

The second question concerning sterilisation was whether it constituted 'loss of reproductive capability'. Gynaecologists assumed that, if operations in general were legal, then operations which resulted in the loss of reproduction were also legal, so long as that was the intended effect of the operation and not the result of malpractice. However, this was a medical opinion that was not shared by jurists, who argued that sterilisation had to occur in a manner not offensive to common decency if it was to be legally acceptable. The purpose of the operation determined its legality, and operations were defined as medical procedures for therapeutic purposes.[45]

This placed the onus on doctors to define the acceptable therapeutic purposes which could be met by sterilisation. Certain internal diseases aggravated by pregnancy met this condition: manifest tuberculosis of the lungs or larynx, heart disease (especially mitral stenosis), nephritis, diabetes, chronic anaemia, epilepsy, dementia praecox, multiple sclerosis, myelitis, morbus basedowii and osteomalacia (which required castration). Toxaemias of pregnancy occur only rarely and could be treated by therapeutic abortion. But because these indications were intended to provide justification for therapeutic sterilisation in order to prevent the worsening of a patient's condition during pregnancy, none of them could justify male sterilisation.[46]

Once doctors started listing acceptable indications for therapeutic sterilisation, some 'stretching' of standards occurred. Eugenic indications were advocated on the grounds that the purpose of procreation was to produce healthy children. Eugenicists saw sterilisation as an appropriate social prophylaxis against defective offspring. They set out to promote qualitative rather than quantitative population growth. American and Swiss laws providing for compulsory sterilisation were their model. In 1907 the insane asylum in Wil became the first European institution to perform sterilisation on psychiatric indication. But the United States was the most significant social 'laboratory' for eugenic policy. Social workers, criminologists, and other progressive-minded professionals secured the passage of sterilisation laws in more than thirty states, starting with Indiana in 1907. (In Kansas Hoyt Pilcher couldn't wait for legislation; he castrated 58 boys and girls on his own initiative during the 1890s.) By 1935 some 20,000 people had been sterilised in the United States, nearly half of them in California.[47]

In Germany, too, eugenicists overwhelmingly recommended sterilisation; 214 out of 300 pre-war publications on the subject advocated sterilisation. For most of them voluntary sterilisation, together with an extensive campaign for public enlightenment on the social implications of eugenics, constituted a sufficient policy, but a persistent minority argued that any policy of eugenic sterilisation would have to be imposed on all concerned in order to be genuinely effective.[48]

The medical profession generally remained reluctant to embrace eugenic guidelines, feeling that such proposals were premature: 'Whether we doctors should seek the enactment of such legislation, only time will tell.'[49] Senior gynaecologists insisted that any eugenic sterilisation should be limited to cases of serious and incurable hereditary illnesses present in the mother and her children, such as epilepsy, Huntington's chorea, retinitis pigmentosa and some mental illnesses. Eugenic sterilisation to prevent the birth of prospective 'welfare bums' remained a minority concern. August Hegar, although sympathetic to eugenic sterilisation, argued that 'criminal behaviour should not be used as an indication for eugenic sterilisation'.[50] A more basic objection was voiced by Dr Haberda:

> I cannot propose that anyone should be castrated for reasons of state. I hope doctors never lend themselves to that. We know so little about heredity that we must not get involved with it. I consider the whole business to be typically American.[51]

Social indications for sterilisation also constituted a legal grey area. Doctors normally took a patient's economic situation into account, as this affected her ability to obtain adequate treatment. They felt more comfortable performing sterilisation on women who already had children. But doctors and jurists both rejected sterilisation for the purpose of birth control: the woman who 'did not want to be bothered with children', or the man who got a vasectomy because 'he knows that in certain circles of women sterilised men are highly prized and highly paid for their "untainted" sexuality'. Yet even among senior gynaecologists there were some who accepted sterilisation for birth control as readily as any other form of contraception.[52]

Some insight into the extent of 'social' sterilisation was shed in an investigation by the Prussian Ministry of the Interior on the eve of the First World War. Doctors from all parts of the state reported their impression that sterilisation was widespread, as attested by the large numbers of women coming to them to request the operation. Naturally, the doctors who did sterilise patients for birth control seldom reported the fact for fear of professional censure. But Dr Krohne, a staff member of the Ministry, recounted how colleagues informed him that, when their wives consulted certain specialists for any reason they frequently received advice along these lines: 'Listen, ma'am, you have one child already; why risk the dangers of another pregnancy? It would be much better for you to be sterilized. I often perform this operation on young women, and then they are through with it once and for all.'[53]

For most people sterilisation remained a drastic — and expensive — last resort. Mechanical and chemical contraceptives, on the other hand, were readily available at a reasonable price. Advertising brought products to public attention in a manner reminiscent of patent medicines; some advertisements even combined the old with the new:

> + Women's Protection +
> Schweitzer's and Unger's Security Tablets — both recommended by doctors; Mensinga and Haase Diaphragms; Condoms. Quality in all rubber articles and devices. Regina drops and Minerva powder for blood stasis and menstrual irregularity.[54]

All of the ads promised a 'worry-free marriage' and offered 'tips' for those who want 'the surest way to wealth'.

> Clever Couples
> Move up in life with small families and demand the newest hygienic discovery. Legally protected in Germany and abroad. No rubber, no book, no douche. 2 Marks each; lasts one year. Instructions enclosed. Strictest confidence.[55]

Advertisers utilised cheap mass-circulation newspapers and magazines reaching into more and more homes to spread their messages. Advertisements appeared most frequently in the large weekend editions; popular *Witzblätter* and satirical papers like *Simplicissimus* were also favoured. Advertisers preferred metropolitan papers because they reached both a large home market and widely scattered rural areas, saving the cost of printing advertisements in every local paper without sacrificing a potentially lucrative mail-order market: 'Immoral newspaper ads have ensured that in many areas rubber devices and condoms are as well known among the country lads as among the big city playboys.'[56]

Promoters did not rely solely on the fortuitous attention of newspaper readers. Some energetic firms scoured the daily papers for notices of weddings and births, then checked the names against records in city registry offices to obtain addresses of likely prospects to whom they sent catalogues listing — and sometimes illustrating — a range of contraceptive products.[57]

Retailers sold contraceptives in medical and rubber goods stores, drug stores, pharmacies, barber shops and reform houses. Pedlars carried them to the countryside. Armed with a licence to sell housewares, pedlars loaded their carts and knapsacks with condoms, diaphragms, and Steriletts. They wandered from village to village, evading the midwives and district medical officers who might report their activities. Pedlars dropped in on rural women while their husbands were out at work in the fields. They displayed their pots and pans, asked how things were going, descried the 'tough times', and then offered a ray of hope for the long-suffering housewife. Customers who were not convinced were given a chance to try out the product and pay for it on the pedlar's next round.[58] An abortion trial in a small East Prussian village illustrates the success of these tactics. The abortionist in question was found to have an array of birth-control devices in stock, including douches, powder sprays, diaphragms and contraceptive jellies — all for a community of less than 800 people. She had obtained them from a local innkeeper who in turn had purchased them from a pedlar for the purpose of reselling them locally.[59]

Until 1900 no law specifically regulated the marketing of contraceptives. But on 25 June of that year the *Lex Heinze* came into effect, incorporating among other changes to the Criminal Code the following clause:

Whoever displays objects which are suited for obscene use in places which are accessible to the public, or who advertises or promotes such objects to the public will be punished with prison for up to one year and with fines up to 1000 Marks or with one of these penalties.[60]

Contraceptives were affected by this law because of several previous decisions by the *Reichsgericht* which had defined obscenity as 'anything which offends the public's sense of shame in a sexual sense'.[61] Contraceptives were deemed to be obscene because they circumvented the 'natural consequences' of intercourse; it did not matter whether this occurred within or without wedlock: 'In conjugal intercourse the use of rubber articles could be intended for obscene purposes wherein pleasure is enhanced while the natural consequences are evaded.'[62] Apparently the joy of sex was only for those who accepted the pain of labour.

Contraceptives which were affected by court decisions between 1900 and 1914 included condoms (which were doubly damned because the prophylactic function also encouraged 'obscene' sexual relations), diaphragms, syringes, suppositories and contraceptive jellies. Items which were arguably hygienic in basic purpose by virtue of their particular construction were not involved. But for all proscribed items the law forbade the public display or promotion of contraceptives in wholesale or retail trade. Brochures and other promotional literature could not be sent to doctors, pharmacists, druggists, wholesalers, or retailers because each of these groups constituted a 'public'. Nor could catalogues, brochures, or sample wares be sent to the general public, even if the distribution was limited to married couples. The promotion of specific contraceptives at public lectures was illegal, although talks on sex, even illustrated lectures, were acceptable. Promoters got around these provisions by advertising catalogues for 'hygienic articles'; in the catalogues they noted that other catalogues were available on request for 'items not shown here'.[63] Retailers could not display contraceptives in store windows or even within the store, nor could they post signs indicating that contraceptives were available. But the actual sale of contraceptives by retailers and by pedlars was legal on a one-to-one basis.[64]

Social networks supplemented market forces to make contraceptives available to the general public. Countryfolk who made their way to the city frequently learned about contraceptives from fellow workers, and passed the information to friends back home.[65] A singularly effective enculturating agency for men was the army. Conscription acquainted tens of thousands of young men with the prophylactic use of condoms every year. The Prussian army was especially active in this process because it preferred rural conscripts, whom it then concentrated in urban garrisons.[66] The impact of the military as a social learning experience was most pervasive during wartime: 'Knowledge of birth control seems to me to be one of the unholy fruits of 1870–71. Almost exclusively it is the men who were called up, and their friends, who have just one or two children.'[67]

The First World War had an even greater impact by virtue of the larger scale of conscription; the more widespread public awareness of birth control; and the concerted efforts of state, medical and military authorities to check the incidence of venereal disease. The War Ministry prepared informational brochures, provided condoms and prophylactic salves, and arranged for medical inspection and treatment in the barracks. Men readily transferred the use of condoms from prophylaxis to contraception; as Max Marcuse found, many admitted that they 'got smarter in the army'.[68]

Domestic service played the same educational role for young women as conscription did for men. Thirty per cent of working women in the late nineteenth century were domestic servants. Most of them came from rural or small-town backgrounds. In the cities they learned to emulate the values and lifestyle of their employers. In the process they became acquainted with a broad range of consumer goods, including the 'hygienic' devices belonging to their mistresses. The need that they felt to maintain their single status persuaded many of them to adopt contraception.[69]

Medical personnel were another important source of contraceptive information and equipment. In rural areas midwives sold diaphragms and chemical contraceptives, and inserted intra-uterine devices for fees ranging from 10 to 40 Marks. In the cities some doctors provided contraceptives or performed sterilisation. Women from the city and the country soon learned which doctors were willing to provide assistance; rural women sometimes preferred to go to the city for the sake of anonymity.[70]

Not all doctors were sympathetic to birth control, however. Some questioned whether there was 'any difference between coitus where the genitals are covered with rubber or chemicals and anal intercourse'. Others wondered whether it was a sign of progress to 'become enslaved to sponges and sheaths'.[71] Part of the problem was that doctors seldom received any birth-control instruction in medical school, and their lack of knowledge redounded to the disadvantage of their patients. Women reported 'thousands of times' that doctors would advise them to avoid further pregnancy, yet when asked how to accomplish this they would respond only with a shrug.[72]

Professional ignorance might also be wilful. The older generation renounced any medical role in birth control:

> To say anything from a medical perspective about contraception other than a loud 'Pfui!' was until recently considered professionally unworthy. Distinguished doctors declined to do anything in response to the wishes of their patients because this was considered beyond the bounds of their expertise, the purpose of which was simply to heal.[73]

Beyond narrow professional concerns lay a larger social perspective. Doctors were keenly aware of the high social standing of their profession, and regarded birth control as immoral and therefore inappropriate. As Dr Paul Zweifel stated at the 1900 meeting of the Leipzig Society for Obstetrics:

> It is thus clear that the use of contraceptives of any sort can only serve lust, and every doctor, out of concern for public opinion, must not place himself in the position of abetting such behaviour. Whoever does so forfeits the respect of society.[74]

These doctors had little respect for women who wanted to control fertility for social reasons: 'A German mother should be proud to raise her child, even if she must give up a party or two.'[75]

Opponents of birth control also pointed to the drastic political, economic, social and military impact which widespread birth control portended.

> As the son of my Fatherland, whose military capacity would be ruined by such illegal, degenerate practices; as a German man, who still has a glimmer of respect for the divine and natural duties of women; as a counsellor to a strong *Volk* which rejects and condemns cowardice in the struggle for survival; I stand against this decrepid Malthusian egoism. I protest against such a view of the joys and duties of conjugal life. All Christian husbands should realise that these practices lead not to stronger marital bonds but to the morality of the brothel.[76]

A second school within the medical profession argued for the acceptance of birth control on therapeutic indications. In a tradition starting with Wilde and continuing past Mensinga into the twentieth century, these doctors argued that contraception was simpler and safer than abortion in cases where the health or life of the woman was threatened, and ought to be the preferred option, supplemented by sterilisation in extreme cases.[77] But such therapeutic birth control should remain under strict medical supervision; these doctors resented the loss of control over patients which easy access to commercial contraceptives made possible: 'If the medical profession could develop an effective and practical method which as much as possible could only be applied by doctors, the whole sad story of contraception could be brought under proper control.'[78]

Finally, a growing number of doctors supported birth control on demand for all who wanted it for whatever reason, arguing that women were 'more than baby machines'. These physicians argued that, far from being immoral, birth control demonstrated 'the elevation of ordinary morality', as parents adjusted family size to their social and economic circumstances. Doctors should aid them in this effort: 'This is not a medical question, it is a human question.'[79] In 1898 the *Deutsche Medicinische Presse* published a discussion on the topic of birth control in which the majority of correspondents favoured social indications for birth control. For other doctors, birth control was acceptable simply as part of the new sexual morality which they saw taking shape in the new century. And besides, doctors were the last ones who should complain: 'Has anyone seen a colleague lately with eight or ten children?'[80]

Doctors involved with the Health Insurance Programme were especially likely to be sympathetic to birth control:

> The thundering Philippics against any awareness of contraception among the public prompts me to discuss this topic. They consider it to be the moral duty of women to bear children until the uterus wears out. I have seen the consequences of this in my Health Insurance practice. The good colleagues speak of the ruin of military capability. They should look sometime at the number of recruits rejected each year for poor health; wouldn't it be better to have fewer but healthier men?[81]

As the preceding comment suggests, the Health Insurance Programme played a positive role in the distribution of contraception to the working class. Starting in the 1890s Insurance Funds in the larger cities initiated prophylactic measures in an effort to reduce soaring costs for treatment. They promoted public awareness of health and disease with lectures, demonstrations and publications. Funds provided free prophylactics and contraceptives to members. The popular acceptance of these activities was facilitated by the fact that members were allowed to vote for representatives on the boards of directors of local Funds, and these positions quickly came under socialist control. The Social Democrats used these positions to promote programmes of benefit to workers, and to ensure that the physicians retained by the Funds were sympathetic to the needs of workers.[82]

The activity of the Health Insurance Programme to distribute contraceptives was supplemented by three political movements which independently promoted the practice of birth control. Although each organisation targeted different social groups and presented its message in its own ideological guise, all contributed to the growing public awareness of contraceptives and all accelerated popular acceptance of birth control.

In February 1892, a small circle of doctors, teachers and civil servants met in Stuttgart at the suggestion of the banker Max Hausmeister to discuss Neo-Malthusianism. They decided to establish the Social-Harmony Union in order to promote awareness of the lessons of political economy in general, and in particular to further public understanding of the population question. Like Neo-Malthusians elsewhere, Hausmeister advocated the proper coordination of income, lifestyle and family size as the answer to the 'social question'.

> The conflict between marriage and upward mobility is due simply to the lack of family planning, and would cease if couples took matters in their own hands and decided when to have children. If the blessings of Neo-Malthusianism were only known and accepted, the resulting decrease in children would raise wages and lower costs. The foolish strife between capital and labour would end, and both would be better off.[83]

The Union published a paper, *Social Harmony*, and distributed a pamphlet, 'The Methods of Preventing Conception', which contained a discussion of the population question, a review of contraceptives and advice on where to obtain them. The pamphlet was given to doctors on request and to married couples who agreed to inform the Union of their success with birth control (few did). The medical consultant to the Union, Dr Eugen Bilfinger, conducted a lecture tour throughout Germany which helped to spread the message. But after the turn of the century the Union could no longer compete with other institutions promoting birth control which avoided the bourgeois proselytising associated with 'social harmony'. The Union folded in 1911.[84]

The Social Democratic Party (SPD) played an important if ambivalent role in the diffusion of birth control within the working class. SPD educational programmes encouraged rationalism at the expense of tradition and custom. Starting in the 1890s, local SPD organisations sponsored courses and lectures on topics of interest to workers. By 1913 there were nearly 800 local education committees which offered more than 400 courses and 600 lectures that were attended by 220,000 workers. SPD locals also operated 1,147 workers' libraries which stocked thousands of books, not all of them on socialist ideology.[85]

Socialists naturally rejected the Malthusian analysis of proletarian fecundity as the cause of working-class poverty, and blamed the capitlist system instead. They consequently rejected Neo-Malthusian notions of individual self-help through family limitation. Yet Social Democrats could not help but be aware of the dire living conditions of many workers; to suggest that they wait for the Revolution before seeking help seemed callous. In practice, therefore, the SPD contributed to the spread of birth control in several ways. The Party published a 'Workers' Health Library' which included pamphlets on contraception. Local education committees sponsored lectures on sex, female hygiene, birth control and venereal disease. One frequent lecturer was Frau Alma Wartenburg of Hamburg, who was eventually indicted for giving a public lecture with slides illustrating contraceptive techniques; her activities prompted a Centrist Deputy in the Prussian *Landtag* to denounce her as 'more dangerous than a wild animal'. Party newspapers reported the heated debate over the 'Birth Strike' issue in 1913, in which socialist physicians led by Alfred Bernstein and Julius Moses advocated 'birth control as a tactical weapon of the proletariat'. And in the *Reichstag* the party consistently opposed legislative attempts to restrict access to birth control.[86]

Feminism provided further ideological support for birth control. Internal wrangling within the Federation of German Women's Associations over proper tactics in the fight against police regulation of prostitution spawned a radical group of feminists who advocated a libertarian sexual morality that downplayed marriage and emphasised the right of women to a full and unencumbered sex life. Contraception and even abortion were seen as essential prerequisites for this new morality. The vehicle for the radical feminists was the League for the Protection of Motherhood, an organisation that attracted widespread left-liberal support for its work on behalf of unwed mothers. The League provided counselling for young mothers and established maternity homes in larger cities where single mothers and their children could receive care.[87]

The League's mandate transcended welfare, however, for it also sought to prevent unwed motherhood by promoting birth control through public lectures. Helene Stöcker, director of the League, participated in the 1911 International Neo-Malthusian Congress in Dresdsen. The League fought against attempts in the *Reichstag* to outlaw contraceptives. But a similar campaign against the abortion laws backfired; most League members were not ready to support the legalisation of abortion, and the issue split the organisation.[88]

The efforts of the League merged gradually with the similar efforts of several other sex-reform organisations that arose on the basis of a new social science, sexology, which orginated with the pioneering work of Krafft-Ebing and Freud and which was quickly popularised by Iwan Bloch, Max Marcuse, Albert Moll and Havelock Ellis. In addition to the League, sex reformers founded the Society for Sex Reform and the Medical Society for Sexology. Several journals appeared, including *Sex and Society, Yearbook for Sexual Intermediates, Motherhood, New Generation, Sexual Problems* and the *Journal for Sexology*. Together they contributed to the growing public awareness of sexual issues and the 'right to control one's body'.[89]

The battle waged by these organisations to promote modern birth control achieved partial success by 1914. On the eve of the First World War most people in most areas had heard of contraceptives, and many people from all classes and regions used them. Failure to use modern contraceptives stemmed from psychological resistance or economic constraint.

Young people often put off use of contraceptives in the belief that 'nothing will happen'. Country folk, especially Catholics, regarded mechanical and chemical products as artificial, unnatural, and immoral:

In the country one doesn't know as much as in the city.

One doesn't talk about such things in the country.

They do that in the city — it's not our custom.[90]

Yet others who learned of the new techniques regretted their earlier ignorance: 'I won't be such a dumb wretch again.'[91]

'Male chauvinism' also delayed the popular acceptance of contraception. This was the first generation that had heard of sex education, let alone experienced it; many men and women remained ignorant of their own physiology, not to mention that of their spouses. Tradition-minded men resisted any constraint on their own sexual pleasure; for them birth control, if it was practised at all, was 'women's business':

I don't concern myself with that.

I don't want to know.

What my wife did, I don't know.

Women know what to do.[92]

In such relationships birth control might be implemented by the woman acting alone, with or without the knowledge of the husband. Diaphragms, cervical caps and intra-uterine devices were often marketed with the claim that they could be used by women alone.[93]

For many people who knew of contraceptives, financial considerations delayed their use. Some of the mechanical devices required accurate measurement and proper insertion, and this involved regular fees for a doctor or midwife. Chemical products and condoms entailed constant expenses which could strain working-class budgets, although it could just as easily prompt a couple to switch from one modern method to another that was equally safe but less expensive. Women who were advised against pregnancy on therapeutic grounds received contraceptives free from the Health Insurance Programme.[94] And for those women who knew of modern contraception and who accepted the principle of birth control but who, for whatever reason, were unable to use modern contraceptives consistently and successfully, these same years saw the development of effective methods of abortion. Once they experienced the certainty of birth control which abortion provided, these women would switch over to contraception, secure in the knowledge that abortion was always available as back-up.

NOTES

1. Norman Himes, *Medical history of contraception* (Gamut Press, New York, 1936, reprinted 1963), p. 187; David Glass and E. Grebenik, 'World population, 1800–1950', in H.J. Habakkuk and M. Postan (eds), *Cambridge economic history of Europe*, vol. VI: *The industrial revolutions and after: Incomes, population and technological change* (Cambridge University Press, Cambridge, 1965), pp. 116–17, 118n; Dr Jorns, 'Zur willkürlichen Beschränkung der Geburtenzahl', *ZMB*, 24 (1911), p. 53; O. Krohne,

'Empfängnisverhütung, künstliche Unfruchtbarkeit und Schwangerschaftsunterbrechung vom bevölkerungspolitischen und ärztlichen Standpunkt', *ZAF*, 14 (1917), p. 343; James Reed, *From private vice to public virtue: the birth control movement and American society since 1830* (Basic Books, New York, 1978), pp. 13-15; John Peel, 'The manufacturing and retailing of contraceptives in England', *PS*, 17 (1963), pp. 114-17.

2. Angus McLaren, *Birth Control in nineteenth century England: a social and intellectual history* (Holmes and Meier, New York, 1978), pp. 43, 51-2; Angus McLaren, 'Contraception and the working classes; the social ideology of the English birth control movement in its early years', *CSSH*, 18 (1976), pp. 237-44; H.A. Boner, *Hungry generations: the nineteenth century case against Malthusianism* (King's Crown, New York, 1955), pp. 128-30, 158-60; Rosanna Ledbetter, *A history of the Malthusian League, 1877-1927* (Ohio State University Press, Columbus, 1976),pp. 6-8, 13-19, 25; Joseph Banks, *Victorian values: secularism and size of families* (Routledge and Kegan Paul, London, 1981); Oscar Wingen, *Die Bevölkerungstheorien der letzten Jahre* (Cotta, Berlin, 1915), p. 195.

3. Ledbetter, *History, passim*; McLaren, 'Contraception', p. 244; McLaren, *Birth control*, p. 107; F.H. Amphlett-Micklewright, 'Rise and decline of English Neo-Malthusianism', *PS*, 15 (1961), pp. 36-9.

4. Gustav Rümelin, 'Zur Übervölkerungsfrage' in his *Reden und Schriften, Neue Folge* (Mohr, Freiburg, 1881), p. 569; see also John Knodel, 'Law, marriage and illegitimacy in nineteenth-century Germany', *PS*, 20 (1967), pp. 279-82. On the political economist Gustav Rümelin see Gustav Schmoller, 'Gustav Rümelin', in Gustav Schmoller, *Charakterbilder* (Duncker and Humblot, Munich, 1913), pp. 141-88; and James Sheehan, *German liberalism in the nineteenth century* (University of Chicago Press, Chicago, 1978), p. 197.

5. Gustav Rümelin, 'Über die Malthus'schen Lehren' in his *Reden und Aufsätze* (Laup, Tübingen, 1875), pp. 308-10.

6. Rümelin, 'Übervölkerungsfrage', pp. 608, 612-14. See also Otto Zacharias, *Die Bevölkerungsfrage in ihrer Beziehung zu den sociale Notständen der Gegenwart*, 4th edn (Mauke, Jena, 1883), pp. 75-6; Jakob Stern, *Unbeschränkte Volksvermehrung* (Scheible, Stuttgart, 1883), pp. 6, 30-2, 50. German attention was drawn to English developments in part by Gustav Stille's translation of Annie Besant's *Law of population* under the title, *Das Gesetz der Bevölkerung* (Luckhardt, Berlin, 1881).

7. Gustav Stille, *Der Neo-malthusianismus, das Heilmittel der Pauperismus* (Luckhardt, Berlin, 1880), p. 12; Rümelin, 'Übervölkerungsfrage', pp. 612-14; Fritz Baum, *Über den praktischen Malthusianismus, Neo-Malthusianismus, und Sozialdarwinismus* (Schmersow, Leipzig, 1928), p. 69.

8. Zacharias, *Bevölkerungsfrage*, p. 16.

9. Ibid., p. 73.

10. Stille, *Neo-Malthusianismus*, p. 68; Ledbetter, *History*, p. 123.

11. H. Gerlach, *Die Einschränkung der Kinderzahl durch Verhütung der Empfängnis* (Cassirer and Danziger, Berlin, 1893), p. 27; A. Grotjahn, *Geburtenrückgang und Geburtenregelungim Lichte des Individuellen und der sozialen Hygiene* (Marcus, Berlin, 1914), p. 242; Reed, *Private vice*, p. 15; Peel, 'Manufacturing', p. 117; Johann Karl Proksch, *Die Vorbauung der*

Venerischen Krankheiten vom sanitätspolitischen, ärztlichen und padägogischen Standpunkt aus betrachtet (Medicinisch-Chirurgische Centralblatt, Vienna, 1872), pp. 50-1. On the manufacture of condoms see also Dr Bertherand and Dr Duchesne, 'Des préservatifs, de leur fabrication et de leur influence sur le dévéloppement de la maladie vénériènne', *Lyon Medicale*, 9 (1877), pp. 269-72. On the rubber industry in Germany see Julius Ausbüttel, 'Die deutsche Kautschukwarenindustrie' Phd dissertation, University of Würzburg, 1922.

12. Friedrich Hinz, *Der Wert der antikonzeptionellen Mittel* (Konegen, Leipzig, 1898) p. 353; Grotjahn, *Geburtenrückgang*, pp. 101-2. See also Ludwig Fraenkel, *Die Empfängnisverhütung* (Enke, Stuttgart, 1932), pp. 136-7. The quality of condoms improved to the extent that they were subject to government inspection. In the United States the Food and Drug Administration began checking on quality in 1938: Robert L. Dickinson and L.S. Bryant, *The Control of Conception*, 2nd edn (Williams and Wilkins, 1938), p. 125; Reed, *Private vice*, p. 244; Christopher Tietze, 'History of contraceptive techniques', *Journal of Sex Research*, 1 (1965), pp. 70-1. Faced with domestic controls, some manufacturers dumped inferior products on the foreign market: H. Sjovall, 'Abortion and contraception in Sweden, 1870-1970', *Zeitschrift für Rechtsmedizin*, 70 (1972), pp. 197-209.

13. Grotjahn, *Geburtenrückgang*, p. 102; Gerlach, *Einschränkung*, p. 27; Roderick Hellmann, *Über Geschlechtsfreiheit* (Staude, Berlin, 1878), p. 206; Hans Ferdy, *Die Mittel zur Verhütung der Conception*, 8th edn (Max Spohr, Leipzig, 1907), p. 119; Fraenkel, *Empfängnisverhutung*, pp. 136-7, 139; Otto von Franqué, *Geburtenrückgang, Arzt, und Geburtshelfer*, (Abhandlungen aus dem Gesamtgebiet der praktischen Medizin, Würzburg, 1916), p. 103; Artur Streich, 'Zur Geschichte des Condoms', *Sudhoffs Archiv für Geschichte der Medizin*, 22 (1929), p. 210.

14. Grotjahn, *Geburtenrückgang*, p. 101; Fraenkel, *Empfängnisverhütung*, p. 137; Anne-Marie Durand-Wever, 'Die ärztlichen Erfahrungen über medizinisch indizierte Konzeptionsverhütung', *MW*, 5 (1931), p. 759; Magnus Hirschfeld and Richard Linsert, *Empfängnisverhütung: Mittel und Methoden* (Neuer deutscher Verlag, Berlin, 1928), pp. 38, 40; Manfred Stürzbecher, 'Die Bekämkpfung des Geburtenrückganges und der Säuglingssterblichkeit im Spiegel der Reichstagsdebatten, 1900-1930' PhD dissertation, University of Berlin, 1954, p. 131.

15. Max Marcuse, 'Zur Frage der Verbreitung und Methodik der willkurlichen Geburtenbeschrankung in Berliner Proletarierkreisen', *SP*, 9 (1913), case nos. 79, 100; Bauer, 'Kritik', p. 964; Hermann Gebhardt, *Zur Bäuerlichen Glaubens- und Sittenlehre*, 3rd edn (Gustav Schlossmann, Gotha, 1895), p. 101; Allgemeine Konferenz der Deutschen Sittlichkeitsvereine, *Die geschlechtlich-sittlichen Verhältnisse der evangelischen Landbewohner im Deutschen Reiche*, ed. C. Wagner (2 vols, Reinhold Werther, Leipzig, 1895-6), vol. II, p. 598; Fritz Meder, 'Die Konzeptionsverhütung in der Hand des freipraktizierenden Arztes', *ZGyn*, 55 (1931), p. 2563; Robert Engelsmann, 'Die Ursache des Geburtenrückganges', PhD dissertation, University of Münster, 1937, p. 143. Cf. Ronald Lesthaeghe, *The decline of Belgian fertility, 1800-1970* (Princeton University Press, Princeton, 1977), p. 136.

16. Mensinga quoted by Magnus Hirschfeld, *Geschlechtskunde* (2 vols, Püttmann, Stuttgart, 1926-7), vol. II, p. 441; Wilhelm Mensinga, *Facultative*

Sterilität, 2nd edn (Heuser, Neuwied; 1885), p. 30.

17. Gerlach, *Einschränkung*, pp. 24-6; Olga Zschommler, *Malthusianismus: Verhütung der Empfängnis und ihre gesundheitlichen Folgen* (Wilhem Möller, Berlin, 1891), p. 22; Grotjahn, *Geburtenrückgang*, p. 242; Fraenkel, *Empfängnisverhütung*, p. 142; Le Mon Clark, *The vaginal diaphragm* (Mosby, St Louis, 1936).

18. Ferdy, *Mittel*, pp. 91-2; Ulrich Linse, 'Arbeiterschaft und Geburtenentwicklung im deutschen Kaiserreich vom 1871', *ASG*, 12 (1972), p. 226; Gebhardt, *Sittenlehre*, pp. 123-5; Allgemeine Konferenz, *Verhältnisse*, vol. I, p. 119, vol. II, pp. 43, 121; Jean Bornträger, *Der Geburtenrückgang in Deutschland: seine Bewertung und seine Bekämpfung* (Kabitzsch, Würzburg, 1913), p. 53; Theresa McBride, *The domestic revolution* (Holmes and Meier, New York, 1976), p. 12.

19. F. Lehmann, 'Über Antikonzeptionelle Mittel', *BKW*, 46 (1909), p. 879; Sarwey, 'Indikationen', p. 294; Durand-Wever, 'Erfahrungen', p. 937; Hirschfeld and Linsert, *Empfängnisverhütung*, p. 26; Fraenkel, *Empfängnisverhütung*, pp. 140-3; R. Gall, *Ein neues Ballon Occlusiv-Pessar* (Seitz and Schauer, Munich, 1895); Dr Matrisalus, *Den Frauen Schutz!* (Spohr, Leipzig, 1897).

20. Mensinga, *Facultative Sterilität*, p. 30; Ferdy, *Mittel*, p. 95; Hinz, *Wert*, pp. 352-3; Baum, *Künstliche Beschränkung*, p. 60; Zschommler, *Malthusianismus*, p. 26.

21. Carl Capellmann, *Facultative Sterilität ohne Verletzung der Sittengeschichte* (Barth, Aachen, 1884); H. Otto, *Künstliche Unfruchtbarkeit des Weibes*, 1st edn (Heuser, Leipzig, 1884).

22. Friedrich Wilde, *Das Weibliche Gebär-Unvermögen* (Nicolai'sche Verlag, Berlin, 1838), pp. 317-18; Siegfried Scholz, 'Medizinische Geschichte der Empfängnisverhütung', PhD dissertation, University of Munich, 1969, p. 37.

23. Karl Kafka, 'Die Adhäsions-Modellkappe', *WMW*, 58 (1908), pp. 1245-8; Karl Kafka, 'Über Kappenbehandlung', *WMW* 58 (1908), pp. 2272-4; Fraenkel, *Empfängnisverhütung*, pp. 143-5; Hans Lehfeldt, 'Contraceptive methods requiring medical assistance', in World League for Sexual Reform, *Proceedings of the third Congress*, ed. Norman Haire (Kegan Paul, London 1929), p. 130.

24. Kafka, 'Adhäsions-Modellkappe', p. 1248; Bauer, 'Kritik', p. 1005; J. Ferro, *Verhütung der Schwangerschaft* (Rudolphsche Verlagsbuchhandlung, Dresden, 1930), p. 50.

25. M. Graefe, 'Über die Gefahren der Intrauterinpessare', *Der Frauenarzt*, 29 (1914), p. 484. See also Heinrich Gesenius, 'Die Gefährlichkeit der Intrauterinpessare', *ZGyn*, 59 (1935), pp. 2169-70. On the nineteenth century experience with intra-uterine devices see Dr Hartwig, 'Ein neues Intrauterinpessar', *BKW*, 11 (1874), pp. 351-2; J. Holst, 'Conception während Behandlung mit Intrauterinpessar', *AGyn*, 6 (1874), pp. 510-11; Heinrich Fritsch, *Lageveränderungen und die Entzündungen der Gebärmutter* (Enke, Stuttgart, 1885); George Bantock, *On the use and abuse of pessaries*, 2nd edn (H.K. Lewis, London, 1884).

26. Dr Keferstein, 'Verurteilung eines praktischen Arztes wegen fahrlässiger Körperverletzung in fünf Fällen durch Einlegen eines von ihm erfundenen besonderen Intra-Uterin-Pessars als Frauenschutz', *ZGyn*, 26

(1902), pp. 609-14; Graefe, 'Gefahren', pp. 482-3; Gesenius, 'Gefährlichkeit', p. 2170.

27. Lehmann, 'Antikonzeptionelle Mittel', p. 879; Kantor, 'Geburtenrückgang und Kurpfuscherei', *TM*, 30 (1916), p. 567; Durand-Wever, 'Erfahrungen', p. 936; R. Richter, 'Ein Mittel zur Verhütung der Konzeption', *DMW*, 35 (1909), pp. 1525-7.

28. Referat von Dr Knoop, 'Sitzungsbericht, Niederrheinisch-westfälische Gesellschaft für Gynäkologie', *MGG*, 39 (1913), p. 410-12.

29. Referat von Dr Gummert, 'Sitzungbericht, p. 417. See also Dr Streit, 'Diskussion', ibid., pp. 441-2; Graefe, 'Gefahren', pp. 482-3; Gesenius, 'Gefährlichkeit', pp. 2168-70; Jorns, 'Willkürlichen Beschränkung', p. 55; Dr Hanssen, 'Die Abnahme der Geburtenzahlen in den verschiedenen Bevölkerungsklassen und ihre Ursachen', *ASHD*, 7 (1912), p. 395; V. Ohnesorge, 'Gefahren der intrauterinen "Schutzmittel"', *ZGyn*, 59 (1935), pp. 875-80.

30. Gummert, 'Referat', pp. 418-21; Graefe, 'Gefahren', pp. 484-6; Dr Liek, 'Über Fremdkörper in Uterus als Mittel zur Verhütung der Konzeption', *DMW*, 37 (1911), pp. 880-1.

31. Hinz, *Wert*, p. 351; Bauer, 'Kritik', p. 1002; Fraenkel, *Empfängnisverhütung*, pp. 112-13; Dickinson and Bryant, *Control of Conception*, p. 62; Tassilo Antoine, 'Über Konzeptionsverhütung und Sterilisation', *WMW*, 81 (1931), p. 1371; Linda Gordon, *Woman's body, Woman's right: a social history of birth control in America* (Grossman, New York, 1976), p. 42; Cecil Voge, *The Chemistry and physics of contraception* (Jonathan Cape, London, 1933), pp. 82, 195; S. Bruce Schearer, 'The status of technology for contraception' in John Money and Herman Musaph (eds), *Handbook of Sexology*, (Excepta Medica, New York, 1977), p. 590.

32. Gerlach, *Einschränkung*, p. 23; Lehmann, 'Antikonzeptionelle Mittel', p. 878; Grotjahn, *Geburtenrückgang*, pp. 74-7; Kantor, 'Geburtenrückgang', pp. 567-8; Bauer, 'Kritik', p. 1002.

33. Grotjahn, *Geburtenrückgang*, pp.74-5; Kantor, 'Geburtenrückgang', p. 568; Hinz, *Wert*, pp. 350-1; Sarwey, 'Über Indikationen und Methoden der fakultativen Sterilisierung der Frau, *DMW*, 31 (1905), p. 294; Fraenkel, *Empfängnisverhütung*, p. 114.

34. Although *bona fide* manufacturers did not record the ingredients of their products on labels, they did satisfy the requirement for disclosure by listing ingredients in the relevant pharmaceutical registers, such as *Gehe's Codex der Bezeichnungen von Arzneimitteln, kosmetischen Präparaten und wichtigen technischen Produkten*, or *Riedel's Mentor für die Namen, sowie für die Zusammensetzung, Eigenschaften und Anwendung neuerer Arzneimittel, Spezialitäten, und wichtigerer technischer Produkte*. On the problems of inactive ingredients see Hirschfeld and Linsert, *Empfängnisverhütung*, 8th edn (1932), p. 8, and Martha Ruben-Wolf, *Abtreibung oder Verhutung*, 5th edn (International Arbeiter-Verlag, Berlin, 1931), p. 12.

35. Hinz, *Wert*, pp. 350-1; Voge, *Chemistry*, pp. 189, 192, 197-8; Ludwig Fraenkel, 'Sterilisierung und Konzeptionsverhütung', *AGyn* 144 (1931), p. 116.

36. Grotjahn, *Geburtenrückgang*, pp. 74-5; Antoine, 'Konzeptionsverhütung', p. 1372; Fraenkel, *Empfängnisverhütung*, pp. 113-14; Voge, *Chemistry*, pp. 82, 215; O. Pankow, 'Künstliche Sterilisierung', in Josef

Halban and Ludwig Seitz (eds), *Biologie und Pathologie des Weibes* (Urban and Schwarzenberg, Berlin, 1929), vol. III, p. 898; J. Linkner, 'Die Empfängnisverhütung im Lichte der Geschichte', *MW*, 49 (1962), p. 2637.

37. Gustav Günther, 'Über Spermengifte', *Pflugers Archiv für die gesamte Physiologie*, 118 (1907), pp. 551-70; Ruben-Wolf, *Abtreibung*, p. 12.

38. K. Fecht, 'Über die Gefahren der chemischen Mittel zur Schwangerschaftsverhütung', *MMW*, 81 (1934), p. 1764; Antoine, 'Konzeptionsverhütung', p. 1372.

39. Sarwey, 'Indikationen', p. 295; A. Hamm, 'Indikation zur Sterilisierung des Weibes', *MK*, 9 (1913), p. 1422; Rudolf Schreiner, 'Zur Frage der künstliche Sterilisierung der Frau', *ZGyn*, 51 (1927), p. 628.

40. Enoch Kisch, *The sexual life of woman in its physiological, pathological and hygienic aspects*, trans. Eden Paul (Rebman, New York, 1910), pp. 487, 564; Schearer, 'Status', pp. 598-9.

41. Pankow, 'Künstliche Sterilisierung', pp. 901-7; Frederick Taussig, *Abortion, spontaneous and induced* (Mosby, St Louis, 1936), pp. 344-8; Schreiner, 'Frage', pp. 627-9; F.A. Kehrer, 'Sterilisation mittels Tubendurchschneidung', *ZGyn*, 21 (1897), p. 961; Carl Günther, 'Über operative Sterilisation durch Tubenresektion', PhD dissertation, University of Leipzig, 1901; Ernst Isenberg, 'Über die Methoden der künstlichen Sterilisierung des Weibes', PhD dissertation, University of Tübingen, 1911; Wilhelm Hohmann, 'Die künstliche Sterilisierung des Weibes', PhD dissertation, University of Heidelberg, 1910; Hans Naujoks, *Die Technik der Sterilisierung und Kastration* (Enke, Stuttgart, 1934), pp. 22-5.

42. Manfred Fraenkel, *Die Röntgenstrahlen in der Gynäkologie* (Schoetz, Berlin, 1911); L. Fraenkel, *Unfruchtbarmachung durch Roentgenstrahlen bei Verbrechern und Geisteskranken* (Langenscheidt, Berlin, 1914); A. Hirsch, 'Zur Frage der Roentgenbiologie der Ovarien, insbesondere in generativer und eugenetischer Hinsicht', *AFk*, 11 (1925), pp. 377-97; L. Fraenkel, 'Sterilisierung', pp. 97-9.

43. Pankow, 'Künstliche Sterilisierung', p. 859; J.R. Spinner, *Aerztliches Recht* (Springer, Berlin, 1914), p. 190; K. von Lilienthal, 'Künstliche Fehlgeburt und künstliche Unfruchtbarkeit vom Standpunkte des Rechtes', in Siegfried Placzek (ed.), *Künstliche Fehlgeburt und künstliche Unfruchtbarkeit: ihre Indikationen, Technik und Rechtslage* (Thieme, Leipzig, 1918),p. 401; Andreas Hanslmeier, 'Die operative Sterilisation bei der Frau und ihre Erfolg', PhD dissertation, University of Munich, 1927, p. 4; Schreiner, 'Frage', pp. 627-9.

44. Spinner, *Aerztliches Recht*, pp. 186-7, 305-7; Lilienthal, 'Künstliche Fehlgeburt', p. 401; Ludwig Ebermayer, *Arzt und patient in der Rechtsprechung* (Mosse, Berlin, 1925), p. 170; Ludwig Ebermayer, *Fünfzig Jahre Dienst am Recht* (Grethlein, Leipzig, 1930), p. 120; Dr Marx, 'Sind nach dem herrschenden Strafrechtspraxis Sterilisierungsoperationen mit Einwilligung des Operierten straflos?', *ZMB*, 39 (1926),pp. 114-16; August Mayer, 'Medizinisch-juristische Grenzfragen zur operativen Sterilisierung', *MGG*, 90 (1932),pp. 101-2.

45. Marx, 'Strafrechtspraxis', pp. 114-15; Ebermayer, *Fünfzig Jahre*, pp. 120-1; Mayer, 'Grenzfragen', pp. 125-6.

46. Spinner, *Aerztliches Recht*, p. 310 Hamm, 'Indikation', p. 1422; Georg Winter, 'Künstliche Sterilisation der Frau', *DMW*, 46 (1920),

pp. 1–3; Ernst Schwab, 'Technik und Indikationen der künstlichen Sterilisation der Frau', PhD dissertation, University of Freiburg, 1908; David Scherschewer, 'Über die Sterilisation bei tuberkulösen Schwangeren, PhD dissertation, University of Berlin, 1909; Ernst Wetzel, 'Die künstliche Sterilisation der Frau', PhD dissertation, University of Würzburg, 1913, pp. 6, 14–19.

47. Lehmann, 'Antikonzeptionelle Mittel', p. 876; Max Hirsch, 'Über die rassenhygienische Indikation in der gynäkologischen Praxis', *MGG*, 38, (1913), pp. 562–5, 575; Mayer, 'Grenzfragen', p. 107. On sterilisation and eugenics elsewhere see McLaren, *Birth control*, Ch. 8; Gordon, *Woman's body*, Chs 6, 7; Kenneth Ludmerer, *Genetics and American society: a historical appraisal* (Johns Hopkins University Press, Baltimore, 1972), pp. 7–8; E.S. Gosney and Paul Popenoe, *Sterilization for human betterment: a summary of results of 6,000 operations in California 1919–29* (Human Betterment Society, New York, 1930).

48. Geza von Hoffmann, *Die Rassenhygiene in den Vereinigten Staaten von Nordamerika* (1913), cited in Mayer, 'Grenzfragen', p. 107; Friedrich Gerngross, *Sterilisation und Kastration als Heilmittel im Kampfe gegen das Verbrechen* (Lehmann, Munich, 1913); Karl Binding and Alfred Hoche, *Die Freigabe der Vernichtung lebensunwerten Lebens: ihr Mass und ihre Form* (Meiner, Leipzig, 1920).

49. Hamm, 'Indikationen', p. 1424.

50. August Hegar, 'Beitrag zur Frage der Sterilisierung aus rassenhygienischen Gründen', *MMW*, 60 (1913), p. 244.

51. A. Haberda, 'Gerichtsärztliche Erfahrungen über die Fruchtabtreibung in Wien', *VGMOS*, 56 (1914), p. 169; Alfred Ploetz, 'Neomalthusianismus und Rassenhygiene', *ARGB*, 10 (1913), pp. 169–71; W. Strohmayer, 'Zur Frage der künstliche Sterilisierung der Frau aus eugenischer Indikation', *DMW*, 46 (1920), p. 387; Alfred Grotjahn, *Die Hygiene der menschlichen Fortpflanzung: Versuch einer praktischer Eugenik* (Urban and Schwarzenberg, Berlin, 1926), pp. 24–5, 103, 127. Dr Haberda was not alone in his opinion; J.B.S. Haldane called compulsory sterilisation a 'piece of crude Americanism' in 1938: Geoffrey Searle, *Eugenics and politics in Britain, 1900–1914* (Noordhoff International, Leyden, 1976), p. 94.

52. Ebermayer, *Fünfzig Jahre*, p. 122. See also Mayer, 'Grenzfragen', pp. 102–3; Marx, 'Strafrechtspraxis', pp. 115–16; Dr Boeters, 'Sind nach dem herrschenden Strafrechtspraxis Sterilisierungsoperationen mit Einwilligung der Operierten straflos?', *ZMB*, 39 (1926), pp. 217–21; Dr Offergeld, 'Über die Bewertung des "sozialen Faktors" in der Indikationsstellung zur tubaren Sterilisation der Frau', *Würzburger Abhandlungen aus dem Gesamtgebiet der praktischen Medizin*, 11 (1911), p. 105; Otto von Franqué, 'Künstliche Sterilisierung und Geburtenrückgang', *MMW*, 64 (1917), p. 1040; Hamm, 'Indikationen', p. 1422–4; Pankow, 'Steriliserung', p. 862. Dr Dührssen was one of the first to endorse social indications for sterilisation: Hans Ferdy, *Sittliche Selbstbeschränkung* (Verfasser, Hildesheim, 1904), p. 151).

53. Krohne, 'Empfängnisverhütung', p. 344. See also O. Krohne, 'Künstliche Fehlgeburt und künstliche Unfruchtbarkeit vom Standpunkt des Staatsinteresse', in Placzek (ed.), *Künstliche Fehlgeburt*, pp. 370–1, 378–9; G. Winter, 'Sollen wir Bevölkerungspolitik treiben?', *MGG*, 47 (1918), p. 356.

54. Carl Reissig, 'Geheimmittelschwindel und Geschlechtsleben in der Annonce', *Aerztliche Vereinsblatt Deutschland*, 36–8 (1909), p. 10. See also Kriege, 'Abnahme', p. 48.
55. Reissig, 'Geheimmittelschwindel', pp. 10–11.
56. C. Wagner, *Die Sittlichkeit auf dem Lande*, 4th edn. Reinhold Werther, Leipzig, 1896), p. 73. See also Dr Hanssen, 'Die Abnahme der Geburtenzahlen in den verschiedenen Bevölkerungsklassen und ihre Ursachen', *ASHD*, 7 (1912), pp. 394–5; Bornträger, *Geburtenrückgang*, p. 48; Witting and König, 'Der Geburtenrückgang im Bezirk Marienwerder und seine Ursachen', *ZMB*, 26 (1913), Supplement 1, p. 161; Krohne, 'Künstliche Fehlgeburt', p. 369; Ann Taylor Allen, 'Sex and satire in Wilhelmian Germany: "Simplicissimus" looks at family life', *Journal of European Studies*, 7 (1977), pp. 19–40.
57. Kriege, 'Abnahme', pp. 48–9; H. von Hövell, 'Gründe und Bedeutung des Geburtenrückgangs vom Standpunkte der öffentliche Gesundheitspflege: Was kann der Arzt und die Medizinalverwaltung tun, um diesem Übel zu begegnen?', *VGMOS* (3rd series), 51 (1916), p. 284; Manfred Stürzbecher, 'Standesamt und Empfängnisverhütungsmittel. Ein Beitrag zur Geschichte der deutschen Bevölkerungspolitik', *Gesundheitsfürsorge*, 4 (1954).
58. Bornträger, *Geburtenrückgang*, p. 48; Krohne, 'Empfängnisverhütung', p. 343; O. Krohne, *Die Beurteilung des Geburtenrückganges vom volkshygienischen, sittlichen, und nationalen Standpunkt* (Dieterich'sche Verlagsbuchhandlung, Leipzig, 1914), pp. 34–5; Jorns, 'Willkürlichen Beschränkung', p. 53; Hövell, 'Gründe', p. 284; Kriege, 'Abnahme', p. 49; Witting and König, 'Geburtenrückgang', pp. 161–2; Gesenius, 'Gefährlichkeit', p. 2171; O. Polano, 'Beitrag zur Frage der Geburtenbeschränkung', *ZGG*, 79 (1917), p. 569.
59. Jorns, 'Willkürlichen Beschränkung', p. 54.
60. Ernst Huber, *Deutsche Verfassungsgeschichte seit 1789* (6 vols), vol. 4: *Struktur und Krisen des Kaiserreichs* (Kohlhammer, Stuttgart, 1969), p. 284. See also Gary Stark, 'Pornography, society, and the law in Imperial Germany', *CEH*, 14 (1981), p. 217.
61. Stark, 'Pornography', p. 213.
62. Hövell, 'Gründe', p. 305. See also Kantor, 'Geburtenrückgang', p. 564; Rosenberg, 'Das geltende Recht über den Verkehr mit Mitteln zur Verhütung der Geburten', *Berliner Tageblatt*, 129 (1914), p. 21.
63. Hövell, 'Grunde', p. 305; Kantor, 'Geburtenrückgang', p. 564; Rosenberg, 'Verkehr', p. 21.
64. Hövell, 'Grunde', pp. 305–6; Kantor, 'Geburtenrückgang', p. 565.
65. Witting and König, 'Geburtenrückgang', p. 162; Allgemeine Konferenz, *Verhältnisse*, vol. I, pp. 67, 111; vol. II, p. 43.
66. Ferdy, *Sittliche Selbstbeschränkung*, p. 136; Eda Sagarra, *An introduction to nineteenth century Germany* (Longman, London, 1980), p. 161; Linse, 'Arbeiterschaft', pp. 218, 228; Werner Blessing, 'Umwelt und Mentalität im ländlichen Bayern. Eine Skizze zum Alltagswandel im 19. Jahrhundert', *ASG*, 19 (1979), p. 17; Hsi-huey Liang, 'Lower-class immigrants in Wilhelmian Berlin', *CEH*, 3 (1970), p. 95.
67. Allgemeine Konferenz, *Verhältnisse*, vol. I, p. 155; also vol. I, pp. 51–2, 222, and vol. II, p. 598; Gebhardt, *Sittenlehre*, pp. 101, 125; Mirko Kosic, 'Die soziologischen Grundlagen der Geburtenbeschränkung',

ASA, 10 (1916-17), p. 461.

68. Max Marcuse, *Der eheliche Präventivverkehr: Seine Verbreitung, Verursachung und Methodik*, (Enke, Stuttgart, 1917), pp. 16, 133, and case nos 50, 98, 295. See also Engelsmann, 'Ursache', p. 143; Karl Zieler, 'Uber die persönliche Prophylaxe der Geschlechtskrankheiten', *DMW*, 38 (1912), pp. 345-8; P. Scharff, 'Zur Prophylaxe und Therapie der Geschlechtskrankheiten im Felde', *BKW*, 51 (1914), pp. 1816-18; Wilhelm Gennerich, 'Der heutige Stand der Bekämpfung der Geschlechtskrankheiten im Kriege', *Ergebnisse der Hygiene*, 2 (1917), pp. 286-337; W. Fromme, 'Zur Bekämpfung der Geschlechtskrankheiten, mit besonderer Berücksichtigung der sozialhygienischer Verhältnissen', *Zeitschrift für Hygiene*, 90 (1920), pp. 437-77. For later years see Franz Seidler, *Prostitution, Homosexualität, Selbstverstümmelung. Probleme der deutschen Sanitätsführung, 1939-1945* (Vowinckel, Neckargemünd, 1977), pp. 100-26. On the English experience see Peel, 'Manufacturing', pp. 120-2.

69. Allgemeine Konferenz, *Verhältnisse*, vol. II, pp. 121, 349-50, 598; Bornträger, *Geburtenrückgang*, p. 53; Gebhardt, *Sittenlehre*, p. 101; Kosic, 'Grundlagen', p. 461; Regina Schulte, 'Dienstmädchen im herrschaftlichen Haushalt. Zur Genese ihrer Sozialpsychologie', *Zeitschrift für Bayerische Landesgeschichte*, 41 (1978), pp. 888-9.

70. Hanssen, 'Abnahme', p. 395; Spinner, *Aerztliches Recht*, p. 292; Lehmann, 'Antikonzeptionelle Mittel', p. 878; Krohne, 'Empfängnisverhütung', pp. 343-4.

71. Hinz, *Wert*, p. 353; Zacharias, *Bevölkerungsfrage*, p. 75.

72. Braun, 'Neuartiges Intrauterinpessar', p. 250.

73. Lehmann, 'Antikonzeptionelle Mittel', p. 876. See also Bornträger, *Geburtenrückgang*, p. 56; Linse, 'Arbeiterschaft', p. 231. On England see McLaren, *Birth control*, p. 118.

74. Ferdy, *Sittliche Selbstbeschränkung*, p. 147. See also McLaren, *Birth control*, pp. 118-21, 222; Soloway, *Birth control*, p. 112-14; Reed, *Private vice*, pp. 36, 44, 124; Gordon, *Woman's body*, p. 160.

75. Dr 'S' quoted in *SP*, 4 (1908), p. 438. See also W.Thorn, 'Über die Ursachen des Geburtenrückganges und die Mittel zu seiner Bekämpfung', *Praktische Ergebnisse der Geburtshilfe und Gynäkologie*, 5 (1912), p. 36; Dr Schell, 'Die beim weiblichen Geschlecht gebrauchlichen Gummiartikel zur Verhütung und Unterbrechung der Schwangerschaft', *MK*, 13 (1917), p. 543.

76. Dr 'A', *SP*, 4 (1908), pp. 437-8.

77. Ferdy, *Sittliche Selbstbeschränkung*, p. 149; Lehmann, 'Antikonzeptionelle Mittel', p. 876; Sarwey, 'Indikationen', p. 293; Bornträger, *Geburtenrückgang*, p. 56; H. Kraft, 'Die Indikationen und Mittel zur Schwangerschaftsverhütung', *MMW*, 51 (1904), p. 1748; Max Hirsch, 'Frauenheilkunde und Bevölkerungspolitik', *MGG*, 49 (1919), p. 205.

78. Braun, 'Intrauterinpessar', p. 250. See also Gennerich, 'Heutige Stand', p. 313.

79. Line quotes are from Hermann Rohleder, Schwangerschaftsverhütung und Aerztestand', *NG*, 7 (1911), p. 538; Dr Löwenfeld, quoted by Ferdy, *Sittliche Selbstbeschränkung*, p. 150; and Dr 'C', *SP*, 4 (1908), p. 436, respectively. See also Robert Braun and Joseph Winterberg, 'Kritische Bermerkungen über die verschiedenen antikonzeptionellen Massnahmen',

Monatsschrift für Harnkrankheiten und sexuelle Hygiene, 4 (1907), pp. 494-5; and Soloway, *Birth control*, p. 132.

80. Heinz Potthoff, 'Geburtenregelung und Geschlechtsmoral', *SP*, 6 (1910), p. 385. See also Dr 'J.P.', *SP*, 4 (1908), p. 442; Ferdy, *Sittliche Selbstbeschränkung*, pp. 149-51, discussing a series of articles on the theme, 'Die Stellung des Arztes zur Verhinderung der Conception', in the *Deutsche Medicinische Presse*, 2 (1898), nos 15, 16, 20-2.

81. Dr 'G', *SP*, 4 (1908), pp. 439-40.

82. A. Fischer, 'Krankenversicherung', in Alfred Grotjahn and Josef Kaup (eds), *Handwörterbuch der sozialen Hygiene*, (2 vols, Vogel, Leipzig, 1912), vol. I, pp. 650-1; William Dawson, *Social insurance in Germany, 1893-1911: its history, operation, results* (Unwin, London, 1912), pp. 182-4; Gerlach, *Einschränkung*, pp. 20-1; Grotjahn, *Geburtenrückgang*, pp. 70-1, 86, 90; Albin Gladen, *Geschichte der Sozialpolitik in Deutschland. Eine Analyse ihrer Bedingungen, Formen, Zielsetzungen* und *Auswirkungen* (Steiner, Wiesbaden, 1974), pp. 61-2; Florian Tennstedt, 'Sozialgeschichte der Sozialversicherung', in Maria Blohmke (ed.), *Handbuch der Sozialmedizin* (3 vols, Enke, Stuttgart, 1976), vol. III, p. 37. On the role of the Insurance Programme in the prevention and treatment of venereal disease, including the free distribution of condoms, see Dr Uhlmann, 'Geschlechtskrankheiten und Krankenkassen' (Deutsche Gesellschaft zur Bekämpfung der Geschlechtskrankheiten), *Mitteilungen*, 1 (1902-3), pp. 49-58; F. Pinkus, 'Der Kampf gegen die Geschlechtskrankheiten und die Krankenkassen', *Mitteilungen*, 17 (1919-20), pp. 67-77; Paul Kaufmann, 'Träger der Arbeiterversicherung und Bekämpfung der Geschlechtskrankheiten', *Deutsche Arbeit*, 39 (1916), pp. 72-5; Kaufmann, *Krieg, Geschlechtskrankheiten und Arbeiterversicherung* (Vahlen, Berlin, 1916); Kaufmann, *Die Sozialversicherung im Kampfe gegen die Geschlechtskrankheiten* (Springer, Berlin, 1919).

83. Hausmeister, quoted by Gustav Stille in a report to *The Malthusian*, vol. 21 (1897), pp. 65-6; cf. Gustav Stille, 'Malthusianische Bestrebungen in Westeuropa', *ZSW*, 5 (1902), pp. 928-9. See also Rosanna Ledbetter, *A history of the Malthusian League* (Ohio State University Press, Columbus, 1976), pp. 181-2; Heinrich Rubner, 'Familienplanung um 1900', (Historischer Verein von Oberpfalz und Regensburg), *Verhandlungen*, 120 (1980), p. 530.

84. Stille, 'Bestrebungen', pp. 928-9; Stille, Reports to *The Malthusian*, 1892, p. 83; 1897, p. 65; Grotjahn, *Hygiene*, p. 49; Ledbetter, *History*, pp. 181-2; Rubner, 'Familienplanung', pp. 532-3. An even more obscure group, the *Gesellschaft zur Bekämpfung der Übervölkerung Deutschlands*, was founded in Berlin by Ferdinand Goldstein: R. Lewinsohn, 'Die Stellung der Deutschen Sozialdemokratie zur Bevölkerungsfrage', *Schmollers Jahrbuch*, 46 (1922), p. 215.

85. Dieter Langewiesche and Klaus Schönhoven, 'Arbeiterbibliotheken und Arbeiterlektüre im Wilhelminischen Deutschland', *ASG*, 16 (1976), pp. 148, 197; Vernon Lidtke, *The alternative culture: socialist labor in imperial Germany* (Oxford University Press, New York, 1985).

86. Line quotes from Jorns, 'Willkürlichen Beschränkung', pp. 57-8; and Dr Rauch, 'Sozialdemokratie und Geburtenrückgang', *ZMB*, 26 (1913), p. 107, respectively. See also Kriege, 'Abnahme', p. 49; R.P. Neuman, 'The sexual question and social democracy in Imperial Germany', *JSH*, 7 (1974),

p. 280. On the 'Gebärstreik' controversy see Anneliese Bergmann, 'Frauen, Männer, Sexualität, Geburtenkontrolle: Zur "Gebärstreikdebatte" der SPD 1913', in Karin Hausen (ed.), *Frauen suchen ihre Geschichte* (Beck, Munich, 1983); Kurt Nemitz, 'Julius Moses und die Gebärstreikdebatte 1913', *Jahrbuch des Instituts für Deutsche Geschichte*, 2 (1973), pp. 321-35; Karl-Heinz Roth, 'Kontroversen um Geburtenkontrolle am Vorabend des Ersten Weltkriegs: Eine Documentation zur Berliner Gebärstreikdebatte von 1913', *Autonomie: Materialien gegen die Fabrikgesellschaft*, 9 (1978), pp. 78-103.

87. Richard Evans, *The feminist movement in Germany, 1894-1933* (Croom Helm, London, 1976), pp. 17, 115, 117-19, 122-3; C. Wichert, 'Helene Stöcker and the Bund für Mutterschutz', *Women's Studies International Forum*, 5 (1982), pp. 611-13.

88. Evans, *Feminist movement*, pp. 132-8, 162; Wichert, 'Helene Stöcker', pp. 613-14.

89. Evans, *Feminist movement*, pp. 122-4.

90. Marcuse, *Eheliche Präventivverkehr*, case nos 81, 134, 247 respectively; Cf. 161, 172. See also Polano, 'Beitrag', pp. 568, 570; Eugene Sandberg and Ralph Jacobs, 'Psychology of the misuse and rejection of contraception', *American Journal of Obstetrics and Gynaecology*, 110 (1971), pp. 227-37.

91. Marcuse, *Eheliche Präventivverkehr*, case nos. 119, 163, 208; and Peter Stearns, 'Adaptation to industrialization: German workers as a test case', *CEH*, 3 (1970), p. 326.

92. Marcuse, 'Frage', p. 776; Marcuse, *Eheliche Präventivverkehr*, case nos 180, 213; Engelsmann, *Ursache*, p. 143.

93. Marcuse, *Präventivverkehr*, p. 119; Jorns, 'Willkürlichen Beschränkung', p. 54.

94. Marcuse, *Eheliche Präventivverkehr*, case no. 256; E.R. May, 'Zur Frage des Geburtenrückganges', *Schmollers Jahrbuch*, 40 (1916), p. 60.

3

The Abortion Epidemic

Abortion rates exploded after 1900 as women everywhere miscarried on an unprecedented scale. The increase appeared in major cities during the years 1905–1910, but spread quickly throughout Germany. In the years after the First World War even small-town hospitals reported that 'the halls are filled' with abortion cases. Doctors projecting local rates onto the national population estimated 100,000 to 300,000 abortions per year during the pre-war period, half a million per year after the war, and up to one million abortions annually during the Depression. In 1935, when compulsory reporting of abortions was introduced, reliable figures became available on a national scale. Dr Reichert calculated the abortion mortality rate and, using mortality statistics from the 1920s, argued that maximum abortion incidence might have reached half a million per year during the 1920s, but that the level would have dropped afterwards to only 100,000 by 1932. But because of changes in morbidity and mortality during the 1920s, these figures should be regarded as minimal estimates.[1]

All calculations of abortion incidence on a national scale before 1935 are necessarily approximations based on information from midwives, doctors, and hospitals. Midwives were trained in state schools to provide basic obstetric care throughout the country, particularly in rural areas, and were required to submit annual reports to the District Medical Officer. But a woman might not summon a midwife for miscarriage unless complications set in, and the midwives, who received rather skimpy training, might not accurately diagnose the situation. Doctors were better qualified to diagnose and treat miscarriage, but they were not required to report these cases. And hospital records involve the serious cases that could not be treated elsewhere (although by the 1920s women were more willing to present themselves at hospitals for treatment as a result of increasing public confidence in hospitals and the support provided by the Health Insurance Programme). While none of these sources provide conclusive evidence separately, taken together the records add up to a dramatic upsurge in abortion during the early twentieth century, a trend that apparently affected women from all classes and all regions of the country.[2]

Most reported cases of abortion from the late nineteenth century involved young, single women anxious to avoid the social and economic burden of illegitimacy.[3] But in the twentieth century the mass rush to abortion consisted primarily of married women. In pre-war years three-fourths of hospital-treated abortions involved married women. The ratio dropped in large cities, where single women took advantage of new abortion techniques. Cities like Berlin, Munich, Breslau, and Magdeburg reported an even division of marital and non-marital abortions, while smaller centres like Rostock, Bremen, Jena, and Mainz reported more than three-fourths of all abortions as occurring among married women. A brief upsurge in marital abortion during the war years preceded a sustained decline in the 1920s, when marital abortions accounted for less than half of all cases in the larger cities. But in general the first third of the twentieth century was characterised by the predominance of married women in the abortion ranks.[4]

Abortion occurred among women of all ages. In Berlin one-fourth of abortions occurred among women under age 25, another fourth among women aged 26–30, one-fourth in the age group 31–35, and the rest among older women. But this percentage share changed over the years, with women under 25 accounting for 18 per cent of abortions in 1900–1 and 30 per cent in 1930–1. In Breslau and Munich young women constituted 40 per cent of abortion cases. During the 1920s a downward trend in the age of abortion patients took place. In Prussia in 1911 women over age 30 made up 46 per cent of cases while women under 25 comprised 28 per cent; by 1928 the respective figures (for Germany rather than Prussia) were 35 per cent and 37 per cent.[5]

The changing age composition of abortion patients reflected changes in the fertility history of each age cohort. At the turn of the century women having abortions usually had more prior births than abortions; by the 1920s the situation was reversed. As women halted childbearing at ever lower numbers of children, all age groups demonstrated an increased tendency to have abortions rather than births. Young women sometimes had a prior history of abortions only. The 1920s witnessed a downward shift in the age of abortion patients, a greater tendency to have prior abortions, and a sharp increase in the number of *primi-parae* (women having their first delivery) and *primi-gravidae* (women having their first pregnancy) who aborted rather than carry to term.[6]

Abortion occurred in women from every social class, although upper-class women seldom appear in the statistics because they obtained treatment in private clinics.[7] Throughout the period 1900–1930 most of the single women who aborted were domestic servants, maids, cooks, waitresses, sales clerks, seamstresses, factory workers, secretaries and young women living at home.[8] Married women, when not employed themselves, were the wives of artisans, retailers, factory, railway and postal workers, farmers, teachers, civil servants, and white collar workers.[9] Health Insurance records show 10 per cent of female members having abortions, but domestic servants, sales clerks and office workers had much higher rates: 20 per cent, 28 per cent and 34 per cent, respectively.[10] Crime statistics show the same occupational profile, although these figures include both the women getting the abortion and the men or women performing it. Nearly half of all convictions involved people in industry and crafts, with the rest evenly divided among trade and commerce, agriculture and domestic service. All levels of the social ladder were represented, from professionals and civil servants to shopkeepers, sales clerks and servants; unmarried daughters of the lower middle class figured prominently.[11]

Although tens and even hundreds of thousands of abortions occurred annually, not all of them were deliberate. Spontaneous abortion normally occurs among 7 to 10 per cent of all conceptions. In the late nineteenth century clinical estimates put the rate at 11 per cent. After the turn of the century more careful tests in major hospitals led to new results. In Berlin Dr Koblanck found 9 per cent of hospital-treated abortions to be spontaneous, while Dr Bumm traced 5 per cent to natural causes. Rates from other institutions ranged between 8 and 28 per cent; a nation-wide survey in 1929 found 5½ per cent of abortions to be spontaneous. In 1933 Dr Pohlen calculated 7 per cent, and this is near the level accepted today.[12]

Most spontaneous abortions were due to maternal causes, as opposed to foetal malformations which accounted for less than 10 per cent of spontaneous cases. Berlin and Munich reported a somewhat higher incidence of foetal malformation, but still under one-fourth of all cases.[13]

Retroflected uterus was the largest single cause of spontaneous abortion. Tumours and irritation of the endometrium can also inhibit foetal development. Inflammation of the uterus as a result of venereal disease or prior septic abortion can lead to habitual abortion, where serial conceptions would abort, often at the same stage in gestation. Estimates placed the incidence of habitual abortion at 1 per cent of all abortions.[14]

General maternal health affects the development of the foetus as well. Improper nutrition leads to foetal malnutrition, such as vitamin deficiency, while chronic poor health weakens the foetus. Various diseases affecting the mother — smallpox, influenza, cholera, typhoid fever, tuberculosis, syphilis — can be transmitted to the foetus with worse consequences for the less resistant organism. One study of 266 pregnant women with syphilis found 124 abortions (46.6 per cent). Blood toxins acquired at the place of work (e.g lead), external trauma, or internal constriction can all cause abortion. But these conditions are only possible causes of abortion; the overall health of the woman and her general lifestyle determine whether abortion will occur in any particular instance.[15]

Max Hirsch, a Berlin gynaecologist and proponent of the holistic study of women's health, argued that modern life, especially factory employment, contributed to the high incidence of abortion. Sitting, standing, or bending over machinery for long hours placed excessive strain on the lower abdomen. Foul air, dim lighting and loud noises were upsetting, while noxious fumes and glass or metal particles in the air directly affected health. The working conditions aggravated the effect which the poor living conditions of the working class had on women. Hirsch advocated maternity insurance and state spending on housing as measures to improve the physical condition of the working class. But for the most part the medical profession rejected such an ambitious programme and contented itself with investigating the causes of spontaneous abortion to determine whether the aetiology was susceptible to treatment and whether complications which might affect future fecundity could be prevented.[16]

Therapeutic abortion accounted for another 10 per cent of abortions treated in hospitals.[17] Therapeutic abortion presented a two-fold dilemma to doctors. On the one hand, cutting down overall abortion incidence required them to tighten the range of acceptable indications for the procedure. On the other hand therapeutic abortion, as induced abortion, was illegal. Exculpatory justification of therapeutic abortion required clear adherence to 'therapeutic purpose' in the application of guidelines for inducing abortion, as this formula issued by the Prussian government to state prosecutors demonstrates: 'Abortion by a doctor is indicated if, in consequence of a previously existing illness an unquestionably grave danger to the health or life of the mother exists which can only be removed through abortion.'[18] This formula became the standard criterion in other states as well.

In 1927 the *Reichsgericht* confirmed the legal basis of therapeutic abortion. While granting that no provision of the Criminal Code authorised such operations, the Court argued that the intent of the entire corpus of legislation did do so:

> Only when the situation of the woman is such as to justify her own action can her consent to abortion justify the doctor who performs it. . . . An action which is recognised as proper can be taken in an emergency to preserve an objective which is also recognised by the state, such as the health or life of the mother, and in this case the right to life of the foetus is of lesser weight than the right of the mother, and an action which, in circumstances where both rights are at stake, saves the greater even at the expense of the lesser is no longer illegal, and the doctor who acts out of duty to safe the life of the mother and thereby renounces the duty to save the life of the foetus is not acting against the law.[19]

Establishing acceptable indications for abortion was complicated by the individual interpretation of those indications by general practitioners. Clinicians often complained that general practitioners were too casual in referring patients to hospitals for therapeutic abortion with only slight justification. Many cases had to be rejected by the hospitals, and this aroused suspicion of the entire profession among the laity. More than half of all referrals were routinely dismissed by hospitals, two-thirds of referrals in Berlin and Munich. Georg Winter blamed this on the lax standards of practising physicians. Clinicians maintained strict standards, and imparted these to students in medical school. But life altered the attitude of many doctors, a result of being too close to their patients. They did not fully diagnose the situation to ensure that abortion was indeed the only option; they acted on the basis of patient complaints rather than the known characteristics of the illness; and they stretched indications according to their own whim. Winter argued that it was up to senior specialists to spell out acceptable indications for all doctors.[20]

The discussion of guidelines for therapeutic abortion generally followed developments in medical science. The classic barrier to normal birth was extreme contraction of the pelvis, for which the traditional response was morcellation. The rise of operative gynaecology made abortion a feasible alternative, but doctors preferred Caesarian section or symphysiotomy (surgical division of the pubic bone); by

1914 the mortality from Caesarian section had been reduced to less than 5 per cent, and doctors felt that women should be persuaded to have the operation. The choice was theirs, however, and women who had previously had Caesarian section were advised to abort.[21]

Conditions of the uro-genital tract that could affect pregnancy include fixed retrograde uterus and cervical tumour. In Prussian hospitals in 1911 most therapeutic abortions were for uro-genital indications. Toxaemias of pregnancy — eclampsia (which even today accounts for a significant number of maternal deaths) and hyperemesis or acute vomiting — are the direct result of the state of pregnancy. In Prussia in 1911 one in ten therapeutic abortions were for toxaemias.[22]

The two principal illnesses aggravated by pregnancy were pulmonary tuberculosis — which accounted for nearly half of therapeutic abortions in Berlin, Frankfurt and Munich between 1910 and 1930 — and heart disease. Although both had been accepted indications at the end of the nineteenth century, subsequent experience demonstrated that alternative therapy was practical. With proper care, mortality for pregnant women with heart trouble was only 2 or 3 per cent, and most doctors felt that this low rate did not justify therapeutic abortion as a standard policy. Likewise, improvements in sanatoria treatment for tuberculosis led to an equally impressive reduction in the mortality of that disease, which reduced the need for abortion. Better treatment for diabetes, liver and kidney disorders, and blood diseases (leukaemia, pernicious anaemia) also reduced the need for therapeutic abortion, except in those cases where treatment failed.[23]

Some neurological illnesses justified therapeutic abortion: meningitis, multiple sclerosis and epilepsy. Psychological indications included hysteria, dementia praecox, and melancholy, if treatment failed. The risk in these situations was a personality change in the woman. The threat of suicide seemed to justify abortion, but later studies showed that these tendencies waned after the mid-point in pregnancy and the rise of 'maternal instinct'.[24]

Eugenic indications were argued by some doctors: women with mental illness, imbecility, or alcoholism burdened society and could not be expected to raise children properly. In 1924 the Prussian Health Council endorsed eugenic indications for therapeutic abortion if one or both parents had a transmittable disease or came from a family with a history of transmittable diseases. But most doctors rejected eugenic indications on the grounds of insufficient evidence from genetics, and also on moral grounds: 'It would mean the organised murder of human lives.'[25]

Social indications were accepted only in conjunction with medical indications: if a woman could not afford the sanatorium treatment necessary for her illness, then abortion was acceptable as a legitimate alternative. Whether social indications alone — the financial ability to raise chldren — justified abortion was seldom discussed in the medical literature until after the war. Dr Winter argued against social indications on three grounds. First, such abortions would be illegal. Second, doctors swore in the Hippocratic oath not to take life; they certainly should not do so simply because the parents were hard up. And third, there was no practical way to determine the extent of social need that would be required to justify the abortion.[26]

Rape presented a special kind of social indication. Should a woman who conceived against her will be compelled to bear the child? Winter argued that they should, because the law did not specifically allow abortion (the law also did not permit rape, but perhaps Winter believed that two wrongs do not make a right). He also argued that sympathy for the rape victim should not obscure concern for the child's right to life. Winter and others questioned the credibility of women; perhaps they had illicit sexual relations and fabricated a story of rape in order to get an abortion. Dr Kupferberg argued that rape could be admitted as an indication for abortion only after the fact of rape had been established in court. But a woman could not know immediately after rape that she had conceived; to insist that all rape victims undergo curettage after rape added insult to injury. Dr Bacharach argued that since no law required women to become pregnant, rape did justify abortion.[27]

After 1933 standard procedures were set up to determine the propriety of medical indications for therapeutic abortion. Consulting committees for all specialisations were established to determine whether danger to health or life existed in any given case, and whether abortion was necessary. Eugenic abortion was transferred to the jurisdiction of the hereditary courts after promulgation of the sterilisation law. As a result of these strict measures the number of referrals to hospitals dropped dramatically, from 44,000 in 1932 to 4,131 in 1937; the proportion of referrals which were declined fell from 58 per cent to 28 per cent.[28]

Spontaneous and therapeutic abortions together accounted for less than one-fifth of all hospital-treated abortions. Most cases entered the record as 'incomplete abortion'. Doctors suspected that criminal intervention was responsible for most of these, particularly when complications set in. This suspicion was frequently confirmed by the condition of the patient, by the testimony of women, who were increasingly willing to acknowledge deliberate abortion, and by autopsies.[29]

The most common complication was fever. Before 1914 major hospitals reported between one-fourth and one-fifth of all abortions as febrile. The ratio rose to one-third to one-half in the post-war years and then declined steadily; in 1928 30 per cent of hospital-treated abortions in Germany were febrile. Fever presented a much greater risk to the health and life of the patient, and medical consensus blamed criminal abortion for 90 per cent of all febrile abortions. Detailed studies confirmed that at least one-third of febrile abortions were criminally induced, and in larger cities the proportion exceeded two-thirds.[30]

Complications associated with criminal abortion stemmed from the inadequate anatomical knowledge of the abortionists and from their improper techniques — such as excessive force with instruments, or lack of antiseptic precautions — which caused perforations in the uro-genital tract, bleeding and infection. Moreover, lay abortionists usually only induced abortion; if complete evacuation did not occur placental tissue could remain *in utero* and complicate subsequent pregnancies. Products to cause abortion, such as ingested abortifacients or the solutions employed in syringes, sometimes caused gastro-intestinal inflammation, corrosion of tissue, general systemic intoxication, or embolism. Overdoses of poisonous substances were not uncommon, since the dividing line between the degree of toxicity needed to kill the foetus without killing the mother was difficult to gauge in advance. Air bubbles in syringes entered vaginal or uterine blood vessels which opened during the course of the abortion procedure; death was often instantaneous.[31]

Uterine or transuterine infection — endometritis, parametritis, peritonitis, salpingitis, adnexitis, or thrombophlebitis — was the most serious complication attending abortion. Sepsis invariably stemmed from the introduction of bacteria into the uterus by means of unsterilised instruments. Wounds occurring during abortion provided a nesting place for bacteria and a gateway into the body, leading to generalised sepsis.[32]

Perforations of the uro-genital tract increased sharply during the early twentieth century. Wounds occurred wherever instruments could reach: vulva, vagina, fornices, cervix, uterus, or adnexa. Excess force could push instruments through the uterus into the abdominal cavity and penetrate the rectum or intestines. Sometimes the wounds were so severe as to require emergency operations: laparatomy, intestinal resection, nephrectomy, or hysterectomy. Mortality in cases of performation averaged 25 per cent. Even when the damage was not extensive, wounds exacerbated the risk of infection and created the additional risk of extensive bleeding, which could result in death for anaemic women or women with heart disease. As late as 1928 bleeding remained the most frequent complication attending abortion (other than fever).[33]

Perforation clearly resulted from external intervention. The growing use of instruments to induce abortion, especially by doctors, was responsible for this. A review of the medical literature on perforations for the years 1900–1910 turned up 264 cases: 5 due to digital manipulation, in contrast to 174 perforations caused by the curette; other cases were traced to utrine sounds, catheters, dilators, and forceps. A study covering the years 1907–22 discussed 266 cases of perforation by doctors during abortions. In half of these cases the instrument involved was unknown; otherwise the guilty gadgets included forceps, curette, dilatator, catheter, and uterine sound. Mortality averaged 15 per cent.[34]

The incidence of post-abortion complications peaked during the immediate post-war years, then declined during the 1920s as doctors replaced abortionists and as lay abortionists took better precautions. In 1928 only 7 per cent of abortions treated in hospitals had complications, but infection continued to account for two-thirds of abortion deaths.[35]

Long-term consequences of abortion were not infrequent: nearly 8 per cent of all women treated in 1928 left with some after-effect. Alterations in the structure or functioning of the ovaries, tubes, or uterus were not uncommon, and these changes might prevent further conception, or create complications at birth. Among a sample of one hundred women treated for abortion during 1927–32, two-thirds subsequently complained of disruptions in menstruation, anomalies of uterine position, or pathological disorders of the ovaries; one-fourth became sterile. For Germany as a whole, 30 per cent of the women who aborted became sterile.[36]

The ultimate complication was death. Doctors who estimated one million abortions per year also placed mortality at a corresponding level, ranging from 5,000 to 50,000 deaths per year. Such alarming estimates led the Prussian Statistical Office to attempt to calculate the maximum possible number of deaths that could be attributed to abortion. Of 60,000 female deaths in 1927, they calculated that 3,500 could be considered 'hidden' abortion deaths — deaths disguised under other headings. Together with known abortion deaths, this totalled 5,000 possible deaths for Prussia, or 8,300 per year for Germany. Dr

Freudenberg used an alternative procedure, comparing male and female death rates in categories with unusually high female mortality in order to determine the number of hidden abortion-related deaths; he estimated 3,000 in Prussia and 5,000 per year in Germany.[37]

The health risks associated with abortion made it a matter of serious medical concern, but the fact that most of these abortions were deliberate made it a matter of social and even political concern as well. Doctors felt both compelled and qualified to address the question. Medical awareness of the abortion epidemic coincided with public discussion of the *Geburtenrückgangsfrage* (the question of falling births). During the First World War doctors joined with jurists, demographers, academics and politicians to form the German Society for Population Policy, an organisation dedicated to discussion of the causes of the fertility decline and to the formulation of public policy to combat it. Doctors also engaged in a wide-ranging debate in the medical press on the theme, 'Our Role in Population Policy', in an effort to forge a consensus within the profession on the practical steps which they should take to stem the fertility decline. As Ludwig Nürnberger observed, 'War has lifted obstetrics from its narrow specialisation and given it a broader social and demographic significance.'[38]

Dr Winter initiated the discussion in 1916 with an article entitled 'Our tasks in population policy'. Social and economic measures were the responsibility of the state, but Winter argued that doctors, and especially gynaecologists, had an obligation to take all possible medical measures to increase fertility. This included the investigation and treatment of involuntary sterility and spontaneous abortion, restrictions on the incidence of therapeutic abortion, cooperation with authorities in detecting and prosecuting criminal abortion, and promotion of better post-natal care to reduce the high level of infant mortality. Although Winter emphasised medical action, he shared Nürnberger's concern with the larger context:

> Every far-sighted policy-maker recognises the significance of this trend [fertility decline], especially when he considers the slow decline of France and the steady growth of Russia, for the population question is inextricably intertwined with military and political considerations.[39]

Winter's article received a good deal of favourable response from the medical profession. In addition to his programme to 'protect every pregnancy', Jaschke and Fehling stressed the need for better post-natal care.[40]

It was abortion, however, that remained the primary focus of gynaecologists. Their objectives were two-fold. Medically, they sought to diagnose and prevent spontaneous abortion, to reduce the incidence of therapeutic abortion, and to alleviate the risk of complications in cases of septic abortion. Socially, they sought to prevent illicit abortion by promoting maternity insurance, by persuading their patients not to have abortions, by supervising those persons believed responsible for performing illegal abortions, and by banning or controlling the equipment used to induce abortion. But how to accomplish these objectives was an issue on which the profession remained divided.

For conservative physicians abortion was inexcusable. Even therapeutic abortion, with rare exceptions, was rejected.[41] These doctors argued that women should accept the health risks as an 'occupational hazard' of motherhood that was part of their 'duty to the state', just as soldiers faced occupational hazards in the trenches. If women were allowed to have abortions, morality would decline and the demographic, economic, political and military strength of the nation would decline with it. 'The state cannot permit the complete demoralisation of its people, and so it must punish abortion along with other crimes against public morality.'[42] For these reasons the state had the right to protect the foetus, regardless of whether it was considered as a part of the mother or as a separate organism, since the state had the right to designate any part of any body as essential to its survival. If the state could punish men who wounded themselves to avoid military service, then it could punish women who aborted themselves and denied the state its future citizens. Reflecting these views the Prussian *Ehrengerichtshof* took the view that 'it is the moral obligation of the physician to warn the patient against any action which might limit the natural course of pregnancy'.[43]

Moderate opinion appeared first in the debate over therapeutic indications for abortion. Whereas strict constructionists accepted abortion only in cases where an immediate life-threatening situation existed, moderates accepted abortion whenever serious danger could reasonably be expected to arise at some point in gestation or at delivery, or when the continuation of the pregnancy would adversely affect the health of the woman. 'Patients are entitled to demand protection from grave threats to their health, and the doctor is obligated to help them with induced abortion at a time when there is still a chance of success for the woman.'[44] Such concerns easily slid into consideration of social and economic circumstances, and doctors listened to women who claimed they could not endure another child:

'One need only look at these women to see that they are telling the truth.'[45] But however sympathetic they might be, moderates generally preferred to stress social and economic assistance from the state rather than advocate unrestricted abortion: 'Where does it say that doctors can break the law out of sympathy?'[46] Moderate opinion was reflected in the 1925 decision of the German Medical Association to endorse the legalisation of therapeutic abortion.[47]

Finally, a growing liberal group of doctors called for the de-criminalisation of all abortion. These doctors, mostly young and often affiliated with the Health Insurance Programme, had constant contact with women in desperate social and economic conditions and chronic poor health. They argued that until living conditions improved, abortion should be available to those in need, and that these women should not be driven to criminal abortion with all its risks.[48]

Responsible social policy to combat abortion required economic assistance to expectant mothers and their families in order to remove the incentive for abortion. But of more immediate concern to the medical profession were measures to reduce the availability of criminal abortion. Doctors supported legal attempts to restrict the manufacture and sale of items that were used to induce abortion. But since bona fide medical instruments were sometimes involved and since substitutes for other items could easily be found, the profession concentrated on proposals for greater supervision of the persons suspected of performing abortion. The medical profession waged a continuing battle to achieve state regulation of non-certified persons practising health care.[49] But doctors also had to recognise that many legitimate medical practitioners were also involved with abortion.

Controlling midwives became a concern of the medical profession as early as 1881. At that time the focus of interest was on measures to eliminate puerperal fever, but after the turn of the century attention shifted to the role of midwives in the spread of birth control. Several reforms were suggested. First, the education and training of midwives needed improvement. Second, the stipend they received should be increased; if they earned more legally they might be less inclined to supplement their income illegally. Doctors suggested that midwives should be persuaded not to engage in birth control activities by pointing out to them that fewer births in the short run would mean fewer clients in the long run. They should also be reminded of the moral trust which they held as certified medical agents of the state. Prussian 'Instructions to Midwives' included a ban on 'advising or inserting diaphragms, suppositories, or other products which can prevent conception', and on the unauthorised treatment of 'female complaints'.[50]

Doctors did not exclude their own profession from state surveillance. They recognised that some colleagues were lax in their interpretation of indications for therapeutic abortion, and that others freely induced illicit abortion. Proposals included the compulsory reporting of all cases of abortion or, alternatively, compulsory consultation with another physician prior to inducing abortion. Consultation was normal in other situations, and should be required for abortion. Since a doctor who was willing to perform illegal abortions could probably find a like-minded colleague, the state should designate official consultants similar to court-appointed medical experts who testified at trials involving medical issues. But as court experience demonstrated, these experts were usually emeriti who lacked up-to-date awareness of current procedures. Moreover, general practitioners in rural areas should not be expected to wait until the official consultant arrived, nor should the patient suffer while 'paper rituals' were completed.[51] Compulsory consultation would also diminish the reputation of the profession in the eyes of the public, which already suspected doctors of hypocrisy in their attitude toward abortion. For these reasons it would be better for the profession to police itself, starting with clear and strict guidelines for therapeutic abortion. Compulsory reporting of abortions after the fact was another possibility. Reporting would make doctors and patients think twice before going ahead with abortion; presumably any doctor who reported an unusually high number of cases would be investigated by the District Medical Officer.[52]

The purpose of these proposals was to emphasise that abortion should be an exceptional procedure. But as the abortion epidemic demonstrated, abortion was not an exceptional procedure but an everyday occurrence for thousands of women, and one for which they easily found assistance, whether from laity, midwives, or doctors. The force of the law and the righteous indignation of the medical establishment seemed to be powerless to halt the upsurge in abortion. The only effect of such attitudes was to drive abortion further underground, and this presented such risks to health and fecundity that even doctors who opposed abortion were compelled to advocate a relaxation in the penalties for abortion.

NOTES

1. Ludwig Hoche and Hermann Brandenburg, *Der Kampf gegen die Abtreibungsseuche* (Thieme, Leipzig, 1927); Robert Behla, 'Fehlgeburt und Geburtenrückgang', *Medizinal-statistische Nachrichten*, 5 (1913–4), p. 471; Annemarie Niemeyer, 'Zur Statistik der Fehlgeburten', *MW*, 6 (1932), pp. 1514–15; Max Hirsch, *Die Fruchtabtreibung: ihre Ursachen, ihre volkshygienische Bedeutung und die Mittel zu ihrer Bekämpfung* (Enke, Stuttgart, 1921), p. 3; R. Schaeffer, 'Über die Häufigkeit der Fehlgeburten', *Der Frauenarzt*, 29 (1914), pp. 50–9; Hans von Hentig, 'Zur Abtreibungsstatistik', *MKP*, 23 (1932), p. 681; Fritz Kretschmar, *Die medizinische und soziale Indikation für das Recht zur Schwangerschaftsunterbrechung* (Risse Verlag, Dresden, 1932), pp. 23–4; F. Reichert, 'Die Fehlgeburten 1931–38 und ihre Behandlung in Krankenanstalten', *Deutsche Aerzteblatt*, 70 (1940), pp. 520–2.
2. Agnes Bluhm, 'Mutterschaftsfürsorge', in Alfred Grotjahn and Josef Kaup (eds), *Handwörterbuch der sozialen Hygiene* 2 vols, (Vogel, Leipzig, 1912), vol. II, pp. 73–4; Gustav Tugendreich, *Die Mutter- und Säuglinsgfürsorge* (Enke, Stuttgart, 1910), pp. 169, 173–4; W. Weinberg, 'Fehl- und Frühgeburt', in Grotjahn and Kaup, *Handwörterbuch*, vol. I, pp. 342–3; R. Wehmer and W. Pflanz, 'Kurpfuscherei und Geheimmittelwesen' in O. Rapmund (ed.), *Das Preussische Medizinal- und Gesundheitswesen in den Jahren 1883–1903* (Kornfeld, Berlin, 1908), p. 457; Ludwig Ebermayer, *Arzt und Patient in der Rechtsprechung* (Mosse, Berlin, 1925) pp. 27–8, 43–5; Edward Shorter, *A history of women's bodies* (Basic Books, New York, 1982), pp. 35–6, 43–4, 142; Hans-Heinz Eulner, *Die Entwicklung der medizinischen Spezialfächer an den Universitäten des deutschen Sprachgebietes* (Enke, Stuttgart, 1970), pp. 288, 294.
3. Heinrich Fritsch, *Gerichtsärztliche Geburtshülfe* (Enke, Stuttgart, 1901) p. 110; Hans Harmsen, 'Massnahmen zur Steuerung der menschlichen Fruchtbarkeit' in H. Giese (eds.), *Die Sexualität des Menschen. Handbuch der medizinischen Sexualforschung* (2 vols, Enke, Stuttgart, 1968; 1971), vol. I, p. 130.
4. Dr Bleichröder, 'Über die Zunahme der Fehlgeburten in den Berliner Krankenhäusern', *BKW* 51 (1914), pp. 451–3; Kaethe Deen, 'Über die Zunahme der Fehlgeburten in den städtischen Krankenhäusern Alt-Berlins während und nach dem Kriege', PhD dissertation, University of Berlin, 1923, p. 18; Oskar Haken, 'Über die Häufigkeit des Abortes vor, während und nach dem Kriege', PhD dissertation, University of Berlin, 1925, p. 42; Otto-Hermann Seydewitz, 'Die geschichtliche Entwicklung des Abortes vom Jahre 1924 bis zum Jahre 1938 und ihre Beziehung zur gegenwärtigen Zeit', (PhD dissertation, University of Berlin, 1939, p. 18; Alfred Sternberg, 'Erfahrungen an 2617 Aborte', *DMW*, 52 (1926), p, 1548; Andreas Friese, 'Fehlgeburt und Lebensalter' PhD dissertation, University of Berlin, 1935, p. 33; Werner Barasch, 'Sozialhygienische Gesichtspunkte zur Abortfrage unter Zugrundelegung der von 1911 bis 1921 in den Breslauer Kliniken und Polikliniken behandelten Fehlgeburten', PhD dissertation, University of

Breslau, 1922, pp. 5, 13-15; Artur Brandt, 'Gerichtsärztliche Untersuchungen über Häufigkeit und Art des kriminellen Abortus', PhD dissertation, University of Breslau, 1922, p. 28; Max Hempe, 'Zur Therapie und Pathologie des Aborts', PhD dissertation, University of Breslau, 1923, p. 18; Erwin Koehl, 'Über die Behandlung des Abortes mit besonderer Berücksichtigung des fieberhaften Abortes', PhD dissertation, University of Munich, 1919, p. 12; Kaspar Wölfle, 'Über die Häufigkeit des Abortes mit besonderer Berücksichtigung des fieberhaften', PhD dissertation, University of Munich, 1922, p. 9; O. Landsberg, 'Statistik der Fehlgeburten', *ASA*, 7 (1914), p. 58; Hans Hammerschmidt, 'Die Aborte an der Universitäts-Frauenklinik zu Rostock in den Jahren 1907-1922 unter besonderer Berücksichtigung der fieberhaften Abortes', PhD dissertation, University of Rostock, 1926, p. 10; K. Bley, 'Die Aborte in den Jahren 1912-1917', *MGG*, 48 (1918), pp. 393-410; Harald Lorenzen, 'Die Aborte in den Jahren 1910 bis 1918', *MGG*, 53 (1920), pp. 292-5; Ludwig Nebel, 'Über das Verhältnis von Aborten zu Geburten in Mainz in dem letzten Dezennium', *ZGyn*, 45 (1921), pp. 1657-60; F. Prinzing, 'Die Statistik der Fehlgeburten', *AFk*, 1 (1914), p. 23; Karl Hartman, 'Die Häufigkeit des Abortes', PhD dissertation, 1919, University of Marburg, pp. 21-2; Gottlieb Heilmann, 'Über die Häufigkeit der Aborte, insbesondere der fieberhafte, in der letzten Acht Jahren und ihre Behandlung in der Klinik', PhD dissertation, 1920, University of Würzburg, p. 18.

5. Behla, 'Fehlgeburt', p. 471; Dr Dornedden, 'Die Fehlgeburten in den Universitäts- und Landesfrauenkliniken', *Reichsgesundheitsblatt*, 4 (1929), p. 682; Deen, 'Zunahme', p. 18; Sternberg, 'Erfahrungen', p. 1548; Friese, 'Fehlgeburt', p. 33; Brandt, 'Untersuchungen', pp. 30-1; F. Pietrusky, 'Zur Frage der kriminellen Fruchtabtreibung in Deutschland', *DZGGM*, 17 (1930), p. 56; Koehl, 'Behandlung', p. 12; Georg Legl, 'Der fieberhafte Abort und seine Behandlung', PhD dissertation, University of Munich, 1921, p. 5; Wölfle, 'Häufigkeit', p. 9; Hugo Lappin, 'Statistik der Aborte der Universitäts-Frauenklinik München in den Jahren 1925-1926', PhD dissertation, University of Munich, 1927, p. 8; Paul Rosner, 'Zehn Jahre Abortbehandlung an der zweiten Universitätsklinik für Frauenkrankheiten und Geburtshilfe', PhD dissertation, University of Munich, 1930; Justus Graalfs, 'Die Statistik der Fehlgeburten', PhD dissertation, University of Halle, 1924, pp. 84-7; Statisches Reichsamt, Abteilung für Arbeiterstatistik, *Krankheits- und Sterblichkeitsverhältnisse in der Ortskrankenkasse Leipzig* (Berlin, 1910), pp. 256-7; Hammerschmidt, 'Aborte', p. 8; Thomas Hermannssen, 'Über Abortfolgen', PhD dissertation, University of Kiel, 1929, p. 8; Lorenzen, 'Aborte', p. 295; G. Leubuscher, 'Krimineller Abort in Thüringen', *VGMOS* (3rd series), 50 (1915), p. 3; Georg Haas, 'Zahl und Verlauf der Aborte am St Johann-Hospital zu Hamborn in den Jahren 1908 bis 1919', PhD dissertation, University of Erlangen, 1920, pp. 9-10.

6. Bleichröder, 'Zunahme', p. 451; Deen, 'Zunahme', p. 18; Haken, 'Häufigkeit', pp. 42, 45, 49; Friese, 'Fehlgeburt', p. 33; Barasch, 'Gesichtspunkte', p. 19; Koehl, 'Behandlung', p. 12; Legl, 'Aborte', p. 8; Lappin, 'Statistik', p. 7; Wölfle, 'Häufigkeit', p. 11; Lorenzen, 'Aborte', pp. 300-2; Hammerschmidt, 'Aborte', p. 9; E. Roesle, 'Die Magdeburger Fehlgeburtenstatistik vom Jahre 1924', *ASHD*, 1 (1926), p. 193; E. Rosenthal-Deussen, 'Geburtenhäufigkeit, Kindersterblichkeit und Fehlgeburten', *AFk*, 14 (1928), pp. 5-8. On the changes in parity-specific abortion rates over time

see the comparative tables on Berlin, Munich, and Breslau in Gerhard Gramse, 'Die Beziehung des Aborts zum Geburtenrückgang', PhD dissertation, 1918, University of Breslau, pp. 22-3.

    7. Walter Benthin, 'Über kriminelle Fruchtabtreibung: Mit besonderer Berücksichtigung der Verhältnisse in Ostpreussen', *ZGG* 17 (1915), p. 592; Haberda, 'Erfahrungen', p. 65; Otto Rupp, 'Beitrag zum gegenwärtigen Stande der Abortfrage', PhD dissertation, University of Munich, 1914, p. 11.

    8. Behla, 'Fehlgeburt', p. 471; Benthin, 'Kriminelle Fruchtabtreibung', p. 594; Leubuscher, 'Krimineller Fruchtabtreibung', p. 4; Berthold Polag, 'Die Berechtigung des künstlichen Abortus vom medizinischen, juristischen, und national-ökonomischen Standpunkte', PhD dissertation, University of Strassburg, 1909, pp. 67, 71.

    9. Behla, 'Fehlgeburt', p. 471; Deen, 'Zunahme', p. 17; Wolfgang Schumacher, 'Die Beweggründe zum kriminellen Abort', PhD dissertation, University of Berlin, 1934, pp. 11-12; Friedrich Ofterdinger, 'Über das Verhältnis zwischen Aborten und Geburten in Hamburg', PhD dissertation, University of Hamburg, 1925, p. 4; Barasch, 'Gesichtspunkte', p. 16; Brandt, 'Untersuchungen', pp. 28-9; W. Köhler, *Das Delikt der Abtreibung im Landgerichtsbezirk Gera, 1896-1930* (Fromm, Jena, 1935), p. 20; Leubuscher, 'Krimineller Fruchtabtreibung', p. 4; Polag, 'Berechtigung', pp. 67, 71; Graalfs, 'Statistik', pp. 108-9; Helmut Wolff, 'Zur Beobachtung der Fehlgeburten', *ASA*, 14 (1925), p. 361.

    10. Ernst Hirschberg, *Die soziale Lage der arbeitenden Klassen in Berlin* (Liebman, Berlin, 1897), p. 82; Weinberg, 'Fehl- und Fruhgeburt', p. 343; Statistisches Reichsamt, *Krankheits- und Sterblichkeitsverhältnisse*, pp. 256-7; Kurt Pohlen, 'Die Fehlgeburten im deutschen Reich', *Reichsgesundheitsblatt*, 8 (1933), p. 897; Ewald Gemmer, *Das Problem der Geburteneinschränkung und Fehlgeburten vor und nach 1933*, (Tageblatt-Haus, Coburg, 1937), pp. 23, 34.

    11. Kretschmar, *Indikation*, pp. 28-9; Jahns, *Delikt*, pp. 31-2; Konstantin Inderheggen, *Das Delikt der Abtreibung im Landgerichtsbezirk Mönchen-Gladbach in der Zeit von 1908 bis 1938* (Fromman, Jena, 1940), pp. 92-3; Köhler, *Delikt*, p. 20.

    12. Dr Koblanck, in 'Verhandlungen der Gesellschaft für Geburtshilfe und Gynäkologie zu Berlin', *ZGG*, 79 (1917), p. 363; Bumm, cited by Ludwig Nürnberger, 'Die Bedeutung der Fehlgeburten in der Bevölkerungspolitik', *ZGyn*, 41 (1917), p. 839; Prinzing, 'Statistik', pp. 21-3; Statistisches Reichsamt, *Krankheits- und Sterblichkeitsverhältnisse*, pp. 265-7; Wölfle, *Häufigkeit*, p. 13; Legl, *Aborte*, pp. 8-9; Lappin, *Statistik*, p. 3; Dornedden, 'Fehlgeburten', p. 679; Ohlen, 'Fehlgeburten', p. 897; Hans Endlich, 'Zur Pathologie und Therapie des Abortes', PhD dissertation, University of Breslau, 1914, pp. 18-20; Carl Javert, *Spontaneous and habitual abortion* (Blackiston, New York, 1957), p. 3.

    13. Weinberg, 'Fehl- und Frühgeburt', p. 342; Dornedden, 'Fehlgeburten', p. 679.

    14. Leopold Bürger, 'Häufigkeit und gebräuchliche Methoden des Kriminellen Abortus', *Friedrichs Blätter für gerichtliche Medizin und Sanitätspolizei*, 60 (1909), p. 265; Frederik Taussig, *Abortion, spontaneous and induced* (Mosby, St Louis, 1936), p. 103; Theodor Heynemann, 'Fehlgeburt und Frühgeburt: Klinischer Teil', in Josef Halban and Ludwig

Seitz (eds), *Biologie und Pathologie* (Urban and Schwarzenberg, Berlin, 1929), vol. 7, part 1, p. 570; Judel Berliner, 'Zur Therapie und pathologie des Abortes', PhD dissertation, University of Breslau, 1912, pp. 14-15; Endlich, 'Pathologie', pp. 18-21; Ludwig Laband, 'Zur Frequenz, Aetiologie und Pathologie der Fehlgeburt', PhD dissertation, University of Breslau, 1912, pp. 17-22; Rudolf Stiglbauer, 'Die Fehlgeburtenstatistik in Österreich, ihre sozialhygienische Bedeutung und bevölkerungspolitische Auswirkung', *WKW*, 47 (1934), p. 325.

15. Bürger, 'Häufigkeit', pp. 264-5; Weinberg, 'Fehl- und Frühgeburt', p. 342; Frederick Taussig, *The prevention and treatment of abortion* (Mosby, St Louis, 1910), pp. 29-32; Karl Abernethy, 'Neuere Forschungen über die Ursachen des Aborts und der Frühgeburt', PhD dissertation, University of Konigsberg, 1919; H. Stieve, *Unfruchtbarkeit als Folge unnatürlicher Lebensweise* (Bergmann, Munich, 1926). The study on syphilis by Lindheim is cited by Prinzing, 'Statistik', p. 28; cf. Heinz Oeser, 'Lues und Abort', Berlin dissertation, 1936.

16. Max Hirsch, 'Frauenerwerbsarbeit und Frauenkrankheit', *MGG*, 38 (1913), Supplement, pp. 298-322. For a discussion of Hirsch's holistic approach to gynaecology see Robert Lennig, 'Max Hirsch: Sozialgynäkologie und Frauenkunde', PhD dissertation, University of Berlin, 1977.

17. Dornedden, 'Fehlgeburten', p. 629; Pohlen, 'Fehlgeburten', p. 897.

18., Dr Conrad, 'Ist ärztliche Schwangerschaftsunterbrechung auf Grund "medizinischer Indikation" strafbar?', *Deutsche Juristen-Zeitung*, 32 (1927), pp. 873-4. See also H. Heiss, *Die Künstliche Schwangerschaftsunterbrechung und der Kriminelle Abort* (Enke, Stuttgart, 1967), pp. 106-8; Polag, 'Berechtigung', pp. 43-54; Otto Ehinger and Wolfram Kimmig, *Ursprung und Entwicklungsgeschichte der Bestrafung der Fruchtabtreibung* (Ernst Reinhardt, Munich, 1910).

19. Karl Leibig, 'Abtreibung und Unterbrechung der Schwangerschaft', *Bayerische Polizei*, (1929), pp. 19-21. See also Erich Schubart, 'Das Reichsgericht und die ärztliche Schwangerschaftsunterbrechung', *ASHD*, 3 (1928), pp. 150-2; Ernst Cohn, 'Die Abtreibung als rechtspolitisches Problem der Gegenwart', PhD dissertation, 1930, University of Greifswald, pp. 69-70.

20. Georg Winter, 'Unberechtigte Indikationen zur künstlichen Unterbrechung der Schwangerschaft', *MK*, 13 (1917), p. 49; Georg Winter, 'Die Einschränkung des künstlichen Aborts', *ZGyn*, 41 (1917), p. 4; Winter, 'Unsere Aufgaben', p. 101; Georg Winter, *Der künstliche Abort: Indikationen, Methoden und Rechtspflege für den geburtshilflichen Praktiker*, 2nd edn (Enke, Stuttgart, 1926), pp. 1-2, 8; Ernst Bumm, 'Zur Frage des künstlichen Abortus', *MGG*, 43 (1916), p. 391.

21. Friedrich Ahlfeld, 'Über Indikationen zum künstlichen Abort, *ZGyn*, 30 (1906), pp. 658-9; K. Jaffe, 'Zur Indikation des künstlichen Aborts', *Der Frauenarzt*, 9 (1894), pp. 40-6; Dr Lomer, 'Über künstlichen Abortus bei Allgemeinerkrankung der Mutter', *Der Frauenarzt*, 9 (1894), pp. 1-15; Georg Winter, 'Die Stellung des Arztes zum künstlichen Abort', *MK*, 13 (1917), p. 86.

22. Behla, 'Fehlgeburt', p. 471; Polag, *Berechtigung*, p. 16; Winter, *Künstliche Abort*, pp. 99-101; Walther Benthin, 'Die Grundlagen der künstlichen Schwangerschaftsunterbrechung', *TG*, 62 (1921), pp. 325-6; Dr Roepke, 'Kriminelle Fruchtabtreibung, künstliche Unterbrechung der

Schwangerschaft und Fürsorge für tuberkulöse Schwangeren', *ZMB*, 29 (1916), p. 292; Dr Kupferberg, 'Ist der artifizielle Abort ärztlich überhaupt berechtigt?', *AGyn*, 117 (1922), p. 292; Hans Naujoks, 'Neuere Gesichtspunkte hinsichtlich der Indikationsstellung zum künstlichen Abortus auf der Grundlage des heutigen Gesetzes', *DZGGM*, 16 (1930), p. 218; Dr Zangemeister, 'Die Indikationsstellung beim künstlichen Abort', *ZMB*, 40 (1927), p. 640.

23. Hans Naujoks, 'Die medizinischen Indikationen zum künstlichen Abort in Gegenwart und Zukunft', *ZGG*, 91 (1927), p. 32; Benthin, 'Grundlagen', pp. 326–7; Winter, *Künstliche Abort*, pp. 48–51, 56–9, 68, 75–8; Max Hirsch, 'Der künstliche Abortus', *AKAK*, 39 (1910), pp. 209–232; R. Hantke, 'Die medizinischen Indikationen zur Unterbrechung der Schwangerschaft', *MGG*, 16 (1902), pp. 382–6; Dr Zinke, 'Zur Frage der Schwangerschaftsunterbrechung bei Lungentuberkulose', *MGG*, 88 (1931), pp. 34–6; Naujoks, 'Neuere Gesichtspunkte', pp. 219–21; Hempe, 'Therapie', p. 30; Endlich, 'Pathologie', p. 26; Helene Busch, 'Zur Indikationsstellung des künstlichen Aborts', *MGG*, 47 (1918), p. 95; Taussig, *Abortion*, pp. 292–7.

24. Benthin, 'Grundlagen', p. 329; Winter, *Künstliche Abort*, p. 80; C. Bucara, 'Die psychiatrische und neurologische Indikation zur Schwangerschaftsunterbrechung', *MGG*, 91 (1932), pp. 24–8.

25. Hirsch, 'Künstliche Abortus', p. 223; Winter, *Künstliche Abort*, pp. 109–11; Zangemeister, 'Indikationsstellung', p. 637; Krohne, 'Zunahme der Fruchtabtreibungen', *VGMV*, 23 (1926), pp. 47–8. The quote is from Dr Kahl, 'Über die Legalisierung des ärztlich indizierten Abortus unter Berücksichtigung eugenischer Gesichtspunkte', *AFk*, 12 (1926), p. 59.

26. A. Kuttner, 'Darf die wirtschaftliche Lage der Schwangeren bei Einleitung des Abortes berücksichtigt werden?', *DMW*, 43 (1917), p. 1482; Winter, *Künstliche Abort*, p. 107. Franz Kisch proposed that women who wanted an abortion for social (economic) reasons declare their intent to the police, who would notarise the declaration; the woman would then present the form to a doctor who would thereby have legal authorisation to induce abortion. Franz Kisch, *Das Problem der Fruchtabtreibung vom ärztlichen und legislativen Standpunkt* (Urban and Schwarzenberg, Berlin, 1921), pp. 64–6.

27. Winter, 'Stellung', p. 1291; Winter, *Künstliche Abort*, pp. 112–13; Dr Bovensiepen, 'Straflosigkeit der Abtreibung', *ZSWSP*, 7 (1921), p. 337; Kupferberg, 'Ist artifizielle Abort ärztlich überhaupt berechtigt', p. 144; Dr Bacharach, '"Kriegskinder" und die Zulässigkeit der Abtreibung im Notzuchtsfallen', *ZGSW*, 37 (1916), pp. 459–62.

28. Hans Stadler (ed.), *Richtlinien für Schwangerschaftsunterbrechung und Unfruchtbarmachung aus gesundheitlichen Gründen*, (Lehmann, Munich, 1936).

29. Dornedden, 'Fehlgeburten', p. 680, 683; Reichert, 'Fehlgeburten', p. 520; Walter Offermann, 'Beitrag zur Behandlung des fieberhaften Abortes und einiges über die kriminellen Aborte überhaupt', *ZGG*, 84 (1922), p. 372. On the willingness of women to discuss past abortions see Ofterdinger, 'Verhältnis', p. 15; Max Marcuse, 'Die Fruchtabtreibung und den Sittlichkeitsempfinden des Volkes', *AKAK*, 55 (1913), pp. 371–2; Kretschmar, *Indikation*, p. 24.

30. The risks associated with febrile abortion occasioned a heated debate

over its proper treatment. From the 1870s until 1910 an active, interventionist approach prevailed. But in 1910 Winter argued that some cases with certain bacteria (hemolytic streptococci) showed higher rates of morbidity and mortality, and he recommended a conservative approach. Others argued that active treatment, by removing the source of infection, would promote faster recovery. Each side marshalled statistics to support its argument, often using conflicting definitions and standards which further confused the issue. By the late 1920s the consensus favoured expectant treatment: an initially conservative approach to permit the fever to subside, followed by active removal of uterine contents. See *inter alia* Hermann Fehling, 'Über die Behandlung der Fehlgeburt', *AGyn*, 13 (1878), pp. 222-9; Georg Winter, 'Zur Prognose und Behandlung des septischen Aborts', *ZGyn*, 35 (1911), pp. 569-76; Georg Winter, 'Über Prophylaxe und Therapie des septischen Abortes', *MK*, 8 (1911), pp. 598-601; Marcel Traugott, 'Die konservative Behandlung des Streptokokkenaborts und ihre Resultate', *MK*, 10 (1913), p. 1067; H. Schmottmüller, 'Streptokokkenaborte und ihre Behandlung', *MMW*, 58 (1911), p. 2052; Walther Benthin, 'Der febrile Abort', *Praktische Ergebnisse der Geburtshilfe und Gynäkologie*, 7 (1917), pp. 129-79; George Winter, 'Die zwölfjährige Diskussion über den fieberhaften Abort', *ZGyn*, 47 (1923), pp. 1490-2; H.A. Dietrich, 'Über die Notwendigkeit einer allgemeinen Statistik der Behandlung des Abortus febrilis', *ZGyn*, 46 (1922), pp. 467-73; Werner Grünstein, 'Beitrag zur Dietrich'schen Sammelstatistik über die Behandlung des fieberhaften Abortes', PhD dissertation, University of Hamburg, 1926, esp. pp. 7-10, 14, 19; Heynemann, 'Fehlgeburt', pp. 626-7, 641-2; A. Bauereisen, 'Der fieberhafte Abort und seine Behandlung', *Jahreskurse für ärztliche Fortbildung*, (1920), p. 13.

31. Louis Lewin, *Die Fruchtabtreibung durch Gifte und andere Mittel*, 4th edn (Stilke, Berlin, 1925), pp. 194, 466; Kurt Garve, 'Über Vierzig in den Jahren 1914-1920 in Berlin unter dem Verdacht tötlichen krimineller Fruchtabtreibung gerichtlich sezierte Fälle', PhD dissertation, University of Berlin, 1922, p. 1; Alfons Grassl, 'Folgezustände der mechanischen Abtreibungen und Abtreibungsversuche in gerichtsärztlicher Beleuchtung', PhD dissertation, University of Münster, 1936, pp. 11, 15, 22; Fritsch, *Geburtshülfe*, p. 112; Johann Georg Meyer, 'Der komplizierte Abort. Ein Zehn-Jahres Übersicht aus der Universitäts-Frauenklinik zu Würzburg', PhD dissertation, University of Würzburg, 1935.

32. Grassl, 'Folgezustände', p. 17; Lewin, *Fruchtabtreibung*, p. 467; Georg Schray, 'Über 45 Todesfälle von kriminellem Abort, die im gerichtsärztlichen Institut in Breslau in den Jahren 1927-1929 zur Sektion gekommen sind', PhD dissertation, 1931, University of Breslau, p. 32; M. Möllenbeck, 'Peritonitis nach krimineller Abtreibung', PhD dissertation, University of Munich, 1925.

33. Grassl, 'Folgezustände', pp. 7, 11; Garve, 'Fruchtabtreibung', p. 1; Dornedden, 'Fehlgeburt', p. 680; Taussig, *Abortion*, pp. 223-5; B. Schweitzer, 'Entstehung, Verhütung und Behandlung der artefiziellen Uterusperforationen bei Abort', *MGG*, 42 (1915), pp. 148-61; Hans Sinning, 'Über die in Hamburg von 1923 bis 1930 vorgekommenen Uterusperforationen bei Abortbehandlung', PhD dissertation, University of Hamburg, 1934.

34. Fritsch, *Geburtshülfe*, p. 112; Taussig, *Abortion*, pp. 225-6; Grassl, 'Folgezustände', p. 10; Heynemann, 'Fehlgeburt', p. 583; A. Mayer, 'Zur

modernen Abortusfrage', *ZGyn*, 42 (1918), p. 856; Rosner, 'Abortebehandlung', pp. 42-3; G. Puppe, 'Die gerichtsärztliche Beurteilung instrumenteller, durch Aerzte bewirkter Uterusperforationen', *MGG*, 36 (1912), p. 295; Emil Ekstein, 'Über die rationelle Abortbehandlung als die beste Prophylaxis gegen die artefizielle Uterusperforation', *MGG*, 43 (1916), p. 250; Schweitzer, 'Enststehung', pp. 150-2, 154, 161.

35. Dornedden, 'Fehlgeburt', p. 681.

36. Dornedden, 'Fehlgeburt', p. 683; Grassl, 'Folgezustände', pp. 21-2.

37. Kretschmar, *Indikation*, p. 40; Taussig, *Abortion*, p. 27; Pohlen, 'Fehlgeburten', pp. 895-6; E. Roesle, 'Puerperalfieber und legalisierter Abortus', *ASHD*, 2 (1927), pp. 152-4; Karl Freudenberg, 'Berechnungen über die Häufigkeit der tödlichen Fehlgeburten in Deutschland', *MMW*, 79 (1932), pp. 758-60.

38. Ludwig Nürnberger, 'Die Stellung des Abortus in der Bevölkerungsfrage', *MGG*, 45 (1917), p. 23; Rudolf von Jaschke, 'Ein Beitrag zu dem Thema: Unsere Aufgaben in der Bevölkerungspolitik', *ZGyn*, 41 (1917), pp. 66-71.

39. Winter, 'Aufgaben', pp. 97-104; Winter, 'Bevökerungspolitik', pp. 351-65.

40. Jaschke, 'Beitrag', pp. 65-81; Winter, 'Bevölkerungspolitik', p. 360; Hermann Fehling, 'Unsere Aufgaben für die Bevölkerungspolitik', *MGG*, 45 (1917), pp. 366-71; Hans Albert Dietrich, 'Zur Bevölkerungspolitik', *MGG*, 49 (1919), pp. 428-37; Ernst Bumm, 'Geburtshilfe und Geburtenrückgang', *MGG*, 46 (1917), pp. 63-73; Ernst Bumm, 'Zur Bevölkerungspolitik', *ZGyn*, 42 (1918), pp. 617-20; E. Kehrer, 'Die Organisation der Mutter-, Säuglings- und Kleinkinderfürsorge', *ZGyn*, 40 (1916).

41. Kupferberg, 'Abort'- pp. 138-42; esp. p. 142, where he accepts therapeutic abortion for perhaps three cases per year of hyperemesis gravidarum in Germany.

42. R. Schaeffer, in 'Verhandlungen der Gesellschaft für Geburtshilfe und Gynäkologie zu Berlin, 1916', *ZGG*, 79 (1917), p. 361; cf. the similar opinion of Theodore Roosevelt on women's duty: Linda Gordon, *Woman's body, woman's right: a social history of birth control in America* (Grossman, New York, 1976) p. 142. On medical attitudes towards the 'debased' sexual morality of contemporary women see Albert Amend, *Die Kriminalität Deutschlands, 1919-1932* (Wiegandt, Leipzig, 1937), p. 59; Kretschmar, *Indikation*, p. 24; Theodor Junker, 'Über die Ursachen der Fehl- und Totgeburten', PhD dissertation, University of Berlin, 1917, p. 12; Rupp, 'Beitrag', pp. 10-11; Graalfs, 'Statistik', pp. 28-29; H. Fehling, 'Die Tätigkeit der Universitäts-Frauenklinik zu Strassburg während des Weltkrieges', *Gynäkologische Rundschau*, 9 (1915), p. 178; Rudolf von Jaschke, 'Zum Kämpfe gegen die Fruchtabtreibung', *ZGyn*, 48 (1924), p. 14.

43. Ebermayer, *Arzt und Patient*, p. 228. See also Roepke, 'Fruchtabtreibung', p. 288; H. von Hövell, 'Gründe und Bedeutung des Geburtenrückgangs vom Standpunkte der öffentliche Gesundheitspflege: Was kann der Artz und die Medizinalverwaltung tun, um diesem Übel zu begegnen?', *VGMOS* (3rd series), 51 (1916) p. 300; F. Lonne, 'Zum Kämpfe gegen die Fruchtabtreibung', *ZGyn*, 48 (1924), p. 1361; Dr Wachenfeld, 'Strafwürdigkeit der Fruchtabtreibung', *Deutsche Zeitschrift für die öffentliche*

Gesundheitspflege, (1925-6), p. 14; Kretschmar, *Indikation*, p. 24.

44. E. Bumm, 'Die Frage der Zulässigkeit der Unterbrechung der Schwangerschaft vom Standpunkt der ärztlichen Wissenschaft und Berufsehre', *VGMV*, 5 (1915-16), p. 635. See also Winter, *Künstliche Abort*, p. 9; Hugo Sellheim, 'Indikationen zur Unterbrechung der Schwangerschaft', *MMW*, 77 (1930), p. 1456.

45. E. Bumm, 'Not und Fruchtabtreibung', *MMW*, 70 (1923), p. 1471.

46. R. Schaeffer, 'Diskussion betreffends der berechtigte und unberechtigte Indikationen zur Schwangerschaftsunterbrechung', *ZGG*, 79 (1917), p. 362. See also Dr Mackenrodt, 'Diskussion betreffends der berechtigte und unberechtigte Indikationen zur Schwangerschaftsunterbrechung', *ZGG*, 79 (1917), pp. 392-3; Paul Näcke, 'Strafrechtsreform und Abtreibung', *AKAK*, 33 (1909), p. 99; Hugo Sellheim, 'Ohne Fortpflanzungsverantwortlichkeit keine Fortpflanzungsregulierung', *ZGyn*, 52 (1928), p. 2564.

47. Cited in A. Thiele (ed.), *Die Praxis der Eheberatung*, (Blätter für Wohlfahrtspflege, Dresden, 1931), p. 7.

48. Ibid., p. 8; Deen, 'Zunahme', p. 23; Cohn, 'Abtreibung', pp. 54-5.

49. Dietrich, 'Bevölkerungspolitik', p. 436; Fehling, 'Aufgabe', pp. 368-9.

50. Tugendreich, *Säuglingsfürsorge*, p. 170. See also Friedrich Ahlfeld, 'Künstlicher Abort', *AGyn*, 18 (1881), pp. 307-18; A. Walther, 'Zur Hebammenfrage', *ZGyn*, 8 (1894), pp. 305-10; Hövell, 'Gründe', pp. 310-11; T. Lochte, 'Die Fruchtabtreibung und ihre Bekämpfung', *VGMOS*, 2 (1923), p. 538; Paul Ruge, 'Über die Zunahme der Aborte', *MGG*, 43 (1916), p. 462; Hermann, Fehling, *Entwicklung der Geburtshilfe und Gynäkologie im neunzehnten Jahrhundert* (Springer, Berlin, 1925), p. 135.

51. Winter, 'Aufgaben', p. 101; Winter, *Künstliche Abort*, pp. 3, 8; Mayer, 'Abortusfrage', p. 858; Ruge, 'Zunahme', p. 461; O. Sarwey, 'Die Fruchtabtreibungsseuche. Eine frauenärztliche, hygienische und strafrechtliche Stellungnahme', *Deutsche Zeitschrift für die öffentliche Gesundheitspflege*, (1926), p. 3; O. Krohne, 'Empfängnisverhütung, Künstliche Unfruchtbarkeit und Schwangerschaftsunterbrechung vom bevölkerungspolitischen und artzlichen Standpunkt', *ZAF*, 14 (1917) p. 373; Walter Benthin, 'Kriminelle Fruchtabtreibung, mit besonderer Berücksichtigung der Verhältnisse in Ostpreussen', *DMW*, 42 (1916), pp. 540-1.

52. Mayer, 'Abortusfrage', pp. 858-63; Benthin, 'Kriminelle Fruchtabtreibung', p. 541. Von Winckel proposed an extreme degree of state surveillance of women from conception to delivery, including strict controls on all possible abortion materials and strict regulation of persons capable of inducing abortion. F. von Winckel, *Die kriminelle Fruchtabtreibung* (Langenscheidt, Berlin, 1911), pp. 60-1. Cf. J.R. Spinner, *Aerztliche Recht* (Springer, Berlin, 1914), pp. 380-1, and S. Placzek, 'Fruchtabtreibung und ärztliche Berufsgeheimnis', *MKP*, 7 (1910-11), pp. 228-9, for criticism of Winckel.

4

The Abortion Underworld

The abortion epidemic of the early twentieth century erupted in response to the sudden development of simple yet effective abortion techniques and the equally sudden emergence of an 'underworld' community in which any woman who wanted an abortion could get one quickly and easily. Around 1900 new products and new medical procedures made abortion on a large scale possible. In the years that followed a professionalisation occurred in the ranks of abortionists as women shunned the *alte Weiber* of by-gone days and increasingly sought out doctors for abortion. A corresponding professionalisation in techniques took place as even 'quack' abortionists started using the modern methods. By the 1920s women everywhere could obtain abortion on demand, and this awareness fuelled the abortion epidemic. The propriety of the act no longer deterred them; once women decided on abortion their only concerns were when to do it, what to use, and who to go to for assistance.

When would a woman seek abortion? Usually a missed period was the best sign of pregnancy. Four out of five women waited until at least the second period in the hope that something else was at fault, but experienced women acted after the first missed period. Consequently, the second and third months of gestation were the peak stages at which abortion occurred — more than half came at this point.[1] Moreover, after two or three missed periods women began to sense some urgency over and above the desire to avoid pregnancy, namely the need to prevent the development of those external manifestations of pregnancy — facial changes, swelling of breasts, gain in weight — whose abrupt disappearance later might be hard to explain: 'R.A. gave his maid — the old whore — a big stomach, and his wife was the angel-maker.'[2]

Some women, preoccupied with the possibility of becoming

pregnant, would wrongly assume that conception had occurred. Out of anxiety any physiological change, however insignificant, would be interpreted as a sign of pregnancy. Such concern could arise particularly in the event of a missed period. Irregularities in the menstrual cycle are not uncommon, especially in very young or much older women, or in cases of myoma and ovarian cyst. And, paradoxically, a woman with the subconscious desire to have a child but with conscious awareness of the social or economic burdens involved might suspect pregnancy where none existed. For any of these reasons women suspecting pregnancy might seek abortion. The great danger here was that, because the woman was not actually pregnant, any attempt at abortion would not produce the desired result and she would then resort to more serious and more dangerous methods. Insertions, for example, could produce damage because they presupposed the extended uterus of gestation.[3]

Women seeking to abort might first attempt it on their own. With no participants there were also no witnesses. Solo abortion efforts began with the simpler, more traditional methods like abortifacients and proceeded to more energetic but not more effective physical methods before risking intra-uterine techniques. Many lower-class women were compelled to try abortion themselves because they could not afford the services of 'professionals', who charged 20 to 70 Marks before the war, 400 to 500 Marks in the immediate post-war years, 20 to 100 Reichsmarks in the mid-1920s, and 200 to 600 Reichsmarks in the early 1930s. Groceries or goods and services — sewing a dress, or cooking some pancakes — were accepted from poorer clients. During the period 1900–33 self-abortion averaged 15 per cent to 20 per cent of known cases of criminal abortion in the Rhine-Ruhr area, Thuringia and Silesia, but in East Prussia half of all pre-war abortions were self-induced.[4]

When she did not want to go it alone, the woman seeking abortion relied on assistance from friends or relatives. Sometimes the man involved in the pregnancy helped; at other times parents, siblings, or neighbours aided in the attempt. In Göttingen, 7 to 10 such cases involved friends, two included the man responsible, and on one occasion the parents of the woman helped. In Duisburg 80 of 463 cases involved lay assistance: 66 by the man, 10 by the parents, and 4 by the woman's brother. In Mönchen-Gladbach in the same period 85 of 250 participants were male relatives, 9 were female relatives of the woman. Parents were especially likely to participate in abortion efforts when the pregnancy was illegitimate, while the men in such cases acted out of financial insecurity.[5]

In the event of a successful abortion, how did people dispose of the foetus? Evidence on this subject is naturally limited, but in most cases the foetus was burned or buried. Many discarded foetuses were found in open areas such as woods, fields, parks, cemeteries, ravines, rivers, train-tracks, or thrown on dung-heaps or slag-heaps in the Ruhr; others were concealed in drainpipes or lavatories, or left in hotel rooms rented under assumed names. One woman brought the foetus to her doctor; another took it to the midwife. One woman had her son take it to a relative 'for safe keeping'; and in one town in Thuringia a bold soul left it at city hall.[6]

Most do-it-yourself abortions were not successful, however, due to the use of ineffective traditional methods or to the improper use of modern methods.[7] When this became obvious the woman had no choice but to turn to 'professional' abortionists for assistance. Finding an abortionist was not hard. Most women living in the larger cities had already heard of at least one local abortionist from friends, relatives, or co-workers long before they needed one. Those who hadn't could go from one midwife or doctor to another until they found someone willing to perform abortion. In small towns word-of-mouth was important because it limited the degree of overt public knowledge — which would be risky for all concerned — and because it carried with it some indication of the merits of the abortionist involved.

Abortionists in small towns preferred to go to the home of the client rather than have neighbours notice the large number of pregnant women visiting them, a fact which could lead to indictment. In Gera Frau F. was charged because young women were 'constantly coming and going'; Frau G. was accused of 'always brewing up someting, and women and girls go to her regularly'.[8] In rural areas abortionists sometimes travelled on regular rounds, always avoiding the local midwife and anyone else who might report their clandestine activity. This tactic proved especially important after 1933.[9]

In modern consumer society, however, the most practical way for abortionists to make themselves known was through advertising. Some printed and distributed business cards, but the standard approach was to place advertisements in newspapers. Usually abortionists chose larger provincial or metropolitan papers rather than local or hometown papers, which were carefully scrutinised by the police. Most large papers carried dozens of advertisements daily which, while couched in language technically within the law, managed to make their real meaning clear to everyone.[10] The content of the messages remained fairly constant from the 1890s to the 1930s, offering 'advice and assistance in discreet feminine ailments':

Confidential! Information for the most intimate matters!

Successful bath cures, herbal baths, douches. Women treated in confidence.

Women! Find advice and assitance in discreet circumstances.

Confidential. Absolute success in discreet matters.

Feminine ailments, menstrual irregularity will be quickly and economically cured in strictest confidence.[11]

Naturally, the abortionists placing these advertisements did not use their real names or addresses, especially if they had a prior conviction for abortion. Advertisements might be placed through an intermediary, or by using a covering address to intercept nosy policemen. Abortionists also used these advertisements as a 'come-on'. Once the customer found no relief from the initial products offered, she might take up offers of 'further assistance' involving more effective measures at a higher price.[12]

Anyone could become an abortionist. Even people with no medical experience could buy a gynaecology textbook and syringe and set up shop. The sex reform organisations were a further source of information. A therapist in Mönchen-Gladbach was local secretary of a Society for Sex Education, and many other abortionists were reported to be members of similar organisations. A painter in Thuringia learned how to perform abortion while a prisoner of war in France; a messenger studied female anatomy from textbooks and practised by examining his wife.[13]

Non-medical abortionists were usually uneducated, lower-class, and possessors of a criminal record for a variety of offences apart from abortion. Female abortionists included widows, unemployed single women and married women. Male abortionists included traders, storekeepers, locksmiths, painters, shoemakers, miners and factory workers. Both men and women became involved with abortion through personal acquaintance with a pregnant friend, neighbour, relative, or spouse; one successful effort gratis led to others for payment.[14]

Whatever the social background, the pecuniary interest determined the procedure. Abortionists not infrequently began with simpler methods before escalating to the more effective uterine measures. Prolonging the treatment increased the fee and filtered out women who were not seriously interested in abortion. If a woman received unsatisfactory attention she could hardly report it to the authorities. Younger, inexperienced abortionists were often reluctant to employ the more effective methods out of concern for possible injury and subsequent prosecution; consequently most women turned to abortionists considerably older than themselves.[15]

Although the occasion for sexual abuse was obviously present, few abortionists exploited their clients in this way. One railroad switcher admitted in court that he had started his abortion activity in order to get women in an intimate situation. A plumber who performed abortions acquired such notoriety that husbands accompanied their wives to his home to prevent abuses. And in Münster the natural therapist H.L. used a variety of excuses to persuade women to have sex with him: they were 'too cold' for abortion, or coitus would 'dilate the cervix'. He also 'taught' women how to avoid pregnancy through alternate sexual practices.[16]

Many abortionists were in health-related fields: homeopathy, naturopathy and massage. Private institutions such as bathing spas or maternity homes eagerly added a new dimension to their repertoire, offering the advantages of discretion and convenience. One bath displayed a sign, 'My baths are only for colds!', which implied, for women customers, 'If you're pregnant, take the baths and keep quiet!' The more reputable centres attracted a better class of clientele which shielded them from undue official attention.[17]

Natural therapy emerged in the nineteenth century as a reaction to the degenerative ailments which seemed to accompany 'civilised' society. Alcohol, tobacco and coffee were seen as bad influences; water, massage and vegetarianism as good counter-measures to promote 'natural' health. Natural therapists opposed the medical profession with its 'poisonous' medications and opted instead for herbal teas, massage and hypnosis. They achieved controversy and acclaim for their opposition to compulsory vaccination (1874) and to the compulsory reporting of contagious diseases (1900).[18]

Naturopaths benefited from a close rapport with the public. Many were no better educated than their clients; only one in four advanced beyond *Volksschule*. Men and women were equally involved. Male therapists tended to be barbers, bath attendants, and male nurses; women were usually nurses or midwives. At the turn of the century there were nearly half as many 'quacks' as doctors in Germany, but by 1925 the ratio had dropped to one in four.[19]

Natural therapists specialised in ailments which doctors were unable to treat effectively — and prior to the 1870s that included just about everything that could go wrong with the average person, from baldness and toothaches to more serious illnesses like tuberculosis. But venereal disease and other sexual maladies — impotence, sterility, female complaints — predominated in their repertoire. Those therapists involved with these 'sensitive' areas often had criminal records, not infrequently for abortion.[20]

Pharmacists and druggists preferred to supply products for home use rather than become directly involved with abortion. Pharmacists had ready access to effective substances, but they were also subject to close scrutiny by the state, which limited their ability to supply restricted products. Druggists were more likely to become involved with the abortion trade. They sold a greater variety of products and paraphernalia, from patent medicines to syringes, and were subject to less supervision than the pharmacists.[21]

The druggist trade originated in the late nineteenth century as the oversupply of pharmacy students exceeded the number of available pharmacy concessions. Those who were unable to set up a pharmacy of their own moved into the related area of retail drug stores, which sold everything except pharmaceutical drugs: spices, condiments, candies, dietetic aids, cosmetics, toiletries, paints and varnishes, and technical chemicals, as well as drugs not regulated by the Imperial Ordinance and other legislation restricting certain products to sale in pharmacies. Indeed, it was precisely this Ordinance that sparked the proliferation of drug stores in Germany, from 1,000 in 1872 to 10,000 in the mid-1920s. The increasingly strict supervision of pharmacies meant that many graduating students were unable to secure stores of their own and were compelled to become druggists. In 1873 more than three-fourths of all druggists were certified pharmacists; this percentage declined gradually. At the same time as the number of pharmacies was being restricted, the dynamic pharmaceutical industry was producing a plethora of ready-made drugs which preempted much of the traditional work of pharmacists. Druggists argued that they should be allowed to sell all medications except those which were specifically prepared for individual customers on prescription.[22]

On this basis it is easy to see the importance of druggists for the trade in abortion-related materials. Drug stores were plentiful and relatively unsupervised. Since few customers came in asking for 'something to induce abortion', druggists could plead ignorance of what customers intended to do with the 'hygienic' equipment, while profiting from the sales.[23]

The growing access of the public to professional health care led to an increasing reliance on bona fide practitioners for abortion. Midwives were especially likely to utilise their medical training for abortion because of the need to supplement their meagre income, and because they easily identified with the women, often their neighbours, who came to them for help. Moreover, their relative lack of education led them to share the common belief that restoration of menses before quickening was not immoral. For their part, women might well prefer abortion at the hands of a competent woman rather than an impersonal man. They frequently travelled from one midwife to another until they found one willing to induce abortion.[24]

Advertisers frequently exploited this preference for their own ends. Advertisements often identified the sponsor as a 'former midwife', implying either expertise or the loss of a previous licence to practise from conviction for a criminal offense, such as abortion. One male abortionist even advertised under the name 'Frau R'.[25]

Menstrual Irregularity / Blood Stasis
Quick and safe help from former midwife.[26]

Midwife. Very discreet. Large practice since 1885. Provides ladies with advice and help in all cases.[27]

Douching apparatus, teas. Sure help for period disruptions. Frau Knop, retired midwife.[28]

Practising midwives did not ordinarily become involved with criminal abortion. Instead, after some years of practice they retired to establish private maternity homes offering 'discreet' delivery, with no report of births to home-town authorities. Some of the more expensive homes were located abroad, and this lent an exotic and surreptitious air to them. Madame Dupont, *sage-femme diplomée*, of Annemasse, France, and the Institute for Discreet Deliveries, Rue du Rhone 6, Geneva, were among the homes which advertised in Germany.[29] Obviously, if the homes could provide for delivery in strict confidence, they could just as easily arrange for abortion. One such institution in Breslau recorded 104 deliveries in one year, of which 94 were abortions or premature births. But this discretion was not cheap; a weekly fee of 500 Reichsmarks kept the homes beyond the reach of most women.[30]

After the turn of the century doctors steadily took over the abortion trade in the cities, while leaving rural areas to the midwives. Women openly approached doctors for abortion, complaining at first of 'delicate health' or painful prior deliveries. By the 1920s women offered no medical excuses; they simply asked for abortion because they could not afford, or did not want, another child.[31]

Doctors consistently employed the effective intra-uterine techniques characteristic of modern abortion. In addition to syringes and uterine sounds they relied on dilatation and curettage, which ensured complete abortion but which carried the risk of internal injury — an especially high risk in Göttingen, where three of the doctors convicted of abortion were 'practically blind'.[32]

Many doctors were sympathetic to the plight of their patients and willingly performed abortions, often disguising them under various medical headings. In Rheydt in 1927 an abortion trial centred on two doctors who treated more abortions in their Health Insurance practice than all other doctors in the area combined. In a small north-central German town during the Depression one doctor induced 426 abortions in one year. Doctors who operated private clinics might induce abortion in their office practice and then refer the woman to the clinic for further treatment. This procedure was especially common for upper- and middle-class women.[33]

Others preferred to be coy about the practice. Sometimes doctors and patients would play little games. A woman might show up and say, 'Oh, Doctor, I have this pain; can you help me?' After a brief examination the doctor would declare that the problem was an 'obstruction' which he then removed with dilatation and curettage. Or, a woman might show up every month for 'preventive curettage', or to have a 'uterine catarrh' cauterised. In the 1920s such games were less necessary. If a doctor declined a woman's request for abortion, she could easily and accurately respond, 'Okay, if you won't do it I'll get it done by someone else.' Hospitals reported cases where women who had been denied an abortion showed up a day or two later for treatment of 'incomplete spontaneous abortion'.[34]

Some doctors developed a kickback arrangement with midwives. When approached by a woman seeking abortion, the midwife would induce bleeding and refer the woman to the doctor for treatment. The advantage of this strategy was that it diffused responsibility for the abortion in the event of detection. After all, the doctor had treated uterine bleeding or incomplete abortion; he had not actually induced abortion but had merely treated a patient in need. The midwife could explain her action in almost any fashion since little trace of her manipulation would remain after the doctor's treatment. The merits of this approach were so great that some midwives not acting in tandem with a doctor would nonetheless induce abortion and refer the woman to a hospital for follow-up treatment. If her action had proceeded smoothly not even an experienced doctor would see anything other than incomplete spontaneous abortion. In the event of detection, the midwife could argue that surely she would not have induced abortion and then referred the woman to a hospital where this could be detected.[35]

The 'professionalisation' of abortionists reflected the increasing importance of modern technology for criminal abortion. The new techniques that became available after 1900 made abortion a relatively safe and invariably successful procedure.

Inserting objects into the uterus continued to be a common method for inducing abortion, but the success of the procedure depended on the technique. Lay people generally utilised household objects like needles or pencils, and such random stabbing in the dark might well do more harm to the woman than to the foetus. Experienced abortionists knew that the later months of gestation were more suited to this approach because the foetus provided a larger target and because it was easier to induce contractions. Midwives and doctors employed medical instruments like bougies and catheters, either to kill the foetus and provoke expulsion or simply to penetrate the cervix and stimulate contractions. Insertion of intra-uterine devices after conception remained a popular method of abortion which women could perform themselves: 'One uses the stem *after* a missed period.'[36]

Dilatation and curettage became an important therapeutic measure for treating incomplete abortion after the 1870s, but it could be equally useful for inducing abortion. It involves digital or instrumental dilation of the cervix and removal of the uterine contents. If properly performed it is safe and completely effective. It requires some degree of skill, however, and remained the prerogative of doctors. When used for illicit abortion, the digital or instrumental manipulation and the blood on the doctor's finger assured the patient that something effective was indeed being done.[37]

The simplest application of technology to criminal abortion was the widespread use of syringes to inject fluids into the uterus, thereby poisoning the foetus and dislodging it. Uterine syringes originated shortly after the turn of the century as modifications of the vaginal douches popular for feminine hygiene. The uterine syringes consisted of a large rubber balloon filled with an appropriate liquid and a long, thin nozzle which was often curved to conform to internal female anatomy; alternately, a thin rubber tube could be inserted through the cervix. The solution most commonly used was soap water, but tar water, glycerine, lysol, petrol, carbolic acid, vinegar, and tincture of iodine solutions were also used.[38]

Syringes were readily available in drug stores or by mail order:[39]

Mutterspritze
The legally protected "*Sorgenlos*" syringe, with instructions. Injury impossible. 3 Marks.

Ladies!
Douches and syringes, with instructions. Harmless. 5, 7, or — best of all — 9 Marks.

Since only minor modifications were required to transform vaginal douches into uterine syringes, and since the devices were 'legally patented' and modelled after legitimate feminine hygiene devices promoted by the Health Insurance Programme, women easily accepted uterine syringes for all possible uses. Women could use them alone, and in some neighbourhoods syringes were passed around from hand to hand, along with neighbourly advice on how to use them.[40]

Injections of various solutions were a favoured technique among abortionists because they involved no physical manipulation within the uterus and thus precluded internal injuries: 'syringes don't testify', in the words of one practitioner.[41] Injections were fast, easy, and economical. If properly performed, abortion followed within hours. The procedure was to require the patient to stand, or to sit between two chairs; this placed the uterus in the most advantageous position. The abortionist then knelt before the woman and inserted the tube through the cervix, using his or her finger to guide the instrument. Usually two or more injections were made. The action was sometimes performed in dim light, or with the woman only partly disrobed; this prevented her from seeing what was done, and consequently from testifying accurately in court. On the other hand, some abortionists explained aspects of the procedure to the woman so that she would know what to expect.[42]

The last technique to become available in Germany before 1933 was intra-uterine salve containing a mixture of traditional and modern drugs in an antiseptic base. The first version of these salves was produced by the Berlin pharmacist Paul Heiser, who operated a salon, *Mutabor*, on Steglitzerstrasse. He fabricated a paste containing rue, rosemary, aloes, saffon and camphor, which was injected from the tube into the uterus where it induced contractions and expulsion. Heiser used the salve on thousands of women with no fatalities. Later in the 1920s a prominent gynaecologist, Hugo Sellheim, employed a variant of Heiser's paste for the rapid and safe induction of therapeutic abortion. Sellheim argued that doctors should not 'hold their noses' in protest over the unorthodox origins of the paste if it could serve legitimate medical needs. This opinion was seconded by Dr Sachs at the 1931 Congress of the German Gynaecology Society; Sachs called Interruptin (Sellheim's product), a 'great step forward in obstetrical technique' and admonished critics of the paste: 'The idea that a product should be rejected just because it was not originally developed by a doctor but by a quack is groundless.'[43] Dr Jonathan Leunbach of Copenhagen developed another paste, Provocol, which contained soap, iodine, thymol and astringents. A fourth paste, Antigravid, incorporated iodine, calcium iodide, eucalyptus oil, rosemary and calcium carbonate.[44]

All of these salves were freely available until 1931, when reports of several deaths from air and fat embolisms persuaded the government to restrict their use to doctors and limited their availability to pharmacies. This reduced but did not eliminate the use of pastes for criminal abortion.[45]

The transition from traditional to modern abortion technology stemmed from the simplicity and effectiveness of the intra-uterine techniques. Syringes were readily available at reasonable cost and were easy to use. Women could successfully induce abortion themselves and then report to a hospital for treatment of 'incomplete spontaneous abortion'. Doctors and midwives induced abortion by means of equally successful intra-uterine insertions and manipulations.

The transition from traditional to modern methods did not occur uniformly across the country. The differential pace reflected both the background and the skill of abortionists and the awareness of options among the women seeking abortion. Thus in Berlin, the 'mecca of modernity', many women continued to rely on abortifacients, baths and jumping off streetcars to induce abortion, while in rural areas like East Prussia or Schleswig-Holstein up to one-half of illicit abortions were due to intra-uterine techniques. But by the 1920s the more modern methods prevailed in all parts of the country.[46]

The transition in technology can best be followed at the local level. In Thuringia nearly two-thirds of the 194 known criminal abortions during the years 1905 to 1915 involved traditional procedures. Half of these were connected with the Musczynski affair and thus involved camomile, while the others involved red wine mixed with cloves, cinnamon, cummel, nutmeg, or camphor; coffee with rum or brandy; saffron, aloes, ergot, savin, thuja, nitrobenzine, lysol, and petroleum; various package preparations for menstrual irregularity; and the occasional glass of raw sewage water. Physical or external methods such as baths, massage, and vaginal douches were also employed, usually without success. The remaining one-third of cases involved uterine injections or insertions.[47]

A follow-up study of Thuringia for the years 1915 to 1926 reported on 231 cases. By this time injection with soap water had become the leading method, especially among commercial abortionists, four-fifths of whom used the syringe. But older abortifacients continued to be used, possibly because Thuringia was a region rich in the plants used in these concoctions.[48]

A detailed study of the Gera district in Thuringia over the first third of the century found the same methods in use that were common elsewhere in Thuringia: savin, cloves, cinnamon, cummel, camphor, camomile, and coffee with rum. Hot baths were tried in twelve cases. But the largest incidence was reserved for injections using soap water, vinegar, lysol, salt water, mercury chloride, or camomile tea.[49]

The shift to modern methods was even sharper in the Rhine-Ruhr area. In Mönchen-Gladbach intra-uterine methods predominated throughout the period from 1908 to 1938, ranging from 61 per cent of all cases before the war to 82 per cent in the 1920s. Injections utilised soap water, soda, camomile tea, salt water, or vinegar. External methods and abortifacients each accounted for 12 per cent of all cases.[50]

In Duisburg between 1906 and 1935 some 280 of the 419 women on trial for abortion relied on injections of lye, vinegar, lysol, alum, or soap water. Insertions with crochet needles, knitting needles, goose feathers, and other such devices were common. Abortifacients included ergot, quinine, savin, cloves in wine, coffee with rum, and a variety of teas and menstrual preparations, notably Dr Scheffer's Monatspulver and Dr Berger's Biodrops.[51]

A similar pattern prevailed in Essen during the 1930s, where intra-uterine methods accounted for two-thirds of all attempted abortions; external measures, abortifacients, and baths accounted for the rest. The persistence of the more traditional methods at such a late date in an industrial area like the Ruhr may be explained in part by the rural origin of many of the inhabitants and, after 1933, by the more successful control established over more effective methods; among other things tighter supervision of advertisements for 'services' compelled many abortionists to leave the cities and take up more migratory patterns of activity in the countryside.[52]

Although newer techniques and more qualified personnel made abortion a safer procedure, it remained an illegal procedure. But the legal risks no more deterred women than did the health risks. Women themselves believed that abortion before quickening was not immoral, and that only the persons assisting them or providing the equipment could be prosecuted:

> This isn't a serious offense.
>
> Everyone does it and no one gets caught.
>
> You just have to be careful.
>
> If you do it early enough the penalty isn't so great.
>
> At the beginning of pregnancy the sin isn't so great.[53]

But abortion was illegal, and prosecution was an ever-present possibility. Between 1900 and 1930 more than 70,000 persons were convicted for abortion.[54]

Because abortion was usually a secretive act it generally came to the attention of authorities in the form of verbal or written allegations from 'one who means well' lamenting 'the things that go on here'.[55]

> A person just can't understand the way young girls of sixteen get abortions. According to the Criminal Code Fräulein G. deserves a harsh sentence. That girl is a menace to her community. Just as abortion is never permissible, so should sentences be imposed on such degenerate punks. All right-thinking and morally decent people would be grateful for the prosecution of this affair, especially since this degeneration of youth in our Germany is getting worse every day.[56]

Concerned citizens dropped by police headquarters to report that 'they had heard . . .', or that 'people say . . .'. Some charges were brought to the attention of the whole community by means of prominently inscribed grafitti: 'Whoever wants an abortion go to H.D. and G.H.: they fixed Widow K.R.' But most accusations arrived in the form of written statements with vague observations like 'first she was big, now she's back to normal'. Others were more specific: 'She's always brewing up some potion, and women and young girls drop by regularly.' But even specifics were not always accurate, however; one woman was wrongly accused because her house smelled of carbolic acid, but the informer neglected to mention that the house was being painted at the time.[57]

Informers usually claimed anonymity because they were known to the woman, but occasionally other excuses were used: 'These people are extremely brutal and dangerous'; 'I learned last time what these Jews can do.'[58] Many letters bore multiple signatures, as if that would provide greater authority:

The occupants of the house at No. 48 L. Street.

Co-workers in the factory.

On behalf of many who want to see some justice in these matters.

Several people who want to see an end to the dirty work of H. and friends.

From many citizens, including nearby towns.

From the whole village.[59]

One writer anticipated the probable reaction of the police: 'I urge you not to disregard this letter just because it's anonymous.'[60]

This sort of denunciation was a part of everyday life for working-class and lower middle-class people. A woman who had an abortion might tell a friend or co-worker, and the story would spread through the gossip mill until it reached the ears of someone — friend, relative, separated spouse or lover, neighbour, or co-worker — who, for whatever reason, held a grudge against the woman. A few women even informed on themselves in order to get revenge on a boyfriend who had jilted them or on a husband on trial for divorce. Indeed, revenge by somebody was so often the motive for these accusations that most of them proved to be completely fabricated. Police dismissed the majority of charges out of hand as 'the idle gossip of some old women'. In Thuringia more than half of the allegations never came to trial; in the Ruhr three-fourths were dropped. But the police did retain a file on the accused, and if further information came to light they would reopen the case.[61]

Dirct evidence — 'smoking syringes' — seldom led to prosecution. The death of a pregnant woman could arouse suspicion; in one case a woman on her death bed named the abortionist. Once police started to investigate a person they could uncover records that would implicate dozens or even hundreds of women. The 1908 raid on Frau Musczynski in Zürich led to scores of indictments throughout

Germany.⁶² The discovery of a foetus was at best circumstantial evidence. In Duisburg and Mönchen-Gladbach dozens of discarded foetuses failed to initiate proceedings, although fourteen such discoveries in Thuringia did result in court action. Prosecution was more likely to occur when a foetus could be linked to one specific person. A foetus found in the drainpipe of an apartment building led police to focus on a young, single tenant. When blood-stained clothing was found in her apartment she — perhaps unwisely — denied having menstruated. This led to a court-ordered medical examination which revealed some afterbirth *in utero*, and the trial began.⁶³

One reason why so few cases came to court was the difficulty of prosecution. The state had to demonstrate that the woman believed herself to be pregnant and that she had deliberately resorted to specific measures to terminate that pregnancy. When other persons were charged along with the woman, the state had to show that they were aware that the woman was, or considered herself to be, pregnant, and that they offered to, or did, provide the means for, or perform the procedure for abortion. It did not matter whether the woman was actually pregnant, so long as she believed herself to be; nor did it matter whether the procedure was potentially effective or utterly innocuous, as long as the woman procured it with the intention of abortion or the supplier provided it in response to the woman's desire for abortion.⁶⁴

First of all, then, the prosecution had to prove that the woman thought she was pregnant. Unless gestation had reached a point where external manifestations were evident, it would be difficult to controvert a defendant's statement that she did not consider herself pregnant. But if she claimed concern over a missed period and had written away for a 'menstrual tea' rather than seek bona fide medical treatment, then awareness of pregnancy could be inferred.⁶⁵

Proof of attempted abortion was equally problematic. The standard procedure was to determine what technique had been employed, whether that technique was suitable for abortion, and whether the woman or other participant was capable of properly implementing that technique. Although police investigation supplied the evidence, courts relied on medical consultants to determine whether a particular technique was suited for abortion or whether it was a legitimate 'feminine hygiene appliance'. These consultants would also comment on whether the fees charged by the participant were commensurate with legitimate therapy or exorbitant.⁶⁶

Defendants confronted with evidence of procedures they had employed typically tried at first to deny that they had been pregnant, or that they were aware of their pregnancy. If some characteristic of pregnancy had been observed, the woman might blame it on chlorosis or some other condition which duplicated some symptoms of pregnancy. She would often claim further that any procedure that had been used was intended to restore menstrual regularity or to treat some other condition: colds, blood stasis, or venereal disease. More commonly women claimed that the douches or syringes had been used for hygiene or for contraception. Two men who had sex with a woman on different occasions testified that injections of soap water had been performed immediately after coitus to avoid pregnancy; the court accepted this argument.[67] When the fact of abortion could not be denied, women usually blamed it on hard work — especially during the First World War — and claimed that it had been spontaneous.[68]

Professional abortionists, who were more familiar with legal loopholes and courtroom procedures, objected whenever possible to the arguments of the prosecution. They declared that devices or procedures had been used only for hygienic or therapeutic purposes. Rare and unusual medical conditions were also cited, and the court consultants could not always exclude these possibilities. Defendants everywhere realised that if they raised any doubts in the mind of the judge they would probably go free.[69]

When the accused were convicted, it became necessary to apportion responsibility. Did another person assist the woman or perform the entire abortion? Did the person act only in this case, or on a regular basis for compensation? Was the person adequately trained for abortion (a doctor or midwife), or was he or she a quack acting in an irresponsible manner which could threaten the health or life of the woman? The court also had to decide whether mitigating circumstances were present. Social and economic concerns, psychiatric problems, and the possibility of rape or incest could all influence the final decision, even though none excused the act.[70]

As a result of these considerations acquittal occurred in one-fifth to one-sixth of all cases in the communities investigated. Duisburg presented a striking exception with an acquittal rate of 58.3 per cent, which was credited to the greater skill of big-city lawyers, 'four-fifths of whom were non-Aryan'.[71] Most acquittals resulted from lack of evidence rather than proof of innocence. In some cases the excuses offered by defendants — therapy, hygiene, contraception — could not be gainsaid. A woman who had an affair, became pregnant, and then miscarried after two mysterious visits during which the windows had been covered claimed that the visitor was a shoe saleswoman, and since no one could prove otherwise she was acquitted. Legal technicalities also secured acquittal. In one case a man gave his pregnant girlfiend a card with recipes for various abortion concoctions, but, since the card lacked the words 'take' or 'drink', advising to procure abortion could not be proven.[72]

Sentences handed out to persons convicted of abortion reflected the general social perception of abortion as a fact of life rather than a major crime. Even before the First World War, 96 per cent of all sentences were for simple imprisonment; penal servitude was reserved for only a small handful of professional abortionists. This was even truer after the law reform of 1926. Thus in 1925 there were 481 convictions for 'commercial abortion', but in 1927 only 184 for 'career abortion'. The women accused of getting an abortion were punished less severely than the persons who performed abortion, but in neither situation did the courts ordinarily impose the full sentence. Moreover, less than half of the sentences imposed were actually served in full; most were pardoned or suspended, while others were cancelled by amnesties in 1918, 1922, and 1932.[73]

Despite the legal consequences, abortion remained the predominant form of birth control for many people. Whether because some of the techniques seemed reassuringly familiar, being based on traditional patent medicines or everyday hygienic devices; or because the personnel were familiar, being primarily doctors, midwives, and naturopaths; or because the rationale for abortion seemed reasonable, whether it was the folk belief in quickening as the true sign of pregnancy or the modern feminist rhetoric of women's right to control their bodies; or simply because of indolence — the fact that it was easier to do something once the need arose than to bother with endless precautions on every coital occasion on the off-chance that something might happen — for any of these reasons or for all of them thousands of women ignored the law and procured abortion.[74]

Yet reliance on abortion remained relatively short-lived. Abortion proved to women that they could control births; once they realised that, it became possible to think in terms of an ounce of prevention rather than a pound of cure. By the 1920s most women realised that modern contraceptives were as reliable as abortion, much safer, and less expensive. As a result they switched to the use of contraceptives almost as rapidly as they had taken up modern abortion, secure in the knowledge that abortion was always available 'just in case'.

NOTES

1. Jahns, *Delikt*, p. 55; Konstantin Inderheggen, *Das Delikt der Abtreibung im Landgerichtsbezirk Mönchen-Gladbach in der Zeit von 1908 bis 1938* (Fromman, Jena, 1940), p. 35; W. Köhler, *Das Delikt der Abtreibung im Landgerichtsbezirk Gera, 1896-1930* (Fromm, Jena, 1936), p. 36; Werner Barasch, 'Sozialhygienische Gesichtspunkte zur Abortfrage unter Zugrundelegung der von 1911 bis 1921 in den Breslauer Kliniken und Polikliniken behandelten Fehlgeburten', PhD dissertation, University of Breslau, 1922, pp. 14-18; Thomas Hermannssen, 'Über Abortfolgen', PhD dissertation, University of Kiel, 1929, p. 8; Rettberg, 'Gerichtlichmedizinische Untersuchung von 133 Strafverfahren wegen Abtreibung in Landgerichtsbezirk Göttingen, 1930-1939', PhD dissertation, University of Göttingen, 1942, p. 19.
2. Köhler, *Delikt*, pp. 31, 36. See also Inderheggen, *Delikt*, pp. 36, 59; Ludwig Kleinwächter, 'Die maskierte kriminelle Schwangerschaftsunterbrechung', *AKAK*, 5 (1900), p. 201.
3. J.R. Spinner, 'Abtreibungshandlungen bei nicht schwangeren Uterus', *VGMOS*, 58 (1919), p. 220; Alfred Stensch, 'Strafbarkeit des Versuchs der Abtreibung bei vermeintlich Schwangeren', PhD dissertation, University of Würzburg, 1920, pp. 3, 8.
4. Leopold Bürger, 'Häufigkeit und gebräuchliche Methoden des kriminellen Abortus', *Friedrichs Blätter für gerichtliche Medizin und Sanitätspolizei*, 60 (1909), p. 197; Jahns, *Delikt*, pp. 25-6; Inderheggen, *Delikt*, pp. 25-8; Köhler, *Delikt*, p. 13; Hans Reichling, 'Abortivmittel und Methode des kriminellen Aborts im Landgerichtsbezirk Essen', PhD dissertation, University of Münster, 1940, p. 16; Georg Strassmann, 'Abortivmittel', p. 80; F. Peitrusky, 'Zur Frage der kriminellen Fruchtabtreibung in Deutschland', *DZGGM*, 17 (1930), pp. 57-8; Angus McLaren, 'Abortion in France: women and the regulation of family size', *French Historical Studies*, 10 (1978), p. 474; Edward Shorter, *A history of women's bodies* (Basic Books, New York, 1982), p. 178. For representative prices see G. Puppe, 'Über kriminellen Abort', *MGG*, 21 (1905), p. 315; Dr Horvat, 'Beitrag zur Statistik krimineller Aborte', *MGG*, 59 (1922), p. 282; Puppel, 'Kriminelle Abort', p. 583; Dr Meisinger, 'Die Bekämpfung der Abtreibung als politische Aufgabe', *DZGGM*, 32 (1939-40), p. 235.
5. Hellmuth Hahn, 'Gerichtsärztliche Erfahrungen über den kriminellen Abort am Landericht Göttingen in den Jahren 1910 bis 1919', PhD dissertation, University of Göttingen, 1920, p. 4; Jahns, *Delikt*, p. 26.
6. Jahns, *Delikt*, p. 16; Inderheggen, *Delikt*, p. 50; Köhler, *Delikt*, p. 32; Hahn, 'Erfahrungen', pp. 7-8.
7. Inderheggen, *Delikt*, p. 25; Jahns, *Delikt*, p. 24; Köhler, *Delikt*, p. 12.
8. Jahns, *Delikt*, p. 25. See also Hahn, 'Erfahrungen', pp. 4-6; Hans Schneickert, 'Die gewerbsmässige Abtreibung und deren Bekämpfung', *MKP*, 2 (1906), p. 628; A. Brun, 'Der Kampf gegen die kriminelle Fruchtabtreibung', *ZGyn*, 36 (1912), p. 702. On working-class lines of communication see Gerhard A. Ritter, 'Workers' culture in Imperial Germany:

problems and points of departure', *Journal of Contemporary History*, 13 (1978), p. 172.

9. Werb, 'Wandlung', p. 26; Meisinger, 'Bekämpfung', p. 236.

10. Schneickert, 'Abtreibung', pp. 628-9; Köhler, *Delikt*, p. 44; Carl Reissig, 'Geheimmittelschwindel und Geschlechtsleben in der Annonce', *Aerztliche Vereinsblatt Deutschland*, 36-8 (1909), pp. 6-7; Puppe, 'Abort', p. 314.

11. Bürger, 'Häufigkeit', p. 201. See also Raimond Werb, 'Die Wandlung der Abtreibungsmethoden und ihre forensische Bedeutung', PhD dissertation, University of Marburg, 1936, p. 25.

12. Schneickert, 'Abtreibung', p. 629; Puppe, 'Abort', p. 314; Dr Kantor, 'Geburtenrückgang und Kurpfuscherei', *TH*, 30 (1916), p. 518.

13. Hugo Sellheim, 'Eheberatung', *ZGyn*, 52 (1928), p. 668; Inderheggen, *Delikt*, pp. 21, 114, 116, 118, 121; Köhler, *Delikt*, p. 45.

14. A. Haberda, 'Gerichtsärztliche Erfahrungen über die Fruchtabtreibung in Wien', *VGMOS*, 56 (1914), p. 66; Jahns, *Delikt*, pp. 64, 69.

15. Kleinwächter, 'Schwangerschaftsunterbrechung', p. 202; Schneickert, 'Abtreibung', pp. 624-6; Inderheggen, *Delikt*, pp. 86-7; Kantor, 'Geburtenrückgang', p. 563. In England the Chrimes brothers blackmailed thousands of women to whom they had sold abortifacients. Angus McLaren, *Birth control in nineteenth century England: a social and intellectual history* (Holmes and Meier, New York, 1978), pp. 234-8.

16. Jahns, *Delikt*, p. 69; Inderheggen, *Delikt*, pp. 111-14; Hermann Schmid, 'Beiträge zur Psychologie der Abtreibenden', PhD dissertation, University of Münster, 1940, pp. 10-15; Meisinger, 'Bekämpfung', p. 234.

17. Schneickert, 'Abtreibung', p. 630n.

18. Hugo Magnus, *Das Kurpfuscherthum: Eine medicingeschichtliche Studie* (Müller, Breslau, 1908); Wolfgang Krabbe, *Gesellschaftsveränderung durch Lebensreform. Strukturmerkmale einer sozialreformerischen Bewegung im Deutschland der Industrialisierung* (Vandenhoek and Rupprecht, Göttingen, 1974), p. 79; Karin Bergmann-Gorski, 'Aerztliche Standes- und Berufspolitik in Deutschland von 1900 bis 1920', PhD dissertation, University of Berlin, 1966, p. 53; Carl Ludwig and Paul Trüb, 'Die Gegner der Pockenschutzimpfung und ihre Propaganda im neunzehnten Jahrhundert und später', *Medizinische Monatsschrift*, 27 (1973), pp. 68-77.

19. Bergmann-Gorski, 'Berfuspolitik', pp. 46, 98; Tennstedt, 'Krankenversicherung', p. 388; Krabbe, *Gesellschaftsveränderung*, p. 86; E. Hesse, 'Kurpfuschereibekämpfung und Verkehr mit Geheimmitteln im Deutschen Reiche, *ASHD*, 3 (1928), p. 365.

20. Bergmann-Gorski, 'Berufspolitik', pp. 46, 53; Krabbe, *Gesellschaftsveränderung*, p. 83.

21. Böttger, *Giftverkaufbuch*, passim; W. Bernsmann, 'Arzneimittelforschung und Arzneientwicklung in Deutschland in zweiten Hälfte des neunzehnten Jahrhunderts', *Pharmazeutische Industrie*, 29 (1967), pp. 449, 669-71; Ulla Meinecke, 'Apothekenbindung, und Freiverkauflichkeit von Arzneimitteln', PhD dissertation, University of Marburg, 1971, pp. 170-1.

22. Meinecke, 'Apothekenbindung', pp. 145, 158-61, 170-1; Johannes Thiessen, *Die deutsche Drogisten. Geschichte des Deutschen Drogisten-Verbandes, 1873-1926* (Müller, Berlin 1926), pp. 10, 18.

23. Meinecke, 'Apothekenbindung', pp. 170-1; Dr Wollenweber,

'Diskussion. Original Sitzungsbericht, Niederrheinisch-westfälische Gesellschaft für Gynäkologie und Geburtshilfe, 1913', *MGG*, 39 (1913), p. 442.

24. Schneickert, 'Abtreibung', p. 626; Jahns, *Delikt*, p. 69; Brun, 'Kampf', p. 702.

25. Köhler, *Delikt*, pp. 44–5; Schneickert, 'Abtreibung', pp. 627–30.

26. Reissig, 'Geheimmittelschwindel', pp. 6–7.

27. Ibid.

28. Ibid.

29. Paul Cattani, 'Die Medizin in der politischen Presse', PhD dissertation, University of Zurich, 1913, p. 52; Arthur Müller, 'Diskrete Entbindungen in Frankreich und der Schweiz, ein Krebsschaden für das deutsche Volk', *Bayerische Hebammenzeitung* 15 (1913), p. 184.

30. Kantor, 'Geburtenrückgang', p. 519; Pietrusky, 'Frage', pp. 57–8; Cattani, 'Medizin', p. 54.

31. Haberda, 'Erfahrungen', p. 56; Kleinwächter, 'Schwangerschaftsunterbrechung', pp. 205–6; Walther Benthin, 'Kriminelle Fruchtabtreibung mit besonderer Berücksichtigung der Verhältnisse in Ostpreussen', *DMW*, 42 (1916), pp. 577–8.

32. Rettberg, 'Untersuchung', p. 21.

33. Inderheggen, *Delikt*, pp. 20, 33; Haberda, 'Erfahrungen', p. 65; O. Krohne, 'Empfängnisverhütung, künstliche Unfruchtbarkeit und Schwangerschaftsunterbrechung vom bervölkerungspolitischen und ärztlichen Standpunkt', *ZAF*, 14 (1917) pp. 367–9; Meisinger, 'Bekämpfung', pp. 232–3, 235; A. Grotjahn, *Eine Karthothek zu Paragraph 218. Berichte aus eine Kleinstadtpraxis über 426 künstliche Aborte in einem Jahr* (Metzner, Berlin, 1932), pp. 9–14.

34. Kleinwächter, 'Schwangerschaftsunterbrechung', p. 201; Inderheggen, *Delikt*, p. 20; Dr Reifferscheid, 'Über den Geburtenrückgang und die Zunahme der Fruchtabtreibung in Deutschland', *Allgemeine Deutsche Hebammenwesen*, 40 (1925), p. 3; A. Niedermeyer, 'Der Paragraph 218 und die Reform des Strafgesetzbuches', *AFk*, 13 (1927), p. 287n; Ruge, 'Zunahme, pp. 459–60; Shorter, *Women's Bodies*, p. 206.

35. Haberda, 'Erfahrungen', pp. 74–6; Pietrusky, 'Frage', p. 57; Meisinger, 'Bekämpfung', p. 235.

36. Bürger, 'Häufigkeit', p. 393; Werb, 'Wandlung', pp. 30–3; Jahns, *Delikt*, p. 36; Reichling, 'Abortivmittel', p. 31; Paul Strassmann, 'Die Gefährlichkeit intrauteriner empfängnisverhütender Apparate', *DZGGM*, 12 (1928), p. 278.

37. Hermann Fehling, 'Über die Behandlung der Fehlgeburt', *AGyn*, 13 (1878), pp. 222–9; J.R. Spinner, *Aerztliches Recht* (Springer, Berlin, 1914), p. 375; Frederick Taussig, *Abortion, spontaneous and induced* (Mosby, St Louis, 1936), p. 158; Fritz Engelmann, 'Curette und Abortbehandlung', *ZGyn*, 32 (1908), pp. 1139–41; James Ricci, *The development of gynecological surgery and instruments* (Blackiston, Philadelphia, 1949), pp. 327–8.

38. Werb, 'Wandlung', pp. 26–8; Bürger, 'Häufigkeit', pp. 390–1; Anneliese Bergmann, 'Frauen, Männer, Sexualität, Geburtenkontrolle: Zur "Gebärstreikdebatte" der SPD 1913', in Karin Hausen (ed.), *Frauen suchen ihre Geschichte* (Beck, Munich, 1983), p. 84; Shorter, *Women's Bodies*, pp. 199–200.

39. Jahns, *Delikt*, p. 36; Inderheggen, *Delikt*, pp. 32, 39; G. Leubuscher,

'Krimineller Abort' in Thüringen', *VGMOS* (3rd series), 50 (1915), pp. 13-14; Reissig, 'Geheimmittelschwindel', p. 7; Ernst Cohn, 'Die Abtreibung als rechtspolitisches Problem der Gegenwart', PhD dissertation, University of Griefswald, 1930, p. 26.

40. Leubuscher, 'Krimineller Abort', pp. 10, 13-14; G. Strassmann, 'Abortivmittel', p. 79; Puppel, 'Kriminelle Abort', pp. 578-9; Peter Rixen, 'Zur Statistik der Fruchtabtreibung', *AKAK*, 23 (1906), p. 326; Paul Ruge, 'Über die Zunahme der Aborte', *MGG*, 43 (1916), p. 458; Reifferscheid, 'Geburtenrückgang', p. 3; Meisinger, 'Bekämpfung', p. 232.

41. Bürger, 'Häufigkeit', p. 1660; Fritz Hehl, 'Ein Beitrag zur Frage der mechanischen Fruchtabtreibung', *ZGyn*, 30 (1906), p. 835; Haberda, 'Erfahrungen', pp. 82-3.

42. Puppel, 'Kriminelle Abort', p. 579; Werb, 'Wandlung', p. 27; Jahns, *Delikt*, pp. 58-60; Reichling, 'Abortivmittel', p. 17.

43. Dr Sachs, Comment, *AGyn*, 144 (1931), pp. 557-8.

44. H. Sellheim, 'Schwangerschaftszerstörung mittels Salbeninjektion, ihre Gefahren und Versuche, sie dieser Gefahren zu entkleiden', *MGG*, 90 (1932), pp. 441-2; Dr Sachs, 'Über die Verwendung des 'Interruptins' in der Geburtshilfe', *AGyn*, 144 (1931), pp. 548-53, and Comment, pp. 557-8; Dr Dührssen, 'Die Reform der Paragraphen 218-19', *Sexus*, 4 (1926), pp. 77-8; J. Leunbach, 'Provokol: Ein abortive Salbe', *MGG*, 87 (1932), pp. 509-20; Herbert Wolf, 'Einleitung des Abortes durch intrauterine Salbenapplikation', *MGG*, 88 (1931), pp. 442-7; F. Engelmann, 'Über die Gefahren der sogenannten operationslosen Schwangerschaftsunterbrechung', *DMW*, 54 (1932), pp. 166-9; Werb, 'Wandlung', p. 29; Taussig, *Abortion*, p. 323.

45. Werb, 'Wandlung', p. 30; Inderheggen, *Delikt*, p. 41; Reichling, Abortivmittel, p. 14.

46. Benthin, 'Kriminelle Fruchtabtreibung', pp. 595-6; E. Bumm, 'Die Frage der Zulässigkeit der Unterbrechung der Schwangerschaft vom Standpunkt der ärztlichen Wissenschaft und Berufsehre', *VGMV*, 5 (1915-16), p. 387; Dr Hanssen, 'Die Abnahme der Geburtenzahlen in den verschiedenen Bevölkerungsklassen und ihre Ursachen', *ASHD*, 7 (1912), p. 393; Max Marcuse, 'Zur Frage der Verbreitung und Methodik der willkürlichen Geburtenbeschränkung in Berliner Proletarierkreisen', *SP*, 9 (1913), case nos 20, 30, 40, 46, 49, 63, 72, 85, 91; Puppe, 'Abort', pp. 316, 323; Walter Offermann, 'Beitrag zur Behandlung des fieberhaften Abortes und einiges über die kriminellen Abort überhaupt', *ZGG*, 84 (1922), p. 383; Horvat, 'Beitrag', p. 278; Artur Brandt, 'Gerichtsärztliche Untersuchungen über Häufigkeit und Art des kriminellen Abortus', PhD dissertation, University of Breslau, 1922, pp. 38, 41; Pietrusky, 'Frage', p. 58.

47. Leubuscher, 'Krimineller Abort', pp. 6, 9; Werb, 'Wandlung', p. 38.

48. Puppel, 'Kriminelle Abort', pp. 578, 583.

49. Köhler, *Delikt*, pp. 37-8.

50. Inderheggen, *Delikt*, pp. 37-41.

51. Jahns, *Delikt*, p. 50.

52. Reichling, Abortivmittel, pp. 14, 19-20, 23, 26-9; Meisinger, 'Bekämpfung', p. 236.

53. Egon Weinzierl, *Die uneheliche Mutterschaft. Eine sozialgynäkologische Studie, zugleich ein Beitrag zum Problem der Fruchtabtreibung* (Urban and Schwarzenberg, Berlin, 1925), pp. 47-9. See also Cohn,

'Abtreibung', pp. 35-6; Pietrusky, 'Frage', pp. 55-7; Jahns, *Delikt*, pp. 15-18; Inderheggen, *Delikt*, p. 58; Benthin, 'Kriminelle Fruchtabtreibung', pp. 616-17; Puppel, 'Kriminelle Abort', pp. 577, 580.

54. Louis Lewin, *Die Fruchtabtreibung durch Gifte und andere Mittel*, 4th edn (Stilke, Berlin, 1925), p. 26; Köhler, *Delikt*, p. 17; Inderheggen, *Delikt*, pp. 10, 87; S. Weinberg, 'Abtreibungen in die neueste Kriminalstatistik', *NG*, 23 (1927), p. 201.

55. Köhler, *Delikt*, p. 30; Inderheggen, *Delikt*, p. 51.

56. Köhler, *Delikt*, p. 31.

57. Line quotes are from Köhler, *Delikt*, pp. 31-3; and Inderheggen, *Delikt*, p. 59 respectively.

58. Inderheggen, *Delikt*, pp. 50-2; Köhler, *Delikt*, p. 30; Leubuscher, 'Krimineller Abort', p. 31.

59. Inderheggen, *Delikt*, p. 52; Köhler, *Delikt*, p. 31.

60. Inderheggen, *Delikt*, p. 52.

61. Köhler, *Delikt*, pp. 29-31; Inderheggen, *Delikt*, pp. 53, 57-9; Jahns, *Delikt*, p. 14; Hahn, *Erfahrungen*, p. 8.

62. Inderheggen, *Delikt*, pp. 22, 34; Heinrich Fritsch, *Gerichtsärztliche Geburtshülfe* (Enke, Stuttgart, 1901), p. 110; Cohn, 'Abtreibung', pp. 35-6; Köhler, *Delikt*, p. 43; Leubuscher, 'Krimineller Abort', pp. 18-19.

63. Inderheggen, *Delikt*, pp. 50, 60, 65; Cohn, *Abtreibung*, pp. 35-6.

64. Inderheggen, *Delikt*, p. 49; Köhler, *Delikt*, p. 29; Leubuscher, 'Krimineller Abort', p. 31; Lewin, *Fruchtabtreibung*, p. 129.

65. Fritsch, *Geburtshülfe*, p. 115; Leubuscher, 'Krimineller Abort', pp. 31-2; Werner Göhler, 'Statistische Erkenntnisse zum kriminellen Abort', PhD University of Leipzig, 1924, p. 36.

66. Fritsch, *Geburtshülfe*, p. 114; Leubuscher, 'Krimineller Abort', pp. 10, 13-14; Puppel, 'Kriminelle Abort', p. 578; Göhler, 'Erkenntnisse', p. 36-7. On the problems with court medical consultants see W. Liepmann, 'Gerichtsarzt und Gynäkologie', *MMW*, 77 (1930), p. 231.

67. Göhler, 'Erkenntnisse, p. 37; Hahn, 'Erfahrungen', p. 8; Köhler, *Delikt*, p. 35; Puppel, 'Kriminelle Abort', pp. 578-9; Inderheggen, *Delikt*, p. 70; Rixen, 'Statistik', p. 326.

68. Fritsch, *Geburtshülfe*, p. 115; Köhler, *Delikt*, p. 35; Haberda, 'Erfahrungen', p. 88; Hahn, 'Erfahrungen', p. 8; Horvat, 'Beitrag', p. 279; G. Strassmann, 'Abtreibungsmittel', p. 80; Moritz Mayer, 'Landwirtschaftliche Erntearbeit und Fehlgeburten', *Aerztliche Sachverständigen-Zeitung*, 19 (1913), pp. 378-80.

69. Göhler, 'Erkenntnisse, pp. 36-7; Fritsch, *Geburtshülfe*, pp. 112, 115; Rixen, 'Statistik', p. 326; Schneickert, 'Abtreibung', p. 630n; Jahns, *Delikt*, p. 16; Inderheggen, *Delikt*, pp. 63-4; Otto Rupp, 'Beitrag zum gegenwärtigen Stande der Abortfrage', PhD dissertation, University of Munich, 1914, p. 5.

70. Göhler, 'Erkenntnisse, pp. 36-7.

71. Inderheggen, *Delikt*, pp. 67-8; Jahns, *Delikt*, pp. 12, 16, 19-20; Puppel, 'Kriminelle Abort', p. 577; Rixen, 'Statistik', p. 326.

72. Jahns, *Delikt*, pp. 19-20. See also Inderheggen, *Delikt*, pp. 66, 69-70; Köhler, *Delikt*, p. 27.

73. Inderheggen, *Delikt*, pp. 133-4, 139-41, 148, 150-1, 156; Jahns,

Delikt, pp. 8–12; Köhler, *Delikt*, pp. 24–6; Puppel, 'Kriminelle Abort', p. 577; Lewin, *Fruchtabtreibung*, pp. 30, 120.

74. Hirsch, *Fruchtabtreibung*, p. 32; Jahns, *Delikt*, pp. 30–1; Rupp, 'Beitrag', p. 5.

5

The Mass Acceptance of Modern Contraception

The advent of modern contraception involved the application of modern technology to birth control. This made reliable family planning available to those who could afford the new products and who were willing to use them for this purpose. But for many other people social, cultural and economic considerations limited the use of modern contraceptives. In the post-war years, then, the decisive new factor in the history of birth control is the spread of modern techniques of contraception to people of all classes in Germany. During the 1920s public and private organisations mounted a concerted effort to persuade people to use modern contraceptive technology, and to provide these products to those who could not otherwise afford them.

With few exceptions, technological innovation in contraception was slight during the 1920s. Condoms continued to be one of the most popular contraceptives. This trend was accelerated by the wartime experience of millions of conscripts who were issued condoms for prophylaxis against venereal disease. Some barracks even set up dispensers. Because of the greater public awareness of birth control by wartime, more and more men freely transferred the use of condoms to birth control after the war.[1] But even though millions of condoms were sold each year, the commercial marketing still suffered from the limits which the Criminal Code placed on the advertising of contraceptives.[2] Ever since 1900 Paragraph 184, Section 3 read:

> Whoever displays objects suited for obscene use in places which are accessible to the public, or advertises or promotes such objects to the public will be punished with prison for up to one year and with fines up to 1,000 Marks or with one of these penalties.[3]

In 1927 a new law permitted the 'responsible' advertising of prophylactics. The Law to Combat Venereal Diseases included a provision that directly affected condoms:

> Whoever advertises or promotes remedies, objects, or therapies for the purpose of healing or preventing venereal disease in public or through the dissemination of publications, illustrations, or representations, even if in a circumspect manner, or who displays such remedies or objects in a publicly accessible place, will be punished with prison up to six months or with fines or with one of these penalties.[4]

This law necessitated a revision of the obscenity law to remove condoms from the category of obscene items:

> Whoever publicly advertises or promotes objects or procedures which serve to prevent venereal disease in a manner which offends morality or decency, or who displays such objects and products in a publicly accessible place, will be punished with prison up to one year or with fines up to 1,000 Marks or with one of these penalties.[5]

In other words, condoms themselves were no longer deemed intrinsically obscene, and only the 'offensive' or 'indecent' marketing of condoms was punishable.[6]

Since condoms were both a prophylactic and a contraceptive, sales benefited enormously. One Berlin firm alone produced 25 million condoms per year; together all German firms manufactured more than 100 million units annually. Even though half of these were exported, there were still one million condoms per week available in Germany. The 'Venereal Disease' law permitted the erection of vending machines in public places to facilitate the sale of condoms. At first they were installed in railway stations and police stations, but by 1929 they appeared in other locations. By 1932 there were more than 1,600 machines in Germany: 1,000 in restaurants, cafes, and nightclubs; 300 in public lavatories; 250 in railway stations; and 130 for the protection of *Reichswehr* and *Schupo* barracks. The machines stocked condoms or Dublosan salve, made by the German Dublosan Company, an affiliate of the Merz-Werke in Frankfurt. One Mark bought three condoms, but in the Depression the price was reduced to fifty pfennigs for two. Sales in calendar 1931 totalled 171,000 Marks, with twice as many condoms (116,188 units) as salve (55,575 tubes) purchased. Berliners bought more than ten times as many condoms as tubes of salve. As the Depression continued sales of condoms increased dramatically, while sales of salve were cut by half. Not infrequently, condoms were acquired with slugs or by breaking the machines.[7]

Female contraceptives also retained their popularity during the 1920s, but with a marked trend towards the most effective products. Dozens of brands of diaphragms were available; the Ramses model was the most common. Cervical caps proliferated even more rapidly; the Pust and Kafka caps outsold diaphragms by four to one in some cities.[8] IUDs underwent substantial modifications and found greater acceptance as a result. The Gohmann Obturator was patterned after pre-war stem models, although advertisements for the product denied this and promised 'the secret to a happy marriage unlocked forever'. The most successful of the post-war IUDs involved major modification or rejection of the stem pattern. Dr Braun denied that the inter-cervical stem presented any risk of infection, but admitted the risk of penetration by sperm. He added a zigzag strand of silk along the stem, and attached a fan of silk spirals to the uterine portion of the device; together these obstacles would catch any sperm that got through the cervix, while the fan would also catch the monthly ovum as it barrelled down the tube and out into the uterus. Braun claimed hundreds of successful insertions of his device, and argued that success stories seldom made it into print, so that an exaggerated picture of the hazards emerged from the few bad accounts in the literature. A similar IUD was devised by Dr Pust in Jena. The cervical stem was lined with silk strands woven into a pattern that would 'tire out' any sperm that got past the cervical block. The uterine portion contained a silk-wreath to catch any surviving sperm. By 1930 more than 140,000 units of the Pust IUD were in use.[9]

The stem model intra-uterine devices continued in circulation throughout the 1920s, but as reports of harmful effects continued, doctors shifted their interest to another IUD, the Gräfenberg ring. Gräfenberg originally experimented with a silkworm IUD that omitted the controversial inter-cervical stem; it was entirely intra-uterine. Eventually he developed a coil of gold or silver wire which resisted corrosion and facilitated location (by X-ray) and removal. The *modus operandi* of the ring appears to be the local effect (hyperdecidual reaction) which prevents the ovum from attaching to the uterine wall. If the device is removed, fertility is restored. Gräfenberg's ring found widespread acceptance at first, and more than 100,000 rings were in use by 1930, but occasional reports of injury and continued medical opposition to the ring method of contraception removed it from public awareness after 1933.[10]

Chemical contraceptives also proliferated during the 1920s, with more than a hundred brands on the market. Some of the more popular brands included the following:[11]

Ad Acta	Feminex	Patentex
Agonoplasmia	Finil	Patenton
Agressit	For the Malthusian	Pesoletten
Amorkugeln	Gloria	Prophycol
Amuralets	Guttmann's	Rendell's
Antibion	Gynosupp	Schutzpatrone
Anticoncepta	Henke's	Schweitzer's
Antifeconda	Homex	Semori
Antigrava	Ketzer's	Serotonin
Antipart	Kleinwächter's	Speton
Antisperma	Lavagel	Spetonex
Asem	Lugomed	Steriletts
Asepton Morgenrot	Malthus	Steriloform
Atokos	Menschenliebe	Sterilogen
Bellmann's	Mikado	Suppositoire
Cidosperm	Mimi	Timorex
Confidol	Mir-E-Kahl	Tutu
Contrapan	Mitori	Unger's
Damenex	Mutabor	Uxori
Damenlob	Nefi	Vagilen
Einzig	Noffke's	Vaginol
Eta	Omega	Veto
Evau	Ormicetten	Wiba

But consumers faced the same predicament as before the war: how to determine which brands were reliable. Fortunately, several extensive tests shed some light on this problem.

The first examination of brand-name products was made by Steinhäuser in Breslau in 1922. He found that the most effective spermicidal substance was sodium bicarbonate with mercurioxycyanid. The next most effective substances were vinegar, boric acid, sublimat, distilled water and tap water; all worked in ten seconds or less. Less effective substances included alum, citric acid and chinosol (oxychinosulphate). Among brand-name suppositories Semori was the most effective, followed at a distance by other popular brands: Spermathanaton, Patentex, and Noffke's, Schweitzer's, and Unger's pessaries.[12]

Dr Rodecurt of Hannover tested twenty-two items in 1931. He found the most effective products to be Antibion, Prophycols, and Ormicetten; all killed or immoblised sperm immediately. Speton and Agressit required two to three minutes; Unger's, Noffke's, and Schweitzer's pessaries took ten to twenty minutes; and Semori, which most investigators considered highly effective, took nearly an hour. But another study the same year evaluated both the spermicidal effect of the chemicals and the foaming or coating action of the base, and in that study Semori and Asem ranked highest.[13]

The most comprehensive tests on chemical contraceptives were carried out in Britain. John Baker found Semori and Speton to be effective only because of the foam action. Finil, a foam tablet with boric and tartaric acid and dioxyquinolin sulphate, and Rendell's Wife's Friend were the best products. Baker also noted that soap and water was an effective spermicide, and speculated that the increased incidence of indoor baths since the late nineteenth century might have contributed to the fertility decline, at least among the upper and middle classes.[14]

Finally, Dr Cecil Voge prepared a thorough test of virtually all available mechanical and chemical contraceptives for the New York-based Committee for Maternal Health. Voge found that chemical products were unpredictable because of the time required for suppositories to dissolve or the degree of vaginal moisture required to ensure sufficient foam. Nonetheless, several brands were consistently reliable, including Antibion, Prophycols, Patentex, Spetonex, and Semori.[15]

However fortuitously, public consumption of chemical contraceptives favoured the most effective brands. Best-sellers in Germany were Antibion, Confidol, Contrapan, Patentex, Pesoletten, Prophycol, Rendell, Semori, and Speton. Patentex alone sold 30,000 tubes per month in Germany, one-sixth of them in Berlin. Average price for a box of twelve suppositories was 2.65 Marks, while jellies cost 3.95 Marks per tube, with approximately 40 uses per tube.[16]

The 1920s also saw research that foreshadowed the development of oral contraceptives in the 1950s. One line of research believed that the principle of immunisation could be applied to fertility: if women had sperm injected into their bloodstream they might develop antibodies that would resist sperm during coitus. Building on the work of Landsteiner (1899), experimenters achieved temporary sterility in animals through the injection of sperm (Tusknov, 1910, and Dettler, 1920). During the 1920s clinical experiments on humans conducted by Norman Haire in London and by Naiditsch in Russia seemed to indicate that 'spermatoxins' did develop in women and could cause infertility for short periods of time, but this procedure was never applied on a large scale and the experiments remained inconclusive.[17]

A more promising approach was taken by Dr Haberlandt in Austria. Haberlandt sought to produce infertility through a 'hyperhormonalisation' caused by an overdose of oestrogen. His research on animals, funded by the Rockefeller Foundation, demonstrated that ovulation could be suppressed while the hormone was being administered, but returned to normal when injections were discontinued. However significant for the future, Haberlandt's work was ignored in his lifetime, partly because of his early death and partly because of the militant opposition of the medical establishment to this line of research.[18]

There are no reliable statistics on the incidence of operative sterilisation for the purpose of birth control, but Dr Winter observed in 1920 that 'sterilisation is implemented to an unnecessary extent in both private and clinical practice'.[19] Ludwig Fraenkel estimated that if each of the 4,000 gynaecologists in Germany sterilised only one or two women per month, the total would approach 100,000 women per year. Other specialists considered this a conservative estimate. Male sterilisation was apparently less common, but in Austria a sensational trial in 1929 centred on a surgeon from Graz who performed vasectomies on several hundred men in a 'group plan' arranged by the Socialist Party.[20]

Technological innovation was less important than institutional innovations in accounting for the greater diffusion of birth control during the 1920s. These institutional efforts sprang from two not entirely compatible sources. On the one hand, proponents of eugenics argued that society must curb the unrestrained reproduction of the physcially and mentally unfit by means of selective controls on marriage and the provision of contraception, abortion and sterilisation at public expense. On the other hand, advocates of sex reform championed the right of individuals to control their own lives, and in particular supported the right of women to control their own bodies by means of abortion and contraception. Conflict between these two policies arose when the sex reform approach appeared to be more successful in helping 'fit' people to reduce their fertility while eugenicists proved unable to implement effective programmes to curtail the fertility of the 'unfit'.

The Monist League was the first organisation in Germany to advocate a eugenic social policy. The League was founded in 1906 by

Ernst Haeckel, an early convert to Darwin's theory of evolution and to Galton's work on heredity. Haeckel fused materialism, evolution and genetics into a biological philosophy of life, Monism, which he contrasted with the dualistic philosophies that separated man from nature. Monistic eugenics regarded life as a struggle and civilisation as a barrier to true human development. Monists pointed to the growing number of 'defective' individuals in modern society, and urged the adoption of a responsible eugenic policy to discourage or prevent reproduction by inferiors, and to encourage the propagation of the fittest.[21] In 1908 and again in 1910 the League presented a petition to the *Reichstag* calling for mandatory health certificates for all prospective marriage partners that would include notice of potential eugenic risks to offspring. Finding little official response, the League set up its own Eugenic Counselling Centre in Dresden in 1911, but this met with equally little popular response — sixty-four clients in four years — and closed soon after the outbreak of war.[22]

The First World War, with its devastating carnage, aroused eugenic concerns in other organisations which found greater success. The Munich Medical Association set up a Commission to Advise on Questions of Preserving and Improving the Strength of the People, which became the first group to recommend establishing official Marriage Counselling Centres. The Commission suggested that such centres should be empowered to ban questionable marriages, but this idea was rejected by the full Association because it would violate the rights of individuals, and because it would probably lead to more illegitimate births.[23]

The Berlin Society for Racial Hygiene proposed a variation of the Munich idea, namely that spouses should be encouraged to exchange health certificates before marriage. The Society rejected compulsory exchanges, but argued that a voluntary exchange would encourage people to think about the eugenic implications of marriage. The voluntary approach became the basis of official marriage counselling during the Weimar era.[24]

Weimar population policy was enunciated as early as the Constitution of 1919, which defined the importance of the family for society in Article 119:

> Marriage as the foundation of family life and as the cornerstone for the preservation and expansion of the nation stands under the special protection of the Constitution. The integrity, health, and support of the family are the tasks of the state and the municipalities.[25]

Acting on this mandate, the *Reichsgesundheitsamt* prepared guidelines on medical certification before marriage in February 1920:

> 1. In connection with the recovery of the German nation we should seek not only numerical compensation for the losses of the war but also the propagation of healthy and sound offspring.
> 2. Abstention from marriage by those physically and mentally unfit for marriage would be a practical way of preventing racial degeneration.[26]

Late in 1920 the National Assembly acted on these ideas by authorising local registry offices to distribute leaflets to engaged couples calling attention to the importance of medical counselling before marriage.

> The health of husband and wife is a basic pillar of a happy marriage . . . Illness in one has a harmful effect on the other, creates more work, constrains the joy of life, and brings concern and worry into the home . . . Therefore it is a sacred duty of all who want to marry, for their own sake, that of their children, and of the Fatherland, which urgently needs healthy offspring, to determine whether the serious step of marriage is compatible with their state of health . . . If a doctor advises against marriage on grounds of health, the couple should have regard for the future and in conscience delay marriage.[27]

In December 1921, the Prussian *Landtag* called on the Minister of Welfare to prepare a report on the advisability of compulsory health certification before marriage. In February 1922, a memorandum from the Ministry proposed that engaged persons be legally required to file a certificate of health with the local registry office before marriage. This proposal was endorsed by the *Landtag* later that year, but because the proposal fell under *Reich* jurisdiction no further action could be taken.[28]

The first practical steps towards organised marriage counselling were taken by several municipalities which found themselves hard-pressed to meet the financial burdens associated with the large numbers of welfare clients afflicted by hereditary physical or mental illness. Counselling centres were established in Dortmund (1920), Dresden (1923), Frankfurt and Hamburg (both in 1924) to advise young people on the responsibilities of marriage.[29]

The experience of these early municipal centres prompted the

Prussian government to reconsider the subject in 1925. The result was a decree from the Minister of Welfare, Dr Hirtsiefer, on 19 February 1926 which authorised local governments in Prussia to set up marriage counselling centres for engaged couples on a voluntary basis in order to evaluate eugenic suitability for marriage.

> For quite some time now the advisability of encouraging a eugenically sound and healthy offspring through state and other means has been the subject of considerable discussion ... Under the circumstances I consider it appropriate, in view of the exceptional significance of this subject for achieving a strong, healthy offspring, to encourage the establishment of medically supervised marriage counselling centres — such as already exist in some of the larger cities — and to encourage the voluntary patronage of such centres by marriage candidates.[30]

The centres were to advise couples on health-related aspects of marriage, but were barred from dealing with birth control. In later years the Socialists would press for the removal of this restriction.[31]

Local governments responded quickly. Within two years more than 130 centres were in operation across Prussia, including at least one in every administrative district, all linked by the Association of Public Counselling Centres (*Vereinigung für öffentliche Beratungsstellen*). Metropolitan Berlin operated 16 centres. Outside of Prussia, counselling centres appeared in Baden, Bavaria, Hesse, Thuringia, Mecklenburg, and the city-states of Hamburg, Bremen and Lübeck. Here, too, governments generally avoided any involvement with birth control.[32]

The experience of the Frankfurt counselling centre was typical. On 10 November 1924 the City Council passed a resolution establishing a marriage counselling centre to operate out of the Hospital for the Nervous and Emotionally Ill on Stiftstrasse:

> A substantial number of physically inferior individuals, especially the mentally ill, cripples, the blind, deaf, and the dumb impose a heavy burden on society. In view of the favourable experience of other communities, the Municipal Health Committee has resolved to establish a Marriage Counselling Centre which will be limited to these responsibilities and which will not deal with other aspects of married life, since only steadfast concentration in this area will produce useful results.[33]

The Centre opened on 16 November. Posters were mounted in municipal offices; cards were distributed by the registry office; and newspaper articles were placed in an effort to draw public attention to the centre. Unfortunately, it proved to be more difficult to convey an accurate impression of the centre's true function; some people showed up expecting to find a detective agency that would check up on their intended. Two-thirds of the clients had a history of venereal disease; one-fourth of the clients were warned against marriage because of active VD. Yet when all was said and done, less than one hundred people attended each year — in marked contrast to the sex counselling centre operated by the League for the Protection of Motherhood, which did offer information on birth control. In 1930 the City Council accepted the obvious and merged the two centres.[34]

As the Frankfurt experience illustrates, the official marriage counselling centres were soon overshadowed by the sex counselling centres sponsored by various public and private organisation. The first such clinic was established by the Institute for Sexology, which had been founded by Magnus Hirschfeld before the war and was now operated by the Prussian government. The sex counselling centre at the Institute was under the direction of Dr Max Hodann; 90 per cent of the clients came for birth control. Other centres were operated by the League for the Protection of Motherhood, which set up clinics in reaction to the limited mandate of the official centres. The League operated clinics in Hamburg, Frankfurt, Mannheim (all established in 1924); Berlin, Breslau (1926); and Hannover (1928). Each clinic attracted several hundred clients per year.[35]

Saxon policy on counselling centres reflected the new trend. On 21 December 1927 the Saxon Minister for Labour and Welfare issued a memorandum authorising the establishment of centres for marriage and sex counselling. The Saxon government acted more out of concern for the high number of abortions and illegitimate births than out of eugenic considerations. Centres were set up in Dresden, Leipzig, Chemnitz, Plauen, Radeberg, Meissen, Riesa, Pirna, Bautzen and Zittau.[36]

Both the official and the unofficial birth control clinics were subsidised by the Health Insurance Programme. In Berlin the General Health Insurance Fund operated five clinics on its own, and subsidised several municipal clinics. Funds dispensed contraceptives free whenever doctors attested to possible health risks during pregnancy — in other words, on therapeutic indication — and issued condoms to men in an effort to combat venereal disease. Some of the larger Funds also interpreted the 'general prophylaxis' provisions of the

Health Insurance Act to apply to contraception as a prophylaxis against abortion — a roundabout form of social indication, which easily slid into birth control on demand: 'We don't need any special indication; the desire of the woman is sufficient.' As membership in the Health Insurance Programme topped twenty million, the role of the Funds in diffusing birth control became increasingly important.[37]

Clinics attracted thousands of clients each year from a broad social spectrum. Young people especially preferred practical advice on contraception to eugenic preaching about spousal suitability. Both the 'old' and the 'new' middle classes were represented, the former by artisans and shopkeepers, the latter by white collar workers, teachers and civil servants. Skilled workers attended more often than unskilled, but the efforts of the Insurance Programme increasingly reached the unskilled as well. In the early 1930s, however, most clients were unemployed.[38]

The reasons people gave for seeking birth control at a clinic varied. The majority of clients wanted to upgrade their current contraceptive practice, especially if that was coitus interruptus, or switch from abortion to an equally effective form of contraception. Some poorer women reported that they had been advised by doctors or social agencies not to become pregnant, but had not been told how to do this.[39]

Clinics consistently promoted contraceptives that were 'simple, safe, reliable and convenient'. Women received basic sex instruction, and were taught how to insert and remove the diaphragm (Ramses was the most popular model). Only a few clinics issued cervical caps because of a general policy not to make women dependent on doctors for birth control. Condoms were avoided because of the belief that men were less responsible about birth control than women, and because the use of a condom necessitated a break in sexual activity that was considered disconcerting for both partners. No clinic used Steriletts or Obturators, but some experimented with Pust or Gräfenberg IUDs. Along with these mechanical methods clinics prescribed use of a chemical contraceptive in the hope that failure of one method would be compensated by the other. Also, it was easier for people to carry a package of contraceptives than a diaphragm and douche. The most commonly issued chemicals were Patentex, Semori and Speton; Antibion, Contrapan and Pesoletten were also common. Both the mechanical and the chemical contraceptives were given to clients without charge.[40]

In addition to contraception, birth control clinics sometimes arranged for sterilisation. Patients who had been advised against further pregnancy for medical, eugenic, or socio-economic reasons were referred to local hospitals for sterilisation, with costs borne by the Health Insurance Funds. The Frankfurt clinic operated by the League for the Protection of Motherhood had the highest incidence of sterilisation. Between 1925 and 1930 some 420 women were sterilised, most of them on socio-economic indication. If a woman was unable to attend the clinic regularly or was unable or unwilling to use the prescribed contraceptives consistently, then sterilisation was authorised. Most of the women were housewives with three or more living children and one or more prior abortions. In nearly half of the cases the husband was unemployed. The Frankfurt clinic regarded sterilisation as the most practical form of contraception for these people under the circumstances. The operations were funded by Health Insurance and were carried out in the University Women's Hospital.[41]

Elsewhere, sterilisation was performed primarily for therapeutic reasons. A review of the medical literature for the 1920s reported some 1200 cases of therapeutic sterilisation nation-wide: 363 performed in conjunction with some other gynaecological operation, 347 for pulmonary tuberculosis, 103 for contracted pelvis, and 14 for social reasons. Less frequent medical indications — heart and kidney diseases, epilepsy — accounted for the rest. A survey of municipalities in 1931 found that 17 large cities acknowledged subsidising a total of 112 sterilisations, including 83 on medical indication and 29 on eugenic or social indication. Costs were borne by the Health Insurance Programme and the municipal welfare bureaus.[42]

Lay organisations dedicated to practical self-help arose in the 1920s to provide people with effective birth control at low cost. The earliest of these were the various Unions for Sexual Hygiene and Life Reform that emerged around 1923. The Unions promoted sex education, advocated legal reform, and distributed contraceptives (usually spray powders) to members. By emphasising the full range of activities the Unions sought to distance themselves from corporate fronts like Krönig's League of Activists (*Bund der Tätigen*) which had partially discredited birth control organisations in the eyes of the public.[43]

Other organisations that arose in the mid-1920s included the League for Sex Reform, based in Chemnitz but with local chapters in Saxony, Thuringia and Bavaria; the Union for Sexual Hygiene, based in Dresden and active throughout Saxony and Silesia; the People's League for the Protection of Motherhood and for Sexual Hygiene, a splinter group formed by Silesian locals of the Union for Sexual Hygiene; and the Association of Workers' Unions for Birth Control

(*Verband der Arbeiter-Vereine für Geburtenregelung*), which, along with the People's League for Birth Control (*Volksbund für Geburtenregelung*), descended from an organisation established by the Berlin pharmacist Paul Heiser. The largest single organisation was the League for the Protection of Motherhood and for Social Hygiene in the Family (*Liga für Mutterschutz und soziale Familienhygiene*), with chapters all across Germany. Its paper, *Love and Life* (*Liebe und Leben*), had the highest circulation of any independent birth-control paper (60,000) and was available at public news-stands.[44]

As lay birth-control organisations spread across the country, a movement arose to coordinate their efforts. In 1928 the National Association for Birth Control and Sexual Hygiene (*Reichsverband für Geburtenregelung und Sexualhygiene*) emerged as the paramount umbrella organisation. The Association published its own paper, *Sexual Hygiene*, which subsumed the papers of some of the constituent organisations. Monthly lectures were given on topics such as demography, anatomy, reproductive physiology, the manufacture of contraceptives and the theory and practice of contraception. Some of the lectures were illustrated with slides or films. The Association maintained counselling centres in every locale where it was active; these distributed contraceptives to members under medical supervision. In Saxony and Thuringia 'flying centres' were formed to bring birth control to rural districts.[45]

In January 1930, a congress of all sex reform organisations took place in Berlin and adopted a resolution calling for the establishment of a working group of sex reform societies. Such a group eventually met and recommended formation of a unified national organisation for sex reform. A unification congress was called for the summer of 1931, but fell apart because of internal wrangling (over whether the national headquarters should receive 10, 13 or 15 pfennigs from membership dues), and also because of the emergence of a communist-inspired Unity Group for Proletarian Sex Reform and for the Protection of Motherhood (*Einheitsverband für proletarische Sexualreform und Mutterschutz*), which characteristically demanded that all other organisations disband and join it.[46]

The petty manoeuvrings of groups and splinter groups should not obscure the constructive work of these organisations. They reflected the desire of people from all walks of life to inform themselves about sexuality and to obtain effective birth control without relying on the largesse of the state — a matter of some urgency during the crisis years of 1930 to 1932. Their newspapers reached hundreds of thousands of readers; their lectures reached the public in large cities and small hamlets. But their greatest impact was in their example, for they helped persuade the official marriage counselling centres to drop their eugenic orientation and provide birth control to those who needed and wanted it.[47]

One of the reasons for the popularity of birth-control clinics and self-help organisations was the distance people perceived between the public's desire for birth control and the attitude of the medical profession. Although a growing number of doctors sympathised with birth control — if only to reduce the alarming incidence of criminal abortion — and the majority of the directors of medical schools endorsed a proposal for formal instruction on birth control, many others remained aloof if not antagonistic, either from personal ignorance or from professional or political opposition to birth control in general and to the 'diaphragm clinics' in particular.[48]

Whatever is required and reasonable in this area can best be accomplished by the practising physician.
(Northern Medical Union of Berlin, 1924)[49]

Counselling on contraception is the prerogative of the family physician, who must conscientiously evaluate each case with regard to individual circumstances and to the responsibility of the family to reproduce. Marriage counselling centres for this purpose, i.e. sex counselling centres, are unacceptable because they promote non-marital sexual relations which present certain risks no matter what precautions may be taken.
(Bavarian Medical Council, 1931)[50]

The German Society for Gynaecology acknowledges the existence of marriage and sexual counselling centres. It expects that these centres will be conducted along medical lines only by those doctors who are known for their sense of responsibility to the future of the German nation.
(German Society for Gynaecology, Annual Convention, 1931)[51]

The opposition of the medical profession reached its boiling point at the 1931 convention in Frankfurt. Although compelled by circumstances to deal with the subject of contraception, the key report by Ludwig Fraenkel — which constitutes the most lucid and comprehensive survey of mechanical and chemical contraception and of operative, radiological, and hormonal sterilisation from that era — was either ignored or misconstrued by many of the assembled delegates, whom Julian Marcuse fittingly described as a 'synod of revivalists wearing the mask of science'.[52]

Proponents of birth control were repeatedly denounced as 'gravediggers of our nation's future'. Birth control 'sacrifices the future of our people for personal pleasure'. Once 'the forces are unleashed', depopulation would be irreversible. Morality would 'sink even lower than it has already'. Birth control would result in the 'collective arteriosclerosis of the nation', gradual national suicide, and the 'annihilation of the German *Volk*'. Fraenkel could only lament the moralistic remarks of colleagues whose political sentiments led them to read more into his report than he had written: 'They belong more appropriately in a Parliament where applause is cheap.'[53] But Fraenkel's critics had the last word:

> I must raise a moral question which transcends the narrow bounds of his expertise and which addresses the greater and more important question of the welfare, greatness, and purpose of the whole people . . . . The forces of disintegration are strong enough in Germany. So it is deeply regrettable that a German university professor with the full authority of his position acts in such a manner. We cannot urgently enough demand that our university chairs be held by people organically rooted in the German *Volk* and who are prepared to fulfill their responsibilities in a sense of true culture.[54]

Despite such attitudes the popular use of modern contraceptives increased dramatically during the 1920s. The decline in abortion rates was universally attributed to the shift to contraception by thousands of women, a shift credited in large part to the active promotion of contraception by public and private agencies.[55] The desire of eugenicists to encourage rational population policy combined with the efforts of feminists to encourage women to gain control over their own reproductive lives and with the efforts of medical and social agencies to curtail illicit abortion to produce powerful support for contraception. Those who had taken up contraception earlier were encouraged to continue; those who had wanted to control fertility but who had been unable or unwilling to obtain contraceptives now did so; those who had remained ignorant of the new techniques were not only informed of them but were given them without charge. But even though the public attitude towards birth control during the Weimar era was generally more sympathetic than the Imperial era, birth control did not go unchallenged — as the 1931 rhetoric demonstrated. A lingering undercurrent of resentment of the lifestyle which birth control seemed to represent persisted throughout the decade, challenging each new initiative in social policy and supporting those who would call a halt to sexual freedom.

NOTES

1. Robert Engelsmann, 'Die Ursache des Geburtenrückganges', PhD dissertation, University of Münster, 1937, p. 143; Max Marcuse, *Der eheliche Präventivverkehr: seine Verbreitung, Verursachung und Methodik* (Enke, Stuttgart, 1917), p. 16. On the military experience with condoms see P. Mulzer, 'Die Bekämpfung der Geschlechtskrankheiten im Felde und in der Heimat', *Zeitschrift für Dermatologie*, 25 (1918), pp. 221-51; Paul Manteuffel, 'Zur Frage der persönlichen Prophylaxe bei der Bekämpfung der Geschlechtskrankheiten', *Zeitschrift für Hygiene*, 96 (1922), pp. 387-404; Dr Jungblut, 'Die Geschlechtskrankheiten im deutschen Heere während des Weltkrieges, 1914-1918' (Deutsche Gesellschaft zur Bekämpfung der Geschlechtskrankheiten), *Mitteilungen*, 21 (1923), no. 1-2, pp. 2-5, no. 3, pp. 14-15. On the English experience see Angus McLaren, *Birth Control in nineteenth century England: a social and intellectual history* (Holmes and Meier, New York, 1978), p. 136; John Peel, 'The manufacturing and retailing of contraceptives in England', *PS*, 17 (1963), pp. 120, 122.

2. Manfred Stürzbecher, 'Die Bekämpfung des Geburtenrückganges und der Säuglingssterblichkeit im Spiegel der Reichstagsdebatten, 1900-1930', PhD dissertation, University of Berlin, 1954, p. 131.

3. Ernst Urban, *Apotheken-Gesetze nach deutschem Reichs- und Preussischem Landesrecht*, 6th edn (Springer, Berlin, 1927), p. 46.

4. Ibid., p. 241.

5. Ibid., p. 46. See also Ulrich Linse, 'Arbeiterschaft und Geburtenentwicklung im deutschen Kaiserreich von 1871', *ASG*, 12 (1972), p. 258.

6. Linse, 'Arbeiterschaft', p. 258.

7. S. Drucker, 'Schutzmittel-Automaten', *ZGVGF*, 3 (1932), pp. 361-70; Hans Albrecht, 'Über Konzeptionsverhütung', *MMW*, 78 (1931), p. 349; Rudolf Wassermann, 'Schutzmittelautomaten und Jugend', *ZMB*, 42 (1929), pp. 565-8; Ernst Feilchenfeld, 'Erfahrungen über Kenntnis und Benutzung anti-venerischer Prophylaktica', *ZGVGF*, 1 (1930), pp. 578-80.

8. Marcuse, *Eheliche Präventivverkehr*, p. 115; Ludwig Fraenkel, *Die Empfängnisverhütung* (Enke, Stuttgart, 1932), p. 147; Magnus Hirschfeld and Richard Linsert, *Empfängnisverhütung: Mittel und Methoden* (Neudeutscher Verlag, Berlin, 1928), p. 36; *Empfängnisverhütung*, p. 36; Hans Lehfeldt, 'The cervical cap', in Mary Calderone (ed.), *Manual of contraceptive practice*, 2nd edn (Williams and Wilkins, Baltimore, 1970), p. 368n. The Ramses diaphragm was produced by the Weiss and Bässler firm in Berlin.

9. Heinrich Gesenius, 'Die Gefährlichkeit der Intrauterinepessare', *ZGyn*, 59 (1935), pp. 2168-9; Ohnesorge, 'Gefahren', *Der Frauenartzt*, 35 (1920), pp. 876-7; Dr Braun, 'Ein neuartiges Intrauterinpessar', pp. 251-4;

Dr Pust, 'Ein brauchbarer Frauenschutz', *DMW*, 49 (1923), pp. 952-3; Hans Lehfeldt, 'Contraceptive methods requiring medical assistance' in World League for Sexual Reform, *Proceedings of the third congress*, ed. Norman Haire, p. 129.

10. Ernst Gräfenberg, 'The intra-uterine method of contraception', in World League for Sexual Reform, *Proceedings of the third congress*, pp. 611, 616; Ernst Gräfenberg, 'Einfluss der intrauterinen Konzeptionsverhütung auf die Schleimhaut', *AGyn*, 144 (1931), p. 343; Robert L. Dickinson and L.S. Bryant, *Control of conception*, 2nd edn (Williams and Wilkins, 1938), pp. 235, 240; Christopher Tietze, 'History and statistical evaluation of intrauterine contraceptive devices', in M.C. Sheps and J.C. Ridley (eds), *Public Health and Population Change*, (Carnegie Mellon, Pittsburgh, 1965), p. 428.

11. Fraenkel, *Empfängnisverhütung*, p. 132; Hirschfeld and Linsert, *Empfängnisverhütung* (1928), pp. 28-9; A. Grotjahn, *Geburtenrückgang und Geburtenregelung im Lichte der individuellen und der sozialen Hygiene* (Marcus, Berlin, 1914), pp. 76-7; Antoine, 'Über Konzeptionsverhütung und Sterilisation', *WMW*, 81 (1931), p. 1372; Anne-Marie Durand-Wever, 'Die ärztlichen Erfahrungen über medizinisch indizierte Konzeptionsverhütung', *MW*, 5 (1931), p. 829; Bauer, 'Kritik', p. 1002; Martha Ruben-Wolf, *Abtreibung oder Verhütung*, 5th edn (International Arbeiter-Verlag, Berlin, 1931), pp. 12-13.

12. Willi Steinhäuser, 'Über das biologische Verhalten von Spermatozoen in chemischen Reagentien', PhD dissertation, University of Breslau, 1922, pp. 7, 17-19; Fraenkel, *Empfängnisverhütung*, p. 120.

13. M. Rodecurt, 'Experimentelle Untersuchungen über chemische Antikonzipienten', *ZGyn*, 55 (1931), pp. 1458-60; M. Rodecurt, 'Über chemische Kontrazeption', *ZGyn*, 56 (1932), pp. 526-31; A. Poehlmann, 'Zur Frage der Konzeptionsverhütung', *ZGyn*, 55 (1931), p. 3255.

14. J.R. Baker, 'Chemical contraceptives', in International Society for Sex Research, *Proceedings of the second international conference* (Oliver and Boyd, Edinburgh, 1931) pp. 556-7; J.R. Baker, *The chemical control of conception* (Chapman and Hall, London, 1935), pp. 58, 108-10.

15. Cecil Voge, *The chemistry and physics of contraception* (Jonathan Cape, London, 1933) pp. 94, 153-4, 178; James Reed, *From private vice to public virtue: the birth control movement and American society since 1830* (Basic Books, New York, 1978) p. 242; Peel, 'Manufacturing', p. 120.

16. For the chemical composition of these and other contraceptives see Fraenkel, *Empfängnisverhütung*, p. 132; Hirschfeld and Linsert, *Empfängnisverhütung* (1928), pp. 28-9; Durand-Wever, 'Erfahrungen', p. 829; J.R. Baker, 'The spermicidal powers of chemical contraceptives', *Journal of Hygiene*, 31 (1931), pp. 310-18; Voge, *Chemistry*, p. 94.

17. Hirschfeld and Linsert, *Empfängnisverhütung* (1928), p. 22; Fraenkel, *Empfängnisverhütung*, p. 82; Ludwig Fraenkel, 'Sterilisierung und Konzeptionsverhütung', *AGyn* 144 (1931), pp. 101-5; Dr Hauptstein, 'Zur Frage der hormonalen Sterilisierung', *AGyn*, 144 (1931), p. 320; Hans Neumann, 'Experimentelle Untersuchungen zum Antagonismus der Keimdrüse', *AGyn*, 144 (1931), pp. 321-4; C. Vogt, 'Sterilität und Spermaimmunität', *KW*, 1 (1922), pp. 1144-6; Lehfeldt, 'Contraceptive methods', p. 128.

18. Hirschfeld and Linsert, *Empfängnisverhütung* (1928), pp. 22-3; Fraenkel, *Empfängnisverhütung*, pp. 85-92; Dr Gastimirovic, 'Experimentelle

Studie über die hormonale Sterilität. Die Wirkung des Insulins auf die weibliche Keimdrüse', *AGyn*, 144 (1931), p. 325-6; Julius Jarcho, 'Artificial production of sterility', *American Journal of Obstetrics and Gynecology*, 16 (1928), p. 815. For a comprehensive overview of the work of Haberlandt see the following articles by Hans Simmer: 'On the history of hormonal contraception. I: Ludwig Haberlandt (1885-1932) and his concept of "hormonal sterilization" ', *Contraception*, 1 (1970), pp. 3-27; 'On the history of hormonal contraception. II: Otfried Otto Fellner and estrogens as antifertility hormones', *Contraception*, 3 (1971), pp. 1-19; 'Zur Geschichte der hormonalen Empfängnisverhütung', *Geburtshilfe und Frauenheilkunde*, 35 (1975), pp. 688-96; 'Josef Halban (1870-1937), Pionier der Endokrinologie der Fortpflanzung', *WMW*, 121 (1971), pp. 549-52.

19. Wilhelm Liepmann, 'Der Offenburger Aerzteprozess: Die Sterilisierung der Frau zum ersten Male vor Gericht', *MK*, 28 (1932), p. 1224.

20. On Schmerz see Chapter 6. The role of the Austrian Socialists in the railroads was especially strong during the late 1920s. See Charles Gulick, *Austria from Habsburg to Hitler* (2 vols, University of California Press, Berkeley, 1948), vol. 2, pp. 900-2.

21. Daniel Gasman, *The scientific origins of National Socialism. Social Darwinism in Ernst Haeckel and the German Monist League* (American Elsevier, New York, 1971), p. 20; Niles Holt, 'Ernst Haeckel's monistic religion', *Journal of the History of Ideas*, 32 (1971), pp. 268, 277; Alfred Kelly, *The descent of Darwin. The popularization of Darwinism in Germany* (University of North Carolina Press, Chapel Hill, 1981), pp. 24, 103-6, 120.

22. Heinrich Gesenius, *Empfängnisverhütung*, 3rd edn (Urban and Schwarzenberg, Berlin, 1970), p. 163; Hans Nevermann, *Über Eheberatung* (Kabitzsch, Leipzig, 1931), pp. 3-4.

23. Nevermann, *Eheberatung*, pp. 4-5; L.D. Pesl, 'Fruchtabtreibung und Findelhaus', *ZSWSP*, 14 (1928), pp. 189-98. The results of the Munich Commission were published as *Arbeiten der vom Aerztlichen Verein München eingesetzten Kommission zur Beratung von Fragen der Erhaltung und Mehrung der Volkskraft* (Lehmann, Munich, 1917).

24. Nevermann, *Eheberatung*, p. 5; Gesenius, *Empfängnisverhütung*, p. 163.

25. Rene Brunet, *The new German Constitution*, trans. Joseph Gallomb (Knopf, New York, 1928), p. 216; Frederick Blackley and Miriam Oatman, *Government and administration of Germany* (Johns Hopkins University Press, Baltimore, 1928), p. 666.

26. Nevermann, *Eheberatung*, pp. 6, 93-4.

27. Nevermann, *Eheberatung*, pp. 7-9. On the prophylactic work of the Insurance Programme see L. von Zumbusch, 'Krankenkasse und Geschlechtskrankheiten', *Deutsche Krankenkasse*, 12 (1926), p. 191; P. Kaufmann, 'Sozialversicherung im Kampfe gegen die Geschlechtskrankheiten', *Monatsschrift für Arbeiter und Angestellten-Versicherung*, 7 (1924), pp. 137-49; H. Zeisse, 'Die soziale Bedeutung der Vorbeugungsmittel gegen Geschlechtskrankheiten mit Einschluss der Antikonzipienten', *Allgemeine medizinische Central-Zeitung*, 90 (1921), pp. 225-6; Dr Haedenkamp, 'Sozialversicherungsträger im Kampfe gegen die Geschlechtskrankheiten', *Aerztliche Mitteilungen*, 30 (1929), pp. 879-85; R. Fette, 'Geschlechtskrankheiten und Sozialversicherung', *Volkstümliche Zeitschrift für die gesamte Sozialversich-*

erung, 37 (1931), pp. 73-5.

28. Nevermann, *Eheberatung*, p. 10; J. Schwalbe, 'Gesundheitliche Beratung vor der Eheschliessung', *DMW*, 52 (1926), p. 1953.

29. Nevermann, *Eheberatung*, p. 10

30. Nevermann, *Eheberatung*, pp. 92-3; Schwalbe, 'Beratung', p. 1953.

31. Nevermann, *Eheberatung*, p. 63.

32. Nevermann, *Eheberatung*, p. 11; F.K. Scheumann, *Eheberatung als Aufgabe der Kommunen* (Voss, Leipzig, 1932), p. 39; Bund für Mutterschutz, *Enquete über Ehe-und Sexualberatungsstellen in Deutschland*, ed. Lotte Neisser-Schroeter (Nikolassee, Berlin, 1928), p. 15.

33. Frankfurt, Städtisches Archiv, *Akten des Magistrats*, 1536: Report on the Eheberatungsstelle, 1924.

34. Dr Raecke, 'Erfahrungen aus einer Eheberatungsstelle', *KW*, 6 (1927), p. 463.

35. Nevermann, *Eheberatung*, pp. 29, 35, 42, 60; Scheumann, *Eheberatung*, p. 66; Bund für Mutterschutz, *Enquete*, pp. 12-13, 18-19; Alfred Grotjahn, *Der Hygiene der menschlichen Fortpflanzung: Versuch einer praktischer Eugenik* (Urban and Schwarzenberg, Berlin, 1926), p. 329; Dr Knack,'Sexualberatungsstellen in Hamburg', *Die Ortskrankenkasse*, 11 (1924), pp. 944-5; F. Fink, 'Wirkung der Verhütungsmittel. Erfahrungen aus der Ehe-und Sexualberatungsstelle Frankfurt-Main', *AGyn*, 144 (1931), p. 335; Hertha Riese, 'Erfahrungen der Sexualberatungsstelle Frankfurt', *NG*, 21 (1925), p. 97.

36. Nevermann, *Eheberatung*, pp. 100-1; R. Fetscher, 'Eheberatung in Sachsen', *ASHD*, 3 (1928), p. 32.

37. Dr Neufeld, 'Diskussion' in Kurt Bendix (ed.), *Geburtenregelung': Vorträge und Verhandlungen* (Selbstverlag, Berlin, 1929), pp. 91-2; Erna Gläsmer, *Eheberatungsstellen und Geburtenverhütung* (Enke, Stuttgart, 1932), p. 5; Gesenius, *Empfängnisverhütung*, p. 166; Florian Tennstedt, 'Sozialgeschichte der Sozialversicherung' in Maria Blohmke (ed.), *Handbuch der Sozialmedizin* (3 vols, Enke, Stuttgart, 1976), vol III, p. 399; Fraenkel, 'Sterilisierung', pp. 127-8; M. Hirsch, 'Empfängnisverhütung und Sittengesetz', *ZGyn*, 55 (1931), p. 2995.

38. Nevermann, *Eheberatung*, pp. 39-41; Fink, 'Wirkung', p. 335; Knack, 'Sexualberatungsstellen', p. 944; Kurt Bendix, 'Praxis der Berliner Beratungsstellen für Geburtenregelung' in Kurt Bendix (ed.) *Geburtenregelung: Vorträge und Verhandlungen* (Selbstverlag, Berlin, 1929), pp. 46-7.

39. Kurt Bendix, 'Birth control in Berlin', World League for Sexual Reform, *Proceedings of the third congress*, p. 659; R. Fetscher, 'Entwicklung der Eheberatung', *DMW*, 56 (1930), pp. 2138-9; H. Riese, 'Geburtenregelung und Eheberatung', *Erziehung zur Liebe*, (1930), p. 97.

40. Felix Abraham and H. Buber, 'Prüfungsergebnis von Antikonzipienten', *ZGyn*, 56 (1932), pp. 1057-9; Riese, 'Geburtenregelung', pp. 97-8; Dr Dührssen, 'Die Reform der Paragraphen 218-219', *Sexus*, 4 (1926) pp. 77-8; Scheumann, *Eheberatung*, p. 43; Dr Hörnicke, 'Diskussion' in Kurt Bendix (ed.), *Geburtenregelung: Vortrage und Verhandlungen* (Selbstverlag, Berlin, 1929), pp. 92-3; A.W. Bauer, 'Kritik der Konzeptionsverhütungsmittel', *MK*, 26 (1930), p. 964; Proceedings of the Breslau Gynecological Society, *ZGyn*, 55 (1931), p. 1427.

41. Scheumann, *Eheberatung*, p. 43; F. Memelsdorff and F.H. Scheumann, 'Der gegenwärtige Stand der kommunalen Eheberatung in Deutschland', *ZGVGF*, 3 (1932), p. 467; L. Fink, 'Die Tubensterilisation als Mittel der Geburtenregelung', *MW*, 5 (1931), pp. 750–1.

42. S. Hammerschlay, 'Die Sterilität des Weibes', in Max Marcuse (ed.) *Handwörterbuch der Sexualwissenschaften*, 2nd edn (Marcus and Weber, Bonn, 1926), p. 452; Felix Tietze, 'Sterilisierung zur eugenischen Zwecken', *Eugenik. Volksaufartung, Erbkunde, Eheberatung*, 4 (1929), pp. 169–202; R. Fetscher, 'Über den Stand der Sterilisierung im deutschen Reich', *DMW*, 57 (1931), p. 64.

43. Bendix, 'Birth control', pp. 659–60; Scheumann, *Eheberatung*, pp. 43–4; Neufeld,, 'Diskussion', pp. 91–2; Hörnicke, 'Diskussion', pp. 92–4; Fink, 'Wirkung', p. 335; Riese, 'Geburtenregelung', p. 94; Abraham and Buber, 'Prüfungsergebnis', p. 1058.

44. Hans Lehfeldt, 'Die Laienorganisationen für Geburtenregelung', *Archiv für Bevölkerungspolitik*, 1 (1932), pp. 64, 69; Linse, 'Arbeiterschaft', pp. 252–3. The 'Bund der Tätigen' was accused of promoting abortion under the guise of contraception. See Dr Reifferscheid, 'Über den Geburtenrückgang und die Zunahme der Fruchtabtreibung in Deutschland', *Allgemeine Deutsche Hebammenwesen*, 40 (1925), p. 3.

45. Lehfeldt, 'Laienorganisationen', pp. 65–6, 68.

46. Ibid., pp. 73–5, 78–82; Hirsch, 'Empfängnisverhütung', p. 2995.

47. Lehfeldt, 'Laienorganisationen', p. 84. For a representative report on the activities of one local group in Hamburg see Lehfeldt, pp. 65–7.

48. W.Stoeckel, 'Die Konzeptionsverhütung als Gegenstand des klinischen Unterrichts', *ZGyn*, 55 (1931), pp. 1450–8; W. Liepmann, 'Konzeptionsverhütung und klinischer Unterricht', *ZGyn*, 55 (1931), p. 2551; Fritz Meder, 'Die Konzeptionsverhütung in der Hand des freipraktizierenden Arztes', *ZGyn* 55 (1931), p. 2561; Hugo Sellheim, 'Was muss der Arzt von der Regulierung der Fortpflanzung wissen?' *ZSWSP*, 17 (1931), pp. 341–61; Erich Goldberg, 'Darf der Arzt Beratung über Konzeptionsverhütung ablehnen?' *ZGyn*, 55 (1932), pp. 2557–8; Gesenius, *Empfängnisverhütung*, p. 172.

49. Dührssen, 'Reform', p. 119. See also Fraenkel, 'Sterilisierung', p. 309. Grotjahn, *Hygiene*, p. 330; Gläsmer, *Eheberatungsstellen* p. 5.

50. Fraenkel, 'Sterilisierung', p. 309; and Grotjahn, *Hygiene*, p. 330. See also Dührssen, 'Reform', p. 119.

51. Session Report, German Gynecological Society, *AGyn*, 144 (1931), p. 383; and Gläsmer *Eheberatungsstellen*, pp. 6–7.

52. Julian Marcuse, 'Die deutsche Gynäkologen und die Geburtenregelung', *NG*, (1931), pp. 168–9.

53. Line quotes are taken from Gesenius, *Empfängnisverhütung*, p. 12n; Otto von Franqué, 'Die Geburtenverhütung und die Deutsche Gesellschaft für Gynäkologie, *AGyn*, 144 (1931), pp. 353–4; C.J. Gauss, 'Sexualrevolution, Geburtenregelung und die Zukunft unseres Volk', *MW*, 6 (1932), pp. 661–2; Franqué, 'Geburtenverhütung', p. 353; Gauss, 'Sexualrevolution', p. 662; Franqué, 'Geburtenverhütung', p. 353, respectively. See also C.J. Gauss, 'Wohin steuern wir?', *AGyn*, 144 (1931), pp. 360–1; Puppel, 'Diskussion', *AGyn*, 144 (1931), p. 374; Fraenkel, 'Diskussion', *AGyn*, 144 (1931), pp. 381–2.

54. Dr Schneller, 'Arzt und Schwangerschaftsverhütung', *ZMB*, 46 (1933), pp. 1, 8.

55. R. Schaeffer, 'Statistische Beitrag', pp. 636–7; S. Peller, *Fehlgeburt und Bevölkerungsfrage. Eine medizinalstatistische und sozialbiologische Studie* (Hippokrates, Stuttgart, 1930), p. 184; Andreas Friese, 'Fehlgeburt und Lebensalter', PhD dissertation, University of Berlin, 1935, pp. 27–8; Engelsmann, 'Ursache', pp. 87–9; Grotjahn, *Hygiene*, p. 310; Anton Hengge, 'Zum Geburtenrückgang', *MGG*, 46 (1917), p. 183; R. Hofstätter, 'Voreheliche Schwangerschaftsunterbrechungen und Heiratsaussichten', *ARGB*, 30 (1936), pp. 379–84.

6

The Politics of Birth Control

Birth control inevitably became a matter of political controversy. The demographic impact of the fertility decline, the social costs of abortion and illegitimate births, and the sexual morality associated with birth control all ensured that ostensibly private behaviour would become the subject of public debate. Opinions polarised along two lines. One side upheld the right of the individual to run his own life, while the other stressed the duty of the individual to society and the state. Some saw responsible self-control behind birth control; for others it displayed irresponsible self-indulgence. Out of this conflict came two competing policies, with the generally repressive measures of the Imperial era giving way to tolerance and eventually active promotion of birth control in the Weimar Republic.

For conservatives the fertility decline meant first of all demographic stagnation — 'the collective arteriosclerosis of a nation' — that would quickly translate into social, economic and political decline. The aging of the population would reduce the work force, and therewith productivity, at the same time as social costs mounted. The population pool would shrink, curtailing the essential reservoir for natural selection that was necessary to provide leaders without whom 'the masses would be helpless'. Conservatives chastised the upper classes for shirking their racial duty as much as they worried over the excessive fertility of the 'plebs'. Ferdinand Goldstein feared that 'the proles will capture the world'. The result of this would be the 'triumph of mediocrity — as in France today'. And the missing places would be filled by foreigners: 'The only real danger is the mindless breeding of the Slavs.'[1]

Equally ominous was the moral impact of birth control. While moderates like Alfred Grotjahn recognised that birth control reflected a higher degree of parental responsibility towards children, they nonetheless lamented the 'irresponsible' neglect by couples of the total impact which birth control had on society. But for conservatives even the individual practice of birth control was irresponsible and immoral. Birth control 'stripped marriage of its moral integrity, made women the slaves of lust, violated nature, and mocked the will of God'. Marriage was seen not as a partnership of two people on the journey of life, but as a chartered company set up by society for the purpose of raising children. Marriage without children was 'sheer concubinacy', and society should no more recognise such a marriage than it should a homosexual cohabitation.[2]

The waning desire for children was blamed on the moral decay of society. Feminism and its 'pretty words' about respect for the integrity of women and the right of women to control their own bodies were dismissed as covers for a morality of self-indulgence. Neo-Malthusianism was attacked for its individualistic antipathy to the 'organic concept of the *Volk*'; profiteers in industry — some of them foreign — were blamed for the propagation of this ideology. Siebert feared that in the future condoms would be distributed after dinner instead of schnapps.[3]

A domino theory of demography explained this concern: first the two-child family, then one child, then no children — 'thus is the grave of the nation dug!' The collapse of the family would lead to the collapse of society, for the family not only raised but also trained the citizens of tomorrow. As the family goes, so goes the nation.[4]

The truly ominous aspect of the fertility decline lay in its implications for Germany's place in the world. Partly this concern was political: the state was more than the sum of its citizens; it was an entity unto itself, with the right to expect its citizens to cooperate in its perpetuation: 'It is wrong for those who are able to produce to selfishly deny the Fatherland the offspring necessary for its survival.' Partly it was economic: 'Nations whose population continues to grow will usurp our place in the world economy'; Germany would 'lose its place in the sun'.[5] But mainly the threat was military. In the words of Hans Albrecht: 'In the final analysis all the disarmament clauses of the Versailles *Diktat* will not be as fateful as the fact that Germany will simply not have enough men to bear arms.'[6]

Proponents of birth control, on the other hand, argued that reason enabled people to separate procreation from sex; that the purpose of sex was gratification, pure and simple; that non-marital relations could be as fulfilling as marital relations; and that responsible parents should choose to have children only when they could afford to raise them properly. Sex reformers argued that the social acceptance of birth control would reduce illegitimacy, abortion, prostitution and venereal disease.[7] Above all, they argued that sex was a personal rather than a social matter, and should be subject to the guidance of personal reason rather than the dictates of law: 'Once we realise that a common morality — an "objective" morality — does not exist, the possibility of defining morality and immorality by external aspects disappears, and with it the right to punish "immoral" acts as criminal behaviour.'[8]

The political debate over birth-control policy reflected these ideological preconceptions. During the Imperial era the government pursued, with limited success, an essentially conservative policy which sought to curtail public awareness of, and access to, birth control. But liberal and socialist opposition in the *Reichstag* compelled compromise more often than not. In the Weimar era the situation was reversed. Weimar was in many respects an 'experiment with liberty', and as such was tolerant of the new sexual morality and was sympathetic to birth control.[9] But here too governments found themselves compelled by the exigencies of coalition politics to adopt more moderate policies than many would have liked. And because of the unresolved and unassimilated legacy of the Imperial era a good deal of lingering resistance to birth control remained, only to rise to the surface in the politically tense years of the late 1920s and early 1930s. The entire period from 1871 to 1933, then, witnessed an ideological and political seesaw between traditionalism and modernity, rational individualism and 'organic volkish' conservatism.

The attitude of the Prussian government towards the public discussion of 'Neo-Malthusianism' became evident as early as 1866 in the course of disciplinary proceedings against Julius von Kirchmann, Progressive member of the Chamber of Deputies and a member of the judiciary in Silesia. Kirchmann, a native of Saxony, had experienced rapid promotion in the judiciary. In 1848 he was elected to the Prussian assembly from Berlin, and soon ran afoul of the government. As a victim of the Reaction, Kirchmann was reassigned to a judicial position in Ratibor, from which he quickly won re-election. By the 1860s Kirchmann was a leading figure in the Progressive Party, and served on the critical Budget Committee during the crisis years of the early 1860s. In the Chamber of Deputies and in the press Kirchmann voiced his opposition to the policies of Bismarck. In 1865 the government initiated disciplinary proceedings against him for this political activity, but lost.[10]

In 4 Feburary 1866 Kirchmann addressed an assembly of workers in the Alhambra Hall in Berlin on the subject of 'Communism in

Nature'. (Such lectures were a common feature of liberal-labour cooperation during the 1860s.) He focused on what he called the 'Third Communistic Law of Nature': 'Pleasure is separable from its external consequences'. Kirchmann sought to persuade his audience that birth control was responsible behaviour for every couple. All other biological drives were regulated by reason; why should sex be any different? Why is the unregulated indulgence of this drive seen as natural and the resulting oversupply of children seen as a 'gift of God'? Why should this drive be the only one that cannot be questioned without charges of blasphemy? Kirchmann argued that reason enabled people to separate sexual pleasure from reproduction. He noted that upper- and middle-class families controlled their family size, and called on workers to do the same.[11]

Although Kirchmann refrained from any explicit discussion of birth control, the damage had been done. Acting on the basis of the Disciplinary Code of 1851, which authorised the arbitrary dismissal of officials who 'violated the duty of loyalty' or who failed to demonstrate the 'courage' that their office required, the government initiated a hearing to determine whether Kirchmann had acted 'without regard for his special status as a civil servant'. The government charged that Kirchmann had compromised the integrity of his judicial position by arguing in his speech and subsequently in print that married couples should limit their families to two children. Any discussion of this subject was immoral and abominable; for a civil servant to do so was reprehensible and inexcusable.[12]

In his defence Kirchmann argued that the ideas which he had expressed were commonplace among political economists throughout Europe — he specifically referred to Ricardo, Proudhon, Say, Sismondi and John Stuart Mill — and that he had been motivated only by concern for the well-being of the workers. He implied that if birth control was moral for the upper classes, it must be moral for all classes. He noted that he had not specified any particular methods of birth control, even though that information was also part of the literature of political economy. Somewhat perversely, the prosecution argued that not discussing specifics was even worse, since the vague mention conjured up all sorts of immoral images in the minds of the audience.[13]

The result of the hearing was never in question. Kirchmann was dismissed from the Appellate Court for 'violating public morality'. But the real lesson of the proceeding was the insight it offered into the attitude of the Prussian government towards birth control. Kirchmann had discussed neither contraception nor abortion; he had only recommended that people separate procreational from recreational sex, and this is what offended the government.[14] In the words of Karl von Uhden, *Chefpräsident* of the *Obertribunal*:

> What is abominable is the way in which he compared marital to non-marital relations, and took no position against the view of marriage as an excuse for the irresponsible indulgence of sensuality. . . . At the very least it was improper to speak to persons of little education about marriage in this way and thereby weaken their respect for it.[15]

The action against Kirchmann demonstrated that the Prussian government was prepared to move against the dissemination of birth-control information. During the 1850s and 1860s police ordinances had banned advertisements for patent medicines in newspapers. These ordinances were annulled by the new *Reich* Press Law of 1874, which guaranteed freedom of the press in all areas, including advertising. But this freedom extended only to those communications which could only occur in the newsprint medium. If a particular communication, including an advertisement, offended other laws, such as obscenity, then the editors were liable — and liable in every jurisdiction where the paper was distributed, not simply in the place of publication.[16]

The Imperial Ordinance on Trade with Medications provided the basis for renewed police action against drug advertising. Police argued that the restrictions on sales of patent medicines outlined in the Ordinance implied restriction on advertising for these products. Starting in 1887 police imposed regulations to this effect in Berlin and eventually throughout Prussia, until in 1896 the *Bundesrat* issued a nation-wide ban on advertising for patent medicines. In 1903 the *Bundesrat* went further and banned the printing of 'recommendations or testimonials' on packages. Pharmacists were instructed to sell patent medicines only if they were satisfied that the product was not subject to the restrictions in the Imperial Ordinance or the Law on Strong-working Medicines.[17]

These regulations had little effect on birth control, however. Since patent medicines were defined as products with alleged therapeutic benefit in the treatment of illnesses, and since pregnancy was not defined as an illness, contraceptives were not affected by any restriction on patent medicines. Products for 'blood stasis' were only included in the terms of these regulations in 1924. And any manufacturer could claim that his product was not promoted as a 'medication', or deny that it contained pharmaceutical ingredients which were subject to regulation.[18]

Restrictions on the sale or advertising of contraceptives first became possible after the revision of the Criminal Code in 1900, which was prompted by a sensational trial a decade earlier. In the course of his 1890 trial for the murder of a night-watchman a Berlin pimp named Heinze disclosed a good deal more about the seamy side of big city life than a respectable audience cared to hear. The Kaiser was especially offended, and directed the government to expand and enforce the laws on indecency. Because of *Reichstag* resistance and the loss of interest by the mercurial Kaiser, who was miffed by the defeat of the *Mittelland* canal project, the bill was dropped in 1893.[19]

During the 1890s the Centre Party persistently tried to reintroduce the bill, but met with little success until the end of the decade, when mounting concern over the fertility decline led the government to reconsider the proposal. A new draft was presented to the *Reichstag* on 3 February 1899. The revised version contained two new far-reaching provisions, one on obscenity in print and pictures, and one on theatre performances which 'without being obscene grossly offend the sense of shame' — a formula designed to avoid the need to prove obscenity in court. This latter proposal provoked a nation-wide storm of protest — 'a veritable Black Sabbath' — involving public demonstrations and parliamentary delaying tactics by Liberals and Socialists. Finally, after threats from chancellor Hohenlohe, who denounced the attempt to 'legislate morality' and who castigated the 'hypocritical philistines' who supported the bill, and after warnings from the *Bundesrat* that it would veto the bill in its present form, the Centre member Hompesch announced the willingness of his Party to withdraw the controversial section dealing with the theatre.[20]

The '*Lex Heinze*' came into effect 25 June 1900.

> 1. Whoever stocks, sells, or distributes obscene writings, pictures, or representations, or who exhibits, posts, or otherwise disseminates them in places accessible to the public, or who manufactures them for the purpose of distribution, or stocks, advertises, or promotes them for that purpose;
> 2. Sells or offers for sale obscene writings, pictures, or representations to a person under the age of sixteen;
> 3. Displays objects which are suited for obscene use in places which are accessible to the public, or who advertises or promotes such objects to the public;
> 4. Publishes public announcements which are intended to facilitate obscene relations; will be punished with prison for up to one year and with fines up to 1,000 Marks or with one of these

penalties. In addition to prison, the loss of civil rights and the option of police surveillance can be imposed.[21]

Contraceptives immediately fell within the scope of the *Lex Heinze*. In Berlin the chief of police, Windheim, set up a morality squad to check on the public display or hawking of obscene photographs, illustrations, and rubber objects. The squad visited rubber-goods stores, barber shops and drug stores to ensure that trade with these items occurred as inconspicuously as possible. Similar tactics were implemented in other cities. In Lübeck, for instance, a police ordinance not only enforced the letter of the law but banned the use of contraceptives and sex aids in private bathing institutions and sanatoria.[22]

Police also achieved some success in using the new law to restrict newspaper advertisements for abortion services. The Berlin police developed a standard procedure. Editors who accepted such advertisements were advised of the terms of Paragraphs 49, 184, 218, and 219 of the Criminal Code regarding obscenity, abortion and providing assistance to a criminal act, and were reminded of the relevant portions of the Press Law pertaining to their responsibility for all published material and were urged 'in their own best interest' to act prudently. Most editors forwarded copy of their advertisements to the police for advance clarification. The police made their decision on the basis of the content of the advertisement and on their knowledge of the person placing the advertisement — which is why many advertisers used false names. If a paper published an advertisement from a person with a prior conviction for abortion, or if an unconvicted person was later brought to trial on such charges, the editors would 'have their attention drawn to these facts in an appropriate manner'. Police suspicions alone, however, could not compel a paper to refuse any advertisement, but the police could warn editors that if an advertiser was convicted, they might be charged as accomplices. Such tactics worked to reduce the number of advertisements, but so long as the products or services advertised were legal — as was the case with therapy, massage and hygienic douches — the police could not ban them outright.[23]

In the long run effective restraint on birth control necessitated effective control over the persons who provided the products and services. Realising this, the *Reich* government called on the state governments in 1903 to take energetic steps to curb the growth of medical quackery, especially in connection with practices associated with birth control. The Chancellor also called on the medical profession to play a more active role in educating the public about the dangers posed by medical quackery.[24]

Doctors had long sought to control quacks. In the mid-nineteenth century they had secured legislation curtailing or prohibiting quack practices. But the Occupational Code of the North German *Bund*, and later the German *Reich*, extended occupational freedom to health care; any person could offer to provide therapy so long as he or she did not unduly claim certification. Quacks also benefited from the support given to all forms of therapy by the Health Insurance Law of 1883. In 1886 the Saxon government became the first to permit patients to choose treatment by naturopaths, homeopaths, and other non-certified therapists in addition to doctors, and to have this treatment subsidised by the Insurance Funds. Although doctors protested, the *Reich* government confirmed the legality of the Saxon policy.[25] In response, the German Medical Association passed a resolution at its annual convention in 1887 calling on all local medical associations to set up committees to fight health quackery. In 1899 the national association itself established the Committee to Fight Quackery (*Kommission zur Bekämpfung der Kurpfuscherei*). In 1903, in specific response to the *Reich* government's memorandum, other concerned doctors set up the German Society for Combating Quackery (*Deutsche Gesellschaft zur Bekämpfung des Kurpfuschertums*).[26]

In 1908 the government introduced a draft bill in the *Reichstag* entitled 'The Practice of Therapy by Non-Certified Personnel and the Traffic in Patent Medicines'. Of particular interest were Paragraph Five, which would regulate or ban trade with products or objects for the prevention or treatment of illnesses if the use of those items might pose a threat to health, or if fraud or swindle were involved (e.g. overpriced patent medicines), and Paragraph Seven, which would ban the advertising of contraceptives, abortives, sex aids and prophylactics.[27] The bill was opposed by natural therapists and by the medical profession, which argued that it did not go far enough. But doctors made tactical errors in their opposition. They opposed free patient choice of therapist in this context, yet in their own concurrent struggle with the Health Insurance Programme — where local Funds had the right to designate a list of physicians from whom patients could choose — they argued for complete patient freedom. As a result the bill died in committee. The only practical outcome of the agitation was the formation of the League for an Open Health Practice against Medical Compulsion and for the Freedom of all Health Care in Research, Science and Practice (*Bund für freie Heilkunst gegen den Ärztezwang und für die Freiheit der gesamten Heilkunde in Forschung, Wissenschaft, und Praxis*) — an umbrella organisation to coordinate natural therapists in opposition to the medical profession.[28]

In 1910 the government introduced a tougher version of the bill, now renamed 'A Law against Abuses in Health Care'. Paragraph Four would ban the dispensing of medications by non-certified persons — a blow to druggists — while Paragraph Six expanded the scope of Paragraph Five of the earlier proposal. Once again a concerted resistance was mounted by the drug industry (pharmaceutical and patent medicines alike), the press, naturopaths, homeopaths, and even those doctors affiliated with the German Society to Combat Venereal Disease.[29] In the *Reichstag* the only Deputies who supported the bill were members who were doctors themselves; everyone else argued against it. The Conservative, Henning, upheld the right of the public to have a say in the question of patent medicines; the Centrist, Fassbender, feared that the blanket ban would suppress good drugs along with the bad; Socialists shared this sentiment and noted that some doctors did not seem averse to being paid for their 'testimonials' on drug packages; Stresemann of the National Liberals argued that the bill would create a sense of insecurity throughout the entire drug industry; and Müller-Meiningen of the Radical Union noted the practical difficulties for the press in determining which advertisements for which products might fall under the ban envisaged in the bill. For all these reasons the bill failed as ignominiously as its predecessor. Only in 1939 would a Law on Quack Doctors (*Heilpraktikergesetz*) be enacted that would require permission for anyone who wanted to practice therapy.[30]

The failure of these two attempts demonstrated the difficulties which faced the government in its effort to legislate against birth control. But it also demonstrated the continuing anxiety which many felt over the unchecked fertility decline. In a *Reichstag* speech in 1910 the Centrist Deputy Hermann Roeren summed up these feelings:

> The disgusting promotion of certain kinds of rubber goods has not let up despite the *Lex Heinze*. The country is being flooded with these items. Advertisements are posted in every barber shop and drug store. Under such circumstances the widespread use of these products is understandable, and we cannot be surprised that the birth rate has continued to fall in the last few years. This revolting and disgusting trade must be vigorously resisted.[31]

Opponents of birth control wanted stricter regulation of products and devices that could be used for birth control, especially syringes and intra-uterine stems, but also including chemical contraceptives and products for 'menstrual irregularity'. If the manufacture or import of such items was not banned outright, then sales should occur only in pharmacies on a prescription basis, and no sales by druggists or pedlars should be allowed. All advertising for such products or services should be banned.[32]

Some reactionary proposals went even further than these attempts to restrict products and services; extremists wanted to eliminate all public awareness of birth control. Lectures, conferences and meetings dealing with birth control should be banned; press coverage of such events, and of trials involving abortion or contraceptives, should be banned: Jean Bornträger especially lamented the reporting of the Neo-Malthusian Congress held in Dresden in conjunction with the 1911 International Hygienic Exhibition. Popular publications which promoted birth control should be labelled as 'smut' and prosecuted. Public libraries — and SPD libraries in particular — should be cleansed not only of books on birth control and popular hygiene but also of those books on materialism which were considered the seed-bed of birth control.[33] In the final analysis, only a spiritual revival could restore high fertility: 'Respect, renewal, and rejuvenation of the family must be the goal of the reorientation of our public and private life.' Some hope for such a revival arose during the First World War, as observers noted a disenchantment with 'raw materialism' among soldiers back from the front. Whether this disenchantment would spark demographic recovery remained to be seen.[34]

In the meantime, undaunted by the experience of 1908 and 1910, the *Reich* government continued to draft bills designed to curb the spread of birth control. A patent law sought to remove the sanction which patenting seemed to confer on contraceptives in the eyes of the public by denying patents for any device which might offend common decency. Another bill would amend the Commercial Code to prevent pedlars from selling patent medicines and other items for abortion and contraception. The government also sought to prevent registry offices from publishing the names of newly-weds, which were used by firms to select recipients of samples and brochures. Some states enacted legislation to implement these proposals, but most efforts remained unsuccessful. However, in Prussia the Ministry of the Interior sponsored a survey of district medical officers to determine the role of contraceptives in the fertility decline. In the words of the Ministry, 'This is a matter of the highest national interest, and the State can no longer regard the situation passively.'[35]

Frustrated with the pace of governmental efforts, some 213

non-socialist deputies introduced their own draft bill On the Trade with Items for Limiting Births in February 1914.

> 1. The *Bundesrat* may limit or ban trade with objects which are used to interrupt pregnancy. The same applies to objects which are used for contraception, unless consideration of the needs of hygienic protection is involved.
> 2. Anyone who contravenes any restriction or ban on the sale or import of such items will be punished with fines up to 150 Marks or with prison. If sale or import is banned, then in addition to the penalties the objects may be confiscated if they belong to the offender or an accomplice. If prosecution or conviction is not possible, confiscation may proceed independently.
> 3. Anyone who openly advertises or promotes objects which are used to prevent or interrupt pregnancy will be punished with prison up to six months or with fines up to 1,500 Marks, unless other legislation provides for a harsher sentence.
>
> These terms do not apply to announcements or promotions in scientific circles for medicine or pharmacy.[36]

The law in this form was alarmingly vague, and made no distinction between medical and non-medical items, nor between therapeutic and criminal abortion, nor between 'frivolous' and therapeutic contraception, nor between contraception and prophylaxis. The Berlin Society for Obstetrics and Gynaecology urged that the bill be limited to items used by laity to induce abortion, specifically uterine syringes and stem IUDs. Other items should not be subject to blanket restriction.

> It would be a fatal mistake to believe that the lamentable fertility decline can be checked to any significant degree by a ban or restriction on contraceptives. As long as the will to limit births exists, no law can stop it.[37]

A more searching critique of the bill was made by Max Hirsch, who emphasised its impracticality. Any real ban would embrace not only bona fide medical instruments such as catheters, uterine sounds, forceps and curettes, but also hygienic devices. It would have to include a wide range of household items, from sewing needles to goose feathers. A truly comprehensive bill would have to prevent women from jumping, lifting heavy objects, riding on motorcycles, taking hot baths, or getting a massage. The law would have to rescind the popularisation of health care and advice. It would have to strictly control doctors, midwives, natural therapists and anyone else who might possibly assist a woman in abortion. And no law could prevent contraception.[38]

During the First World War concerned physicians were at last able to do something to control contraceptives. Doctors found that the deputy commanding generals appointed to administer martial law were quite sympathetic to their proposals for fighting the fertility decline. Regional medical associations staged conferences to which they invited the generals, senior civil servants, and justices. The commanding generals in several districts responded by invoking provisions of the Law of Siege authorising them to 'maintain public safety'; on this basis they banned or curtailed the advertising, display and sale of contraceptives and abortion aids, and banned offers of 'assistance for female complaints'.[39]

In February, 1918, the *Reich* government tried once again to introduce legislation to combat the fertility decline. The Preamble to the Law against the Limitation of Births set forth the government's rationale:

> The manufacture and sale of contraceptives is not merely a manifestation of the present. Circumstances have changed only in as much as these items were formerly used in non-marital relations to prevent infection, or in marriage on the advice of a doctor. Now, however, these items are used by newly-weds and by healthy and prosperous couples simply to prevent pregnancy. This is due largely to the extensive promotion of these devices by the manufacturers. Promotional brochures present a pseudo-scientific facade encouraging couples to try the devices in the first years of marriage to get a better start.[40]

The government proposed a three-part restriction: items to be banned completely; items restricted to doctors; items available to the general public. Advertisements for all products would receive increased supervision.[41]

A second bill aimed at the dramatic upsurge in abortion and sterilisation. In the view of the *Reich* government:

> Wartime losses and the fertility decline require that every German feel duty bound to reject these operations. The lesson of recent years shows that awareness of this duty among doctors and the public has largely disappeared.[42]

The government blamed improved medical skills for making abortion and sterilisation relatively safe procedures, but recognised that the chief fault lay in the desire of women to avoid having more children. This desire was blamed on selfishness, vanity, convenience, pleasure without responsibility and a rejection of family life. The government proposed the compulsory reporting of abortion and sterilisation as a way of discouraging these operations.[43]

These two bills suggest the direction which social policy might have taken in Germany after the war had things turned out differently. As it happened, neither bill was ever formally introduced in the *Reichstag*. One reason for the decision to drop the proposals was the strong and growing public support for birth control. The *Burgfriede* did not extend to the *Geburtenrückgangsfrage*, and during the war years public assemblies on the theme 'The birth strike as a weapon in the fight for world revolutuion' were sponsored in large cities — and even in military barracks — by leftist and sex-reform organisations.[44]

The move to reform the laws affecting birth control began immediately after the war. Amid the many calls for better treatment of unwed mothers and illegitimate children the *Nationalversammlung*, and later the *Reichstag*, received several petitions for the legal reform of abortion. In 1920 the Social Democratic caucus submitted a resolution to the *Reichstag* recommending legalisation of abortion performed by the woman or by a physician during the first trimester. The Independent Socialists were more direct: 'Paragraphs 218, 219, and 220 are annulled.'[45]

Political disturbances prevented the formulation of any new policy at this time, although the Law Reform Committee of the *Reichstag* did prepare amendments to the Criminal Code which included changes in the abortion law. But before any decision could be taken a major *cause célèbre* intervened to remind politicians of the high degree of public interest in this issue.

In 1918 the Berlin pharmacist Paul Heiser established his 'Mutabor Beauty Salon' on Steglitzerstrasse, where he offered beauty care, massage and baths. A young woman approached him to perform an abortion, which he did by means of a salve he concocted. He subsequently performed more than 11,000 abortions with no ill-effect for the women involved. In 1924 Heiser provoked a trial in order to bring pressure on the government to moderate the abortion laws. He announced that several hundred former clients were willing to testify publicly on his behalf. Heiser also drew attention to the case by publishing a pamphlet, 'How to protect yourself from unwanted children', and by lecturing on the subject.[46]

The trial commenced on 17 May 1924. The prosecution sought to convict Heiser and his wife, and initiated proceedings against 26 of the 400 women who had given their names to the authorities. As was customary in trials like this, a number of experts were called to testify, including Doctors Dührssen, Strassmann, Hirschfeld and Theilhaber; Helene Stöcker of the League for the Protection of Motherhood was permitted to testify as a 'witness' but not as an 'expert'. Many of Heiser's clients claimed that his action had saved them from dire social and economic circumstances after their families and boyfriends had disowned them. Dr Dührssen confirmed much of this testimony and expressed the opinion that if the abortion laws were enforced fairly most of the women in Germany would be in jail.[47]

Heiser was sentenced to two years in prison; his wife received eight months. The Court based its decision on two considerations. First, the prosecution had demonstrated only that Heiser was guilty of attempted abortion; it could not prove any case of completed abortion. Second, the court accepted the defence argument of mitigating circumstances. It recognised that Heiser had acted out of sincere personal and ideological opposition to the abortion law rather than for commercial gain; frequently he had charged his working-class clients no fee. Faced with this relatively lenient sentence for Heiser and the futile prospect of further trials against his clients, the prosecution dropped all charges in September and Heiser was freed.[48]

The year of 1924 also saw new elections which, along with the greater degree of social, economic and political stability in Germany that began with the Dawes Plan and the end of the Ruhr occupation, permitted the *Reichstag* to turn its attention once again to matters of legal reform. In 1925 the Justice Committee commenced reconsideration of the abortion laws. Briefs were solicited from the public, and the medical profession took an active role in debating the issue. Several organisations submitted resolutions to the *Reichstag*.[49]

Doctors argued that the legalisation of abortion would 'remove the last barriers' to sexual indulgence and lead to the 'utter annihilation of morality'. Women would stop having children altogether, and that would mean 'the slow death of the German nation'. The intensification of the fertility decline would undermine military capability, 'something we cannot ignore in spite of the end of conscription', and Germany would forfeit 'great power' status forever. Legalisation was something that should be left to countries like Russia which, 'with its Slavic fertility', could afford the demographic losses; for Germany it would be fatal.⁵⁰ These sentiments were summarised in the brief submitted by the German Medical Association:

> Under wartime conditions the sexual morality of the people has suffered heavily. The virtues of chastity and purity lie mortally weakened . . . Only the fear of pregnancy provides an effective restraint on sensual temptation for many young women. If this last barrier falls there will be no holding back. Sexual degeneracy will run amok and degrade the whole society. Germany's position in the world would suffer enormously.⁵¹

The Association called for the legalisation of therapeutic abortion and proposed reduced penalties for women who obtained illicit abortion, but insisted on the strict punishment of criminal abortionists.⁵²

Once a draft bill was ready, the focus of debate shifted to the *Reichstag*. Conservatives feared the demographic impact of easy access to abortion: 'The implementation of this amendment would mark the final victory of France over Germany.' The Centre Party rejected it on moral grounds: 'The Centre is of the opinion that enactment of the new amendment would make it easier for women to sin.' The *Volkish* Deputy Von Ramin took a racist stand: 'We have no objection to abortion among Jews, but the German people must stick to the old rules.' Leftist and liberal parties took a more tolerant approach to the proposed reform. The right of women to decide their reproduction themselves and the responsibility of society to provide adequate care for mothers and children characterised their attitude. As Frau Lüders of the Democratic Party observed: 'Children must not only be born but also raised.' This sentiment was echoed by Frau Agnes of the Socialist Party: 'The present economic crisis cannot strengthen the joy of children.' Leftists emphasised the connection between adversity and abortion, and argued that one problem could not be solved apart from the other. As a Communist Deputy expressed it early in the abortion debate: 'All the moans and groans of bourgeois society against abortion will remain a hypocritical farce as long as you refuse to give expectant mothers the assistance they need to provide for their children.'⁵³

On 25 May 1926 the new Paragraph 218 was enacted. It demoted abortion from a felony to a misdemeanor and reduced the penalties for both the woman and any third party who assisted her. The law made it more difficult to convict abortionists because the prosecution now had to demonstrate 'career abortion' rather than 'abortion for compensation'. The law continued to regard all abortion — including therapeutic — as illegal.[54]

The reform of 1926, rather than resolving the issue, intensified agitation for complete legalisation. A massive popular groundswell erupted in 1927 as public meetings protested the new law. Felix Theilhaber's Society for Sex Reform produced a short film which served as the basis for consciousness-raising discussions in neighbourhood theatres. Press coverage further inflamed the issue. Governments began to undermine their own justification of the law. The Prussian Ministry for Welfare released a report on the fertility decline which acknowledged the decisive role of economic conditions in the mass resort to birth control. The Saxon *Landtag* drafted a resolution calling on the *Reichstag* to legalise therapeutic abortion and to admit social conditions as an acceptable indication for abortion.[55]

Moved by these and other calls for action, the *Reichstag* Justice Committee started work on a new Criminal Code in 1929, and set up a subcommittee to reconsider the abortion law. Once again medical organisations submitted resolutions to the Committee, but this time several of them called for the acceptance of social indications for therapeutic abortion as a minimum, while others argued for decriminalisation of all abortion. Last but certainly not least, the Catholic Church got involved in the debate through the papal encyclical *Casti Conubbii* (31 December 1930), which reaffirmed the reproductive purpose of sexual relations, stressed the primary reproductive duty of women and their 'proven' subordination to men, condemned abortion and contraception, and called on the state to support the rights of the unborn:

> Since, therefore, the conjugal act is destined primarily by nature for the begetting of children, those who in exercising it frustrate deliberately its natural power and purpose, sin against nature and commit a deed shameful and vicious in itself . . . Any use whatsoever of matrimony exercised in such a way that the act is deliberately frustrated of its natural power to generate life is an offence against the law of God, and those who indulge in such are branded with the guilt of a grave sin.[56]

In Germany the encyclical found a sympathetic response from the Brüning government. But for others *Casti Conubbii* was the last straw. Women's organisations across the country devised a common strategy to oppose the encyclical and to advocate the legalisation of abortion. Several novels treating abortion appeared in the years between 1928 and 1932, including Franz Krey's *Maria und der Paragraph*, which was serialised in working-class papers. Stage plays further dramatised the issue; more than a hundred performances of Friedrich Wolf's *Cyankali* were presented in Berlin and other cities. A film version of the play was heavily censored when not banned outright, and frequently attracted rightist attacks.[57]

In February 1931, Dr Else Kienle and Dr Friedrich Wolf were arrested in Stuttgart for 'commercial abortion' and for issuing false certificates for therapeutic abortion; both were sent to jail. The nascent women's coalition exploded into a crusade on behalf of the two doctors. Newspapers solicited reader opinion; the *Berliner Volkszeitung* received 45,000 letters, of which only 150 supported the law. On 8 March some 1500 rallies and demonstrations were held throughout Germany, starting a process which culminated in a mass rally of 15,000 in the Berlin *Sportpalast* on 15 April. As a result of this agitation — much of it organised by the Communist Party — Dr Wolf was released from jail; Dr Kienle remained incarcerated until a hunger strike won her freedom.[58]

In contrast to the controversy surrounding abortion, contraception enjoyed a relatively high degree of social toleration during the 1920s. Weimar governments generally supported the efforts of sex reform organisations and the Health Insurance Programme to spread the use of contraceptives. There were also no restraints on access to contraceptives, although some limits on advertising remained in force until the 1927 Law to Combat Venereal Diseases legalised the 'tasteful' public promotion of prophylactics (condoms).[59] This general mood of tolerance gradually influenced court decisions regarding birth control, as the 1929 decision of the Chemnitz *Landesgericht* in a case involving the local director of the League for Birth Control demonstrates:

> But the Court is convinced that labelling every non-marital sexual relation as 'obscene' no longer conforms to the general public's interpretation of virtue and morality . . . A change has occurred in public opinion with regard to sex, in that raising children is considered a moral responsibility. Among broad sections of the public it is now considered immoral to bring children into the world when they would face unfavourable physical or economic prospects which would deny them success and happiness. Consequently, in the opinion of the overwhelming majority of the people, contraception is not only not immoral, but in many cases may actually be a moral obligation.[60]

The legal status of sterilisation continued to remain problematic during the 1920s, despite the large number of therapeutic operations performed in various hospitals. The law prohibited 'acts of wounding' which result in the loss of reproductive capability, but confusion clouded attempts to decide whether voluntary sterilisation was the same as 'loss of reproductive capability', or whether therapeutic indications might excuse the act. Many doctors continued to regard genetics as an uncertain science and refused to accept sterilisation for social reasons — a position reaffirmed by the German Medical Association in 1925.[61] Two trials late in the Weimar era shed some light on this question.

In 1929 Dr Schmerz, a surgeon in Graz, was indicted for wounding some 500 to 700 men and for threatening the welfare of the Austrian people. Schmerz had performed vasectomies on the men — most of them railroad workers — after they had attended a lecture on birth control sponsored by the Austrian Socialist Party. The operation was frequently performed on Sundays for the workers' convenience. Workmen were charged 30 shillings; anyone else who wanted the operation paid 300 shillings.[62]

The prosecution charged Schmerz with acts of wounding causing loss of reproductive capability; further, that the operations were conducted on an organised commercial basis; that the patients were not adequately informed of the irreversibility of the procedure; and that the operation was immoral because it resulted in the loss of reproductive capability without the loss of sexual ability (Austria was a Catholic country). Schmerz was convicted and fined 15,000 shillings — an amount equal to the receipts from the operations. He chose prison instead. When the prosecution sought a retrial it was denied and Schmerz was released. The entire affair demonstrated that the court considered vasectomy to be a form of light rather that grave wounding, but did not resolve the question whether patient consent excused sterilisation.[63]

In the spring on 1932 Dr Merck and two assistants from the Municipal Hospital in Kehl (Baden) were charged with dangerous wounding for performing 41 sterilisations along with 42 abortions. The opening statement of the prosecution noted that the issue of wounding for the purpose of sterilisation had not yet come before the courts in Germany; this was attributed to the bona fide therapeutic intent of previous sterilisations, in contrast to the situation in Kehl, where the operation had been performed frequently for socio-economic indications. The defence stressed the distinguished career and personal character of Dr Merck, and noted that the operations had only been performed on married women in dire economic straits, and without any consideration of personal gain. The court accepted these facts as mitigating circumstances, but Merck was sentenced to one year in prison for five counts of abortion, three of attempted abortion, and eight of wounding (sterilisation).[64]

The issues raised in these trials did not resolve the uncertainty over the legality of sterilisation. In Graz concern was as strong over the Socialist conspiracy against the fertility of the *Volk* as over the operation itself, while in Offenburg (the site of the Merck trial) authorities felt compelled to prosecute because of the notoriety associated with the case; common parlance had it that 'in the hospital they can fix it so you won't have children'. Interestingly, Dr Merck was not charged with intentional sterilisation (because the prosecution could not prove the absolute irreversibility of the procedure) but for negligence causing wounding and for grave wounding. The court rejected the consent of the patients as a consideration; it was more concerned that the operation offended common decency by excluding the normal consequences of intercourse and thereby risked creating a nation of uninhibited nymphomaniacs. Since the court also recognised that Merck had acted in good conscience and that the women were all married and in desperate financial circumstances — and thus unlikely to indulge in uninhibited nymphomania — it seems that its main concern was more with upholding morality than with establishing justice on the medical question of sterilisation. The court ominously required specialists to testify whether the accused had attempted to determine in a conscientious and dutiful manner that, according to established medical standards, a clear and present danger to the life or health of the women had existed which could only be alleviated through sterilisation. Such guidelines lent themselves to extremely subjective interpretation which could make all medical operations subject to second-guessing. Given the uncertainty within the medical profession over proper indications for abortion and sterilisation, the legal threat to doctors posed by the Offenburg criteria was serious.[65] Ironically, this verdict was handed down at just the time when a growing consensus in political and scientific circles resulted in a new draft law that would legalise eugenic sterilisation.

The apparent failure of eugenic marriage counselling prompted eugenicists to make a concerted effort to change public policy. They argued that the costs of defective or dangerous persons to society justified sterilisation, or castration for sex offenders. There were 150,000 mentally ill persons in institutions, 100,000 epileptics, 100,000 to 200,000 feeble-minded, 75,000 idiots, 70,000 criminals, and 6,000,000 psychopaths in Germany, all presenting an enormous burden for welfare budgets. Society had the right to be protected, particularly in view of the irresponsible fertility of these people. Sterilisation was the answer: 'The common sense of the people considers it acceptable and demands it of us.' Dr August Mayer related an account of three feeble-minded women in a small town who were seduced and became pregnant; the town mayor and the district health officer both supported sterilisation for the women.[66]

In January, 1932, the German Society for Racial Hygiene presented a resolution to the Prussian government urging greater public awareness of eugenics in general and of its demographic significance in particular. The Prussian Minister for Welfare called a special session of the Prussian Health Council to review the subject. A Subcommittee for Demography and Eugenics discussed the theme 'Eugenics in the Service of the Public Welfare' in its session of 2 July 1932. The consensus of the committee was that the problem was real and immediate. Experts testified that mentally ill people placed an increasing burden on society which was exacerbated by the fertility decline, since fewer healthy people had to subsidise more defective people. 'Irresponsible' birth control was blamed for this, and clarification of the law on sterilisation was requested. The Council recommended that genetics should be taught more widely, and applied through the marriage counselling centres, which should encourage voluntary sterilisation wherever appropriate.[67]

Later that year several other professional organisations debated the eugenics issue and came to similar conclusions. The German Medical Association discussed eugenic indications for sterilisation on two occasions, with considerably more sympathy than in 1925. In September the International Criminology Conference, meeting in Frankfurt, urged adoption of a sterilisation law. In November the Württemberg Chamber of Physicians openly called for legalisation, and this was seconded by the Prussian Chamber in December.[68]

By 1932, then, a substantial consensus of public and professional opinion, including physicians, politicians and theologians, supported some form of eugenic sterilisation. Not even ideology presented an obstacle, as reflected in the comment of the socialist physician Alfred Grotjahn, referring to the American experience:

> It must be assumed that, in the not too distant future, in which consideration of reproductive health is more important than at present, the permanent sterilisation of those individuals from

whom we can expect an inferior offspring will become acceptable among us, too.[69]

As a result of this growing sentiment the government drafted a law on eugenic policy which proposed voluntary sterilisation for persons with a hereditary physical or mental illness, or who carried the genes of such an illness in cases where medical science could reasonably expect the illness to recur in future generations. Special committees were to be established to examine each case to ensure that people were fully informed about the procedure and its consequences and that their consent was voluntary — a condition that was extended to criminals. The government argued that the welfare and penal costs to society justified this policy, and that mass institutionalisation or incarceration of those involved was neither practical nor desirable.[70]

Action on all three fronts — abortion, contraception and sterilisation — came after 1933. The National Socialists had demonstrated their opinion of birth control during the *Reichstag* debate on law reform in 1926, and in a draft Law for the Protection of the Nation, which they proposed in 1930:

> Whoever attempts to constrain the natural fertility of the German *Volk* to the detriment of the nation, or who promotes such efforts in word, letter, publication, picture, or in any other way, or who cooperates in the racial destruction of the German *Volk* through miscegenation with members of the Jewish stock or the coloured races, will be sentenced to prison for racial treason.[71]

Nazi opposition to birth control did not stem from an ethical respect for the right to life of the foetus, but was part of a pragmatic racial policy that sought quantitative and qualitative population growth. The new regime initiated a carrot-and-stick programme to implement its racial policy. Positive economic incentives were extended to large families. Goebbel's Ministry of Public Enlightenement and Propaganda set up a Bureau for Population and Racial Hygiene, and collaborated with the autonomous National Committee for People's Health and the National League for Large Families (*Reichsbund der Kinderreichen Deutschlands zum Schutze der Familie*). Eugenic abortion and sterilisation were complementary components of this policy.[72] The National Socialists also took negative steps. Paragraphs 219 and 220 of the Criminal Code were amended to prohibit the public advertisement, display, or promotion of objects or procedures intended to induce abortion, and to ban the advertising of offers to assist in procedures which might induce abortion. Police cracked down sharply on known abortionists, and closed private institutions which had offered abortion.[73] These efforts were not entirely successful, however, as this letter to the regional leader of the NSDAP in Mönchen-Gladbach illustrates:

> This person has all the equipment needed for abortion. That cannot and should not be permitted in the Third Reich, where our Adolf Hitler is so good for all of us. Therefore it is high time that this business gets cleared up, and you as our *Ortsgruppenleiter* should know about it, and it certainly should not be tolerated that such things occur in our town. Heil Hitler![74]

Nazi moves against abortion were not matched by similar measures against contraception. Police did suppress sex reform organisations and birth-control clinics, while eugenic marriage counselling centres remained open under the framework of the new law on sterilisation (see below). But contraceptives were freely available throughout the 1930s. Not until the Himmler Ordinance of 1941 did the government ban the commercial manufacture, import, advertisement, promotion, stocking for sale, selling, giving, or otherwise bringing into trade of methods, materials, and instruments for the prevention or interruption of pregnancy, and of treatments for these purposes using injection or radiation. In 1943 the abortion law was further amended to provide for capital punishment in cases where abortion resulted in the sterility or death of the woman. Paragraph 219 was amended to prohibit the production, promotion, or sale of any item that could be used for prophylaxis as well as for abortion or contraception.[75]

The National Socialist response to the draft law on eugenic sterilisation was more favourable — and more forceful. The voluntary provisions were dropped and the Law for the Prevention of Hereditary Illness was promulgated on 14 July 1933. Some 1700 Tribunals of Hereditary Health were set up in every large city and in all administrative districts, along with 205 courts and 26 appeal courts. In the first year more than 56,000 persons were sterilised — more than in the United States over a 40-year period. By 1940 more than a quarter million men and women had been sterilised.[76]

So, after a brief liberal interlude, German population policy had come full circle. In 1932 Dr Gauss advocated essentially the same proposals for suppressing birth control and curbing the fertility decline as Jean Bornträger had recommended 20 years earlier. After 1933 the National Socialist government started to implement some of these proposals, although the more draconian measures had to await the emergency circumstances of the war. But by this time it was too late; the fertility decline had cut birth rates by more than 50 per cent, and although Nazi economic policies and repressive measures may have contributed to the brief upward nudge of fertility in the mid-1930s, the downward trend recommenced by 1939. The fertility decline was confirmed as an irreversible facet of modern German society.

NOTES

1. Line quotes are from C.J. Gauss, 'Sexualrevolution, Geburtenregelung und die Zukunft unseres Volk', *MW*, 6 (1932), p. 662; Franz Hitze, *Geburtenrückgang und Sozialreform* (Volksvereinsverlag, Mönchen-Gladbach, 1917), p. 11; Ferdinand Goldstein, *Geburtenbeschränkung: Staatsruin oder Wiederherstellung* (Berger, Berlin, 1924), p. 19; Otto von Franqué, *Geburtenrückgang, Arzt, und Geburtshelfer* (Abhandlungen aus dem Gesamtgebiet der praktischen Medizin, Würzburg, 1916), p. 100; Alfred Grotjahn, *Geburtenrückgang und Geburtenregelung im Lichte der individuellen und der sozialen Hygiene* (Marcus, Berlin, 1914), pp. 327, 336; respectively. See also Hans Albrecht, 'Eheliche Fruchtbarkeit und Geburtenrückgang in Europa', *MGG* 80 (1929), p. 100; Oskar Wingen, *Die Bevölkerungstheorien der letzten Jahre* (Cotta, Stuttgart, 1915), p. 199; Alfred Grotjahn, *Der Hygiene der menschlichen Fortpflanzung: Versuch einer praktischer Eugenik* (Urban and Schwarzenberg, Berlin, 1926) pp. 24–5; F. Siebert, 'Der Neomalthusianismus und die öffentliche Ankundigung der Verhütungsmittel', *ARGB*, 9 (1912), p. 477; W. Stoeckel, 'Geburtshilfe', *Jahreskurse für ärztliche Fortbildung* 5 (1914), p. 3.

2. Line quotes from Hitze, *Geburtenrückgang*, p. 11. See also Grotjahn, *Geburtenrückgang*, pp. 18, 31–2, 52, 247; Grotjahn, *Hygiene*, pp. 49, 57; A. Grotjahn, 'Eheberatungsstellen und Geburtenprävention', *Ergebnisse der soziale Hygiene und Gesundheits-Fürsorge*, 1 (1929),pp. 70–5; Dietrich Tutzke, 'Alfred Grotjahn (1869–1931) und das Hygiene-Institut der Universität Berlin', *NTM Schriftenreihe*, 8 (1917), pp. 81–91; O. Krohne, 'Empfängnisverhütung, Künstliche Unfruchtbarkeit und Schwangerschaftsunterbrechung vom bevölkerungspolitischen und ärztlichen Standpunkt', *ZAF*, 14 (1917), p. 345; O. Krohne, 'Künstliche Fehlgeburt und künstliche Unfruchtbarkeit vom Standpunkt des Staatsinteresse' in Placzek (ed.), *Kunstliche Fehlgeburt*, p. 369; M. Rosenthal, 'Der eheliche Präventivverkehr, insbesondere in ethischer Beziehung', *NG* 14 (1918), pp. 120–1.

3. Siebert, 'Neomalthusianismus', pp. 483–5, 492. See also Hitze, *Geburtenrückgang*, pp. 19, 198; Wingen, *Bevölkerungstheorien*, p. 199; Stoeckel, 'Geburtshilfe', p. 3; Max von Gruber, *Ursachen und Bekämkpfung des Geburtenrückganges im Deutschen Reich* (Viewig, Braunschweig, 1914),

pp. 41-2; August Mayer, *Gedanken zur modernen Sexualmoral* (Enke, Stuttgart, 1930).

4. Hitze, *Geburtenrückgang*, pp. 10-12. See also Friedrich Zahn, 'Die deutsche Familie und der Wiederaufbau unseres Volkes', *ASA*, 16 (1926-7), pp. 2-3; Fritz Burgdörfer, 'Familienstatistik. Ein Beitrag zur Reform der Bevölkerungsstatistik', *ASA*, 10 (1916-17), pp. 484-6.

5. Line quotes are from Hitze, *Geburtenrückgang*, p. 10; Albrecht, 'Fruchtbarkeit', p. 100; and Gauss, 'Sexualrevolution', p. 662. See also Krohne, 'Empfängnisverhütung', p. 346; Krohne, 'Künstliche Fehlgeburt', p. 367; Friedrich Lönne, *Deutschlands Volksvermehrung und Bevölkerungspolitik vom nationalökonomisch-medizinischen Standpunkt* (Bergmann, Wiesbaden, 1917), p. 15.

6. Albrecht, 'Fruchtbarkeit', p. 100.

7. Max Marcuse, *Der eheliche Präventivverkehr: seine Verbreitung, Verursachung und Methodik* (Enke, Stuttgart, 1917), pp. 1-4, 11, 15; Heinz Potthoff, 'Geburtenregelung und Geschlechtsmoral', *Sex Pr*, 10 (1914), p. 385.

8. Helene Stöcker, 'Das Recht über sich selbst', *NG*, 4 (1908), p. 271; cf. Kurt Hiller, *Das Recht über sich selbst* (Winter, Heidelberg, 1908).

9. Eric Kollmann, 'Reinterpreting modern German history: the Weimar Republic', *Journal of Central European Affairs*, 21 (1962), p. 450; Hans-Günter Zmarzlik, 'Das Kaiserreich in neuer Sicht', *Historische Zeitschrift* 222 (1976), pp. 105-26.

10. Julius von Kirchmann, *Aktenstücke zur Amtsentsetzung* (Springer, Berlin, 1867), pp. 72-3; Heinrich Volkmann, *Die Arbeiterfrage im preussischen Abgeordnetenhaus, 1848-1869* (Duncker and Humblot, Berlin, 1968), p. 165. For biographical data on Kirchmann see *Neue Deutsche Biographie* (Duncker and Humblot, Berlin, 1977), vol. 11, pp. 654-5. On the political context see Adalbert Hess, *Das Parlament, das Bismarck widerstrebte* (Westdeutscher Verlag, Köln, 1964), pp. 72, 111, 117n. 7; Gerhard Eisfeld, *Die Entstehung der liberalen Parteien in Deutschland, 1858-1870* (Verlag für Literatur und Zeitgeschichte, Hannover, 1969), pp. 178-88. On the position of civil servants and politics see John Gillis, *The Prussian bureaucracy in crisis, 1840-1860* (Stanford University Press, Stanford, 1971), pp. 107, 113-14.

11. Kirchmann, *Aktenstücke*, pp. 15-16, 77; Vernon Lidtke, *The alternative culture: Socialist Labor in Imperial Germany* (Oxford University Press, New York, 1985), p. 160.

12. Kirchmann, *Aktenstücke*, pp. 18-19; Gillis, *Prussian bureaucracy*, p. 139.

13. Kirchmann, *Aktenstücke*, pp. 41-3.

14. Kirchmann, *Aktenstücke*, p. 43; Hess, *Parlament*, pp. 111, 117 n7.

15. Kirchmann, *Aktenstücke*, pp. 82-4. For data on Karl Albrecht von Uhden see *Allgemeine Deutsche Biographie* (Duncker and Humblot, Leipzig, 1895), vol. 39, pp. 765-7. Compare the fate of Viscount Amberley in England, who was denounced by physicians and politicians alike during the 1868 electoral campaign after publicly expressing agreement with Charles Drysdale on the need for family limitation: Richard Soloway, *Birth control and the population question in England, 1877-1930* (University of North Carolina Press, Chapel Hill, 1982), p. 112.

16. Hermann Böttger, *Die reichsgesetzliche Bestimmungen über den Verkehr mit Arzneimitteln ausserhalb der Apotheken*, 4th edn (Springer, Berlin, 1902), p. 164; Ernst Urban, *Gesetzlichen Bestimmungen* (Springer, Berlin, 1904), pp. 41-2; Elmar Ernst, *Das 'industrielle' Geheimmittel und seine Werbung. Arzneifertigwaren in der zweiten Hälfte des neunzehnten Jahrhunderts in Deutschland* (Jal, Würzburg, 1975) p. 198.

17. Urban, *Gesetzlichen Bestimmungen*, pp. 1-2, 16; Ernst, *Geheimmittel*, pp. 199-200; Heinz Peickert, 'Geheimmittel im deutschen Arzneizverkehr. Ein Beitrag zur Wirtschaftsgeschichte der Pharmazie und zur Arzneispecialitätenfrage', PhD dissertation, University of Leipzig, 1932, pp. 112, 142-5; R. Wehmer and W. Pflanz, 'Kurpfuscherei und Geheimmittelwesen' in O. Rapmund (ed.), *Das Preussische Medizinal- und Gesundheitswesen in den Jahren 1883-1903* (Kornfeld, Berlin, 1908), pp. 458-9; Carola von Littrow, 'Die Stellung des Deutschen Aerztetages zur Kurpfuscherfrage', *Wissenschaftliche Zeitschrift: Mathematisch-Naturwissenschaftliche Reihe*, 19 (1970), pp. 441-2. For a list of regulations in all states see Böttger, *Reichsgesetzliche Bestimmungen*, pp. 164-77.

18. 'Vorschriften über den Verkehr mit Geheimmittel und ähnlichen Arzneimitteln', in Peickert, *Geheimmittel*, p. 112; Urban, *Bestimmungen*, pp. 91-2; Littrow, 'Stellung', p. 442.

19. Alex Hall, *Scandal, sensation and Social Democracy. The SPD press and Wilhelmine Germany, 1890-1914* (Cambridge Univesity Press, New York, 1977), p. 148; Karl Bachem, *Vorgeschichte. Geschichte und Politik der Deutschen Zentrumspartei* (9 vols, J.P. Bachem, Köln, 1929; reprinted Scientia Verlag, Aalen, 1967), vol. 5, p. 422; vol. 6, p. 63; Ernst Huber, *Deutsche Verfassungsgeschichte*, vol. 4, p. 283; Henry Darcy, 'The *Lex Heinze*: an inquiry into the moral and social trends of Germany at the end of the 19th century', PhD dissertation, SUNY-Buffalo, 1976, *passim*. On the politics of the Mittelland canal see Huber, *Verfassungsgeschichte*, pp. 1087-105; Abraham Peck, *Radicals and reactionaries: the crisis of conservatism in Wilhelmine Germany* (University Press of America, Washington, 1978), p. 43; Kenneth Barkin, *The controversy over German industrialization, 1890-1902* (University of Chicago Press, Chicago, 1970), pp. 213-16; Hannelore Horn, *Der Kampf um den Bau des Mittellandkanals* (Westdeutscher Verlag, Köln, 1964).

20. Bachem, *Vorgeschicte*, vol. 6, pp. 63-9, 77; Huber, *Verfassungsgeschicte*, vol. 4, pp. 283-5; G. Bliefert, 'Die Innenpolitik des Reichskanzlers Fürst Chlodwig zu Hohenlohe-Schillingsfürst, 1894-1900', PhD dissertation, University of Kiel, 1949, pp. 220-3; Robin Lenman, 'Art, Society and the Law in Wilhelmine Germany: the Lex Heinze', *Oxford German Studies*, 8 (1973), pp. 88-9. The account in Ellen Evans, *The German Center Party, 1870-1933: a study in political Catholicism* (University of Southern Illinois Press, Carbondale, 1981), p. 139 is unduly sympathetic to the Centre Party.

21. Huber, *Deutsche Verfassungsgeschichte*, vol. 4, p. 284; Gary Stark, 'Pornography', Society and the Law in Imperial Germany, *CEH*, 14 (1981), p. 217.

22. Hans Ferdy, *Sittliche Selbstbeschränkung* (Verfasser, Hildesheim, 1904), p. 57; B. Schlegtendahl, 'Die Empfängnis und ihre Verhütung', *ZMB*, 27 (1914), p. 329; Dr Knoop, 'Referat', (Sitzungsbericht, Niederrheinisch-

westfälische Gesellschaft für Gynäkologie und Geburtshilfe), *MGG*, 39 (1913), pp. 414-15.

23. Hans Schneickert, 'Die gewerbsmässige Abtreibung und deren Bekämpfung', *MKP*, 2 (1906), pp. 632-3.

24. Peickert, 'Geheimmittel', p. 149; Littrow, 'Stellung', p. 437.

25. Dr Springfeld, 'Die Überwachung der Kurpfuscher in Berlin', *Aerztliche Sachverständigen-Zeitung*, 4 (1898), p. 260; Littrow, 'Stellung', pp. 435-6, 439; Bergmann-Gorski, *Berufspolitik*, p. 98; Richard Shryock, *The development of modern medicine. An interpretation of the social and scientific factors involved* (Blackiston, Philadelphia, 1936), p. 244.

26. Littrow, 'Stellung', pp. 434, 436; Karin Bergmann-Gorski, 'Aerztliche Standes- und Berfuspolitik in Deutschland von 1900 bis 1910', PhD dissertation, University of Berlin, 1966, pp. 48-50.

27. Peickert, 'Geheimmittel', pp. 149-50; Dr Kantor, 'Geburtenrückgang und Kurpfuscherei', *TH*, 30 (1916), p. 563.

28. Littrow, 'Stellung', p. 444; Florian Tennstedt, 'Sozialgeschichte der Sozialversicherung' in Maria Blohmke (ed.), *Handbuch der Sozialmedizin* (3 vols, Enke, Stuttgart, 1976) vol. III, p. 394; Claudia Huerkamp, 'Aerzte und Professionalisierung in Deutschland: Überlegungen zum Wandel des Arztberufs im neunzehnten Jahrhundert', *Geschichte und Gesellschaft*, 6 (1980), p. 374. In 1900 militant doctors formed the Verband der Aerzte Deutschlands (Hartmannbund) to campaign against any Fund which discriminated against individual doctors. A series of 'actions' (strikes) in major cities led to a compromise in which patients could select their own physicians, but Funds retained the right to set contracts and fees. Tennstedt, 'Sozialgeschichte', p. 395; Bergmann-Gorski, 'Berufspolitik', pp. 14-29; Hans Schadewaldt, *75 Jahre Hartmannbund. Ein Kapitel deutscher Sozialpolitik* (Bonn, 1975); Arthur Gabriel, *Die Kassenärztliche Frage* (H.A.L. Degener, Leipzig, 1912).

29. Littrow, 'Stellung', p. 444; Peickert, 'Geheimmittel', p. 152; Stürzbecher, *Bekämkpfung*, pp. 151-2; Max Marcuse, 'Die antineomalthusianische Bestimmungen in dem Entwurf eines Gesetzes gegen Missstände im Heilgewerbe', *SP*, 7 (1911), pp. 81-135.

30. Peickert, 'Geheimmittel', p. 153; Littrow, 'Stellung', p. 444.

31. Manfred Stürzbecher, 'Die Bekämpfung des Geburtenrückganges und der Säuglingssterblichkeit im Spiegel der Reichstagsdebatten, 1900-1930', PhD dissertation, University of Berlin, 1954, p. 151. Cf. Hermann Roeren, *Die öffentliche Unsittlichkeit und ihre Bekämkpfung. Flugschrift des Kölner Männervereins zur Bekämpfung der öffentlichen Unsittlichkeit*, (J.P. Bachem, Köln, 1904).

32. Jean Bornträger, *Der Geburtenrückgang in Deutschland: Seine Bewertung und seine Bekämkpfung* (Kabitzsch, Würzburg, 1913), pp. 122-4; H. von Hövell, 'Gründe und Bedeutung des Geburtenrückganges vom Standpunkte der öffentliche Gesundheitspflege: Was kann der Arzt und die Medizinalverwaltung tun, um diesem Übel zu begegnen?' *VGMOS* (3rd series), 51 (1916), pp. 303, 307; W. Thorn, 'Über die Ursachen des Geburtenrückganges und die Mittel zu seiner Bekämpfung', *Praktische Ergebnisse der Geburtshilfe und Gynäkologie*, 5 (1912), p. 46; Hans Albert Dietrich, 'Zur Bevolkerungspolitik', *MGG*, 49 (1919), p. 436; Th. Lochte, 'Die Fruchtabtreibung und ihre Bekämpfung', *VGMOS* (Neue Folge), 2

(1923), p. 536; Paul Ruge, 'Über die Zunahme der Aborte', *MGG*, 43 (1916), p. 462.

33. Bornträger, *Geburtenrückgang*, pp. 119-20, 133, 171-2; Hövell, 'Gründe', pp. 299, 303.

34. Hitze, *Geburtenrückgang*, p. 202. See also Bornträger, *Geburtenrückgang*, pp. 166-7, 173-4; Franqué, *Geburtenrückgang*, p. 96; Ernst Bumm, 'Zur Bevölkerungspolitik', *ZGyn*, 42 (1918), p. 619.

35. Krohne, 'Empfängnisverhütung', p. 343. See also the German Patent Law of 1913 (Washington: Government Printing office, 1914); Stürzbecher, *Bekämpfung*, pp. 158-9; Manfred Stürzbecher, 'Standesamt und Empfängnisverhütungsmittel. Ein Beitrag zur Geschichte der deutschen Bevölkerungspolitik', *Gesundheitsfürsorge*, 4 (1954), p. 142.

36. Berlin Gesellschaft für Geburtshilfe und Gynäkologie, 'Gutachten betreffend den Verkehr mit Mitteln zur Geburtenverhinderung', *ZGyn*, 38 (1914), p. 728. See also A. Blaschko, 'Zum Verbot antikonzeptioneller Mittel', *Deutsche Strafrechts-Zeitung*, 1 (1914), pp. 107-10; M. Vaerting, 'Über den Einfluss des Krieges auf Präventivverkehr und Fruchtabtreibung und seine eugenischen Folgen', *ZSWSP*, 4 (1917), p. 137.

37. Berlin Gesellschaft für Geburtshilfe und Gynäkologie, 'Gutachten betreffend den Verkehr mit Mitteln zur Geburtenverhinderung', pp. 728-30. See also Gesellschaft zur Bekämpfung der Übervölkerung Deutschlands, *Eingabe gegen das Verbot des Handelns mit antikonzeptioneller Mitteln* (n.p., Berlin, 1914).

38. Max Hirsch, *Fruchtabtreibung und Präventivverkehr im Zusammenhang mit dem Geburtenrückgang* (Kabitzsch, Würzburg, 1914), pp. 50-1; Max Hirsch, 'Der Geburtenrückgang. Etwas über seine Ursachen und die gesetzgeberischen Massnahmen zu seiner Bekämpfung', *ARGB*, 8 (1911), pp. 647-8.

39. Dr Schnell, 'Die beim weiblichen Geschlecht gebräuchlichen Gummiartikel zur Verhütung und Unterbrechung der Schwangerschaft', *MK*, 13 (1917), p. 542; Max Marcuse, 'Die Verhandlungen des Preussischen Abgeordnetenhauses über das Medizinalwesen', *DMW*, 43 (1917), pp. 306-7, 340-2; Charlotte Lorenz, *Die gewerbliche Frauenarbeit während des Krieges* (Deutsche VerlagsAnstalt, Stuttgart, 1928), p. 373; Gerald Feldman, *Army, industry and labor in Germany, 1914-1918* (Princeton University Press, Princeton, 1966), pp. 31, 124-5. For some specific military districts in which restrictions were imposed see Schnell, 'Geschlecht', p. 542; Kantor, '*Geburtenrückgang*', pp. 563-5; Franqué, *Geburtenrückgang*, p. 104n; Bergmann-Gorski, 'Berufspolitik', p. 63.

40. Stürzbecher, *Bekämpfung*, pp. 163-4. See also Lewinsohn, 'Stellung', p. 225.

41. Stürzbecher, *Bekämpfung*, pp. 164-6

42. Krohne, 'Empfängnisverhütung', p. 344; Krohne, 'Künstliche Fehlgeburt', pp. 370-1; Georg Winter, 'Sollen wir Bevölkerungspolitik treiben?', *MGG*, 47 (1918), p. 356.

43. Stürzbecher, *Bekämpfung*, pp. 166-8; R. Lewinsohn, 'Die Stellung der Deutschen Sozialdemokratie zur Bevölkerungsfrage', *Schmollers Jahrbuch*, 46 (1922), p. 225.

44. F. Burgdörfer, 'Die Bevölkerungsentwicklung während des Krieges und die kommunistische Propaganda für den Gebärstreik, *MMW*, 66 (1919), p. 433.

45. Stürzbecher, *Bekämpfung*, pp. 236, 242. See also Lewinsohn, 'Stellung', p. 227; Dr Bovensiepen, 'Straflosigkeit der Abtreibung', *ZSWSP*, 7 (1921), p. 14; Max Hirsch, 'Geburtenrückgang und Gesetzgebung nach dem Krieg', *ZSWSP*, 6 (1919–20), p. 241.

46. *Vorwärts*, 18 May 1924, supplement 1, p. 2; Heiser, *Wie schützt man sich gegen unerwünschte Kindersegen* (n.p.).

47. *Vorwärts*, 18 May 1924, Supplement, p. 2.

48. 'Fort mit Paragraph 218! Ein Nachwort zum Prozess Heiser', *Vorwärts*, 20 May 1924, evening edition, p. 1; *Berliner Morgenpost*, 20 May 1924, Supplement 1, p. 2; Dr Dührssen, 'Die Reform der Paragraphen 218-219', *Sexus* 4 (1926), pp. 77–8.

49. Stürzbecher, *Bekämpfung*, p. 239; M. Stritt, 'Frauenbewegung und Paragraph 218', *NG*, 21 (1925), p. 305.

50. Line quotes are from: Dr Reifferscheid, Über den Geburtenrückgang und die Zunahme der Fruchtabtreibung in Deutschland', *Allgemeine Deutsche Hebammenwesen*, 40 (1925), p. 4; K.E. Hoffstaedt, 'Der krimineller Abort, seine medizinische und sozialhygienische Bedeutung', *ZGSW*, 42 (1921), p. 777; Dr Warnekros, cited in Dührssen, 'Reform', p. 72; Dr Wachenfeld, in O. Sarwey, Winkler and Wachenfeld, 'Die Fruchtabtreibungsseuche. Eine frauenärztliche, hygienische und strafrechtliche Stellungnahme', *Deutsche Zeitschrift für die öffentliche Gesundheitspflege*, (1926), pp. 10–11, 16; Hans Naujoks, 'Die Freigabe des kunstlichen Abortes in Sowjetrussland und in Deutschland', *DMW*, 53 (1927), p. 403; respectively. See also Dr Reifferscheid, 'Zum Kampfe gegen die Fruchtabtreibung', *ZGyn*, 48(1924), pp. 518-19.

51. Quoted in Goldstein, *Geburtenbeschränkung*, p. 68.

52. Resolution of the Natural Science and Medical Society of Rostock, in Sarwey, Winkler, and Wachenfeld, 'Fruchtabtreibungsseuche', pp. 16–20.

53. Stürzbecher, *Bekämpfung*, pp. 239–47.

54. H. Heiss, *Die kunstliche Schwangerschaftsunterbrechung und der kriminelle Abort* (Enke, Stuttgart, 1967), p. 92; W. Mittermaier, 'Fruchtabtreibung', *ZSWSP*, 12 (1926), p. 19.

55. Jahns, *Delikt*, p. 10; Dr Meisinger, 'Die Bekämpfung der Abtreibung als politische Aufgabe', *DZGGM*, 32(1939–40), p. 227; Hans Lehfeldt, 'Die Laienorganisationen für Geburtenregelung', *Archiv für Bevölkerungspolitik*, 1(1932), p. 63; Hugo Sellheim, 'Ohne Fortpflanzungsverantwortlichkeit keine Fortepflanzungs regulierung', *ZGyn*, 52(1928), p. 2562; Prussia, Ministry of Welfare, *Der Geburtenrückgang in Deutschland. Folgen und Bekämpfung* (Berlin, 1928); Atina Grossman, 'Abortion and the economic crisis: the 1931 campaign against Paragraph 218 in Germany', *New German Critique*, 14 (1978), p. 122n.

56. J. Poynter, *The popes and social problems* (Watts, London, 1949), pp. 36–7. See also Grossman, 'Abortion', pp. 123, 126–7; Heinrich Gesenius, *Empfängnisverhütung*, 3rd edn (Urban and Schwarzenberg, Berlin, 1970), p. 298; Jahns, *Delikt*, p. 11; M. Rodecurt, 'Die negativen Auswirkungen des Paragraphs 218', *ZGyn*, 55 (1931), p. 3070; A. Kasten, 'Die Stellung der Abtreibung im zukunftigen Strafrecht nach der Entscheidung des Strafrechtsausschusses des Reichstags', *Soziale Praxis*, 39 (1930), pp. 385–7; H. Börner, 'Rundfrage an die Aerztinnen über ihre Stellungnahme zur Schwangerschaftsunterbrechung'. *Die Ärztin*, 8 (1932), p. 3.

57. Grossman, 'Abortion', pp. 127, 129; Renny Harrigan, 'Die Sexualität der Frau in der deutschen Unterhaltungsliteratur', *Geschichte und Gesellschaft* 7 (1981), pp. 430, 433; Petra Schneider, *Weg mit dem Paragraph 218! Die Massenbewegungen gegen das Abtreibungsverbot in der Weimarer Republik* (Oberbaumverlag, Berlin, 1975), p. 84; Istvan Deak, *Weimar Germany's Left-Wing Intellectuals* (University of California Press, Berkeley, 1968), p. 132.

58. Grossman, 'Abortion', pp. 128-30; Friedrich Wolf, *Sturm gegen den Paragraph 218* (Boll, Berlin, 1931); Dr Vollman, 'Der Kampf gegen Paragraph 218: Die Sache Dr Friedrich Wolf', *Deutsches Aerzteblatt* 60 (1931), p. 115; Walther Pollatscheck, *Das Bühnenwerk Friedrich Wolfs. Ein Spiegel der Geschichte des Volkes* (Henschel, Berlin, 1963); W. Jehser, *Friedrich Wolf, sein Leben und Werk* (Verlag Volk und Wissenschaft, Berlin, 1968); Else Kienle, *Frauen. Aus dem Tagebuch einer Aerztin* (Kiepenheuer, Berlin, 1932). For a list of novels, plays, poems, and films produced during the abortion campaign see Harrigan, 'Sexualität', pp. 429-30, and Schneider, *Weg*, p. 80.

59. R. Wassermann, 'Die Verhütung der Empfängnis im Wandel der Zeiten', *ZSWSP*, 16 (1930), pp. 562-3; Erwin Reiche, 'Empfängnisverhütung nach geltendem Deutschen Recht', in Kurt Bendix (ed.), *Geburtenregelung: Vorträge und Verhandlungen* (Selbstverlag, Berlin 1929), pp. 21-2; Max Marcuse, *Der eheliche Präventivverkehr: seine Verbreitung, Verursachung und Methodik* (Enke, Stuttgart, 1917), p. 157; Robert Engelsmann, 'Die Ursache des Geburtenrückganges', PhD dissertation, University of Münster, 1937, p. 93; August Mayer, 'Medizinischjuristische Grenzfragen zur operativen Sterilisierung', *MGG*, 90(1932), p. 115.

60. R. Wasserman, 'Verhütung', pp. 562-3.

61. A. Haberda, 'Gerichtsärztliche Erfahrungen über die Fruchtabtreibung in Wien', *VGMOS*, 56 (1914), p. 169.

62. Mayer, 'Grenzfragen', p. 119; R. Wassermann, 'Der Fall Schmerz', *AKAK*, 88 (1931), p. 254; Erich Goldberg, 'Über Empfängnisverhütung', *ZSWSP*, 17 (1930), p. 284.

63. Goldberg, 'Empfängnisverhütung', p. 284; Max Hodann, *History of modern morals* (Heinemann, London, 1937), pp. 164-5.

64. W. Liepmann, 'Der Offenburger Aerzteprozess: die Sterilisierung der Frau zum ersten Male vor Gericht', *MK*, 28 (1932), pp. 1224-7; Wilhelm Schmitz, 'Ein Strafverfahren in Deutschland wegen Sterilisierung', *Deutsches Aerzteblatt*, 61 (1932), p. 222.

65. Liepmann, 'Offenburger Aerzteprozess', pp. 1225, 1257-8; Schmitz, 'Strafverfahren', pp. 242, 262.

66. Mayer, 'Grenzfragen', pp. 105-6, 111-12; Dr Löffler, 'Sterilisierung, Konzeptionsverhütung und Eugenik', *AGyn*, 144 (1931), p. 355.

67. 'Die Eugenik im Dienste der Volkswohlfahrt, Bericht über die Verhandlungen eines zusammengesetzten Ausschusses des Preussischen Landesgesundheitsrats vom 2 Juli 1932', *VGMV*, 38 (1932); A. DeBary, 'Die Bedeutung der Eugenik in der ärztlichen Praxis und Wissenschaft', *DMW*, 58 (1932), p. 1888; Georg Lilienthal, 'Rassenhygiene im Dritten Reich. Krise und Wende', *Medizin-historisches Journal*, 14 (1979), pp. 118-19.

68. DeBary, 'Bedeutung', p. 1889; Lilienthal, 'Rassenhygiene', p. 119; Mayer, 'Grenzfragen', p. 108; Yves Ternon and Helman Socrate, *Les*

médecins allemands et le national-socialisme (Casterman, Tournai, 1973), p. 160.

69. Grotjahn, *Hygiene*, p. 76. See also Mayer, 'Grenzfragen', pp. 109-10; Lilienthal, 'Rassenhygiene', p. 120.

70. DeBary, 'Bedeutung', p. 1889; Lilienthal, 'Rassenhygiene', p. 119; Ludwig Seitz, 'Weitere Bemerkungen und Vorschläge zum eugenischen Sterilisierungsgesetzentwurf', *MGG*, (1933), pp. 209-22.

71. Stürzbecher, *Bekämpfung*, p. 248.

72. Ewald Gemmer, *Das Problem der Geburteneinschränkung und Fehlgeburten vor und nach 1933* (Tageblatt-Haus, Coburg, 1937), p. 28; Jill Stephenson, ' "Reichsbund der Kinderreichen": the league of large families in the population policy of Nazi Germany', *European Studies Review*, 9 (1979), pp. 352-3; Gisela Bock, ' "Zum Wohle des Volkskörpers": Abtreibung und Sterilisation unterm Nationalsozialismus', *Journal für Geschichte*, 2 (1980), pp. 58-65; Gisela Bock, 'Racism and sexism in Nazi Germany: motherhood, compulsory sterilisation, and the State', *Signs* 8, (1983), pp. 400-21.

73. Stürzbecher, *Bekämpfung*, p. 348, n. 82. The German Society for Juridical and Social Medicine criticised the new law in 1934 for not going far enough in banning all objects which could be used for abortion. Alfons Grassl, 'Folgezustände der mechanischen Abtreibungen und Abtreibungsversuche in gerichtsärztlicher Beleuchtung', PhD dissertation, University of Münster, 1936, p. 34; Meisinger, 'Bekämpfung', pp. 241-2. See also David Glass, *Population policies and movements in Europe* (Oxford University Press, Oxford, 1940), p. 285.

74. Konstantin Inderheggen, *Das Delikt der Abtreibung im Landgerichtsbezirk Mönchen-Gladbach in der Zeit von 1908 bis 1938* (Fromman, Jena, 1940), p. 52.

75. Heinrich Gesenius, 'Die Gefährlichkeit der Intrauterinpessare, *ZGyn*, 59 (1935), pp. 2168-77; Stürzbecher, *Bekämpfung*, p. 349, n. 86; Stephenson, 'Reichsbund', p. 352; Jill Stephenson, *Women in Nazi society* (Croom Helm, London, 1972), p. 61.

76. Lilienthal, 'Rassenhygiene', pp. 123-4; Ternon and Socrate, *Les médecins allemands*, pp. 157, 160; Gesenius, *Empfängnisverhütung*, p. 135.

77. Gauss, 'Sexualrevolution', p. 661.

Conclusion

Birth control cut German fertility by half within two generations. Modern methods of abortion, contraception and sterilisation were crucial for this transition, despite the possible role of traditional birth control in explaining variations in regional birth rates before 1871.[1] Traditional methods are precarious at best, and successful fertility control requires the predictability that characterises modern techniques.

The fact that fertility fell across Europe — and in western societies outside Europe — during the same time period, even though these countries stood at different stages of social, economic and political development, implies that whatever happened after the 1870s was universal, and the one new factor that characterises the fertility decline in all western countries is the diffusion of modern birth control technology. Studies of the fertility decline in Britain, Belgium, Sweden, Germany, Italy and Russia demonstrate that birth rates fell in both industrial and agrarian regions, in areas with high and low levels of literacy, in communities with extensive outside contacts and in isolated backwater areas. In short, no one socio-economic variable, nor any set of variables, explains the fertility decline for all of Europe. Although regional differences affected the pace of the decline, probably due to local cultural factors, they do not explain the cause of the decline.[2] If changes in motivation and mentality do not explain the continent-wide drop in fertility, it seems reasonable to suggest that the new techniques of birth control which appeared in the late nineteenth century and which diffused rapidly throughout western society may have more than coincidental value in explaining the modern fertility decline.

Three factors joined forces to make modern birth control possible. Political economists who discussed the population question sparked the emergence of Neo-Malthusianism, which provided ideological support for those couples who wanted to control fertility and simultaneously drew attention to the latent market for contraceptives. Medical science devised products and procedures for safe and effective therapeutic contraception, abortion and sterilisation. And entrepreneurs exploited these techniques commercially to mass-produce a host of condoms, diaphragms, suppositories, douches, syringes and IUDs which they mass-marketed throughout Germany using retail outlets, pedlars, and mail-order advertising. By the 1890s advertisements for 'rubber goods' appeared in larger newspapers everywhere, and items for abortion and contraception could be found in even the smallest villages. By the 1920s nearly everyone was aware of modern birth control, and anyone who wanted to control fertility had ready access to effective methods for doing so.[3]

Yet there is no technological determinism here; people did not use the new products and services simply because they were new. People must want to control fertility, whether out of greater parental love for each child or from pragmatic concern with balancing family income and expenses; they must be willing to control fertility, which implies a basic awareness of reproductive physiology that should not be taken for granted, especially among young people, and a willingness to use the appropriate measures to achieve that control; and they must be able to control fertility by having ready access to effective techniques.[4] In the late nineteenth century, when western society first experienced national-scale fertility control, each of these conditions represented a radical break with tradition that required more deliberation, more communication, and more persistence than is true now. People raised in large families had to decide that small families were better; people raised in a tradition and custom-bound society had to decide that they alone could and should determine the size of their family; and people raised to believe in 'natural' sex and 'gifts from God' had to decide to separate procreation from recreation by regulating their sexual behaviour artificially and deliberately.[5]

Motivation to control fertility arose from material and ideological factors. The opportunities for mobility and consumer affluence which an expanding and diversifying economy, rising real wages, and compulsory education created prompted millions of people from all classes to limit fertility, whether to enjoy life themselves or to provide well for their children. The rational and secular spirit which permeated western society reinforced the tendency to consider self-interest in planning family size. A more romantic and domestic home life, combined with the greater equality of women at work and at home, helped couples to decide on birth control and to use it successfully.[6]

Motivation, technology, marketing and institutional supports combined to ensure the rapid diffusion of birth control in German society. But because of economic, cultural and other considerations not everyone accepted the new techniques overnight. We can distinguish three distinct stages in the social acceptance of birth control in modern Germany.

During the nineteenth century many couples with property or status became convinced that family limitation was essential if they were to maintain their standard of living. Peasant farmers were pushed and pulled into birth control by their increasing market orientation in both production and consumption, and by population pressures which made a mockery of partible inheritance. Civil servants and free professionals felt compelled to maintain a respectable standard of living for themselves and to provide well for their children, and both tasks were made more difficult by the 'Great Depression' of the late nineteenth century and by the persistent inflation which followed it.[7]

For many individuals in these classes, the motivation to limit family size arose well before 1871, so they were forced to rely on traditional methods of birth control. Since their social standing was at stake, these couples could make abstinence and coitus interruptus work for prolonged periods of time. For other people in society, however, the sexual sacrifice which these methods entailed was too great to allow for consistent success. And the other traditional methods, particularly the tampons, douches and abortifacient preparations available to women, were the least effective or the most capricious, thus condemning traditional birth control to failure.

The experience with traditional birth control should not be slighted, however. Traditional practices demonstrate a traditional interest in birth control; for many people the principle of birth control was quite acceptable, it was the technology that was wanting. Secondly, the experience with traditional procedures predisposed people to accept modern techniques when these became available. Vaginal hygienic douches made uterine syringes seem familiar; tampons presaged diaphragms, suppositories, cervical caps and IUDs; and package abortifacients in the tradition of patent medicines made commercial contraceptive products acceptable.

The second stage of birth control involved the diffusion and acceptance of modern birth-control techniques among all social classes throughout Germany. Although there is no direct correlation between urban industrialisation and the start of the fertility decline, the reshaping of social, cultural and economic life after 1871 inevitably affected family life as well. Urban industrialisation meant opportunity above all else. Millions of people flocked to the cities seeking a better life. Young migrants changed jobs freely in order to find positions that were personally and financially rewarding, while older workers relied on collective bargaining to secure higher wages and shorter hours. Technological and managerial innovations led employers to rationalise hours and improve wages for skilled workers. Diversification created whole new sectors of employment in the form of white-collar, semi-skilled and unskilled work which absorbed millions of men and women. And the steady rise in real wages enabled these workers to share in the material wealth which mass production created.[8]

These changes impacted on family life in several ways. Artisans and skilled workers used their higher wages to obtain better housing in better neighbourhoods, and used their shorter hours to enjoy more leisure time with their families, and especially with their children. Wives who worked to supplement family income acquired a greater sense of personal identity and worth, while their contribution to family income entitled them to equality in decision-making. Parents who enjoyed better living conditions and who saw the opportunity for their children to succeed through education and training invested emotionally and financially in their offspring.[9] These socio-economic dimensions of urban-industrial life contributed directly to the decision to control fertility: 'The demonstration effect of cheap mass-produced goods made available in retail outlets and the real possibilities of upward social mobility intensified the incentives to adopt effective means of birth control within a few generations.'[10]

Couples chose to control fertility for several reasons. Some were so enthralled with commodity fetishism that they shunned children in order to live better themselves.[11]

Kids are a burden.

Children thin the wallet.

One lives freer without kids.

We're young and we want to enjoy life first.

We agreed before marriage that we would live for ourselves and not for kids.

We're a modern couple, we don't need kids. Any idiot can have children, but it's better to have none.

Others who were just managing to get by worried that another child would jeopardise the precarious family budget.[12] Still others saw the opportunities for advancement in modern society, and felt that more children would hold them back:

Too many children are an obstacle to a military career.

My wife could have had a nice porter's job if we didn't have kids.

We want to go up, not down.[13]

And parents who saw opportunity for their children wanted to 'make something' of each child, and realised that when there were too many children 'each steals from the others and none benefits'.[14]

For everyone it was obvious by 1914 that smaller families lived better than large families.[15] And it was equally obvious that birth control was the way to control family size: 'Now the urban populace down to the last proletarian housewife realises that it is easier and more convenient to have fewer children, and that this can be done without giving up sex.'[16]

Motivation, marketing, and ideological support combined to ensure the rapid diffusion of modern contraceptives throughout Germany during the late nineteenth and early twentieth centuries. Upper and middle-class couples quickly embraced new techniques of fertility control because they were more convenient and reliable than traditional practices.[17] Working-class men and women accepted the modern methods just as quickly. In the wake of the Franco-Prussian War former conscripts transferred the use of condoms from prophylaxis to contraception. Men who did not obtain condoms in the army bought rubber 'cigarettes' from pedlars. Later in the century young women working in the cities learned about diaphragms, suppositories and IUDs from their middle-class employers and adopted them for their own use. And, starting in the 1890s, the Health Insurance Programme made condoms available to men in a campaign against venereal disease, and offered contraception, abortion and sterilisation to women on therapeutic indication. Men who had been reluctant to consider birth control were more receptive when the health or life of their spouse was at stake.[18] When men refused birth control, women resorted to those methods which they could use without their partner's knowledge or consent: tampons, diaphragms, cervical caps, intrauterine devices — and abortion.[19]

Dilatation and curettage became a common procedure in the 1890s, and women who could afford a personal physician easily obtained abortion that was safe and effective. Most other women had to wait until the first decade of the new century, when uterine syringes became available. The crucial role of the syringe in the German fertility decline is reflected in the statistics of the 'abortion epidemic' — the sudden upsurge in hospital-treated abortions that occurred throughout

Germany starting in 1905–10. Because only about one-tenth of these abortions could be traced to natural causes, and another one-tenth attributed to therapeutic intervention, the overwhelming majority were regarded as criminal abortion, and the high proportion of septic cases reinforced this impression. Hospital-treated cases were only the tip of the iceberg, since most abortions occurred without complications. But medical and criminal records demonstrate that thousands of women, married and single, young and old, rich and poor, willingly sought abortion each year in order to control fertility. Women chose abortion when their husbands or boyfriends refused to cooperate with contraception, when male or female contraceptives failed, or when neither partner used contraception but the woman, at least, did not want pregnancy.[20]

Socio-economic motivation did not affect everyone at the same time, nor did it persuade all couples to adopt modern methods of birth control. Over and above practical obstacles to their use — cost and access — there remained cultural barriers to the use of modern contraceptives. Some people from isolated areas remained unaware of the new techniques, while others who knew of them opposed their use because they regarded contraceptives as artificial, immoral and sinful. Young people often avoided contraceptives in the belief that 'nothing will happen'. Older couples might be too 'lazy' to use contraceptives regularly and properly.[21]

Tradition was a major obstacle to the use of contraceptives. Religious scruples were one hindrance; male chauvinism was another. Men who worked in physical occupations which put a premium on virility, such as mining or construction, felt that large families were a mark of manhood. Other men resented any interference with natural sensations. Tradition-minded men were frequently reluctant to discuss birth control with anyone else, regarding it as 'women's business'.[22]

These traditional barriers were gradually overcome by the pervasive rationalism of western society. By 1900 a modern outlook pervaded all social classes, though not necessarily all individuals within those classes. Surveys showed that the more 'intelligent' members of all classes were more likely to have smaller families. The rational acceptance of modern birth control was expedited by socialism, which argued that workers were entitled to enjoy the benefits of industrial society as much as the bourgeoisie; and by feminism, which argued that women had the right to control their own bodies. The success of these efforts is reflected in the attitude of a socialist woman in the 1920s:[23]

> I don't think marriage exists to breed as many children as

possible for capitalism, especially since we have so many unemployed today. Why should we workers put a lot of kids into the world when the rich hardly have any?

During the 1920s the third stage of diffusion saw the mass acceptance of modern contraception by people in all classes of society. The impact of war, revolution, and inflation intensified socio-economic pressures to control fertility; more extensive and overt marketing and advertising increased awareness and availability of contraceptives; governmental and voluntary organisation stepped up their efforts to inform people of the proper use of contraceptives and to make them available to those who could not otherwise obtain them; and the constant public discussion of birth control, culminating in the 1931 abortion campaign, further accelerated public awareness and acceptance of contraception. By the 1920s the weight of social attitudes towards birth control had shifted so that peer pressure opposed high fertility. City and country folk alike lost the 'God-given' attitude towards children, and considered anyone who 'let things happen' to be 'stupid and reactionary'. Women who bore too many children were branded as 'rabbit hutches', and those who put off abortion were told they were 'crazy not to do it'. Even young single women started demanding birth control, and men increasingly complied.[24]

The inevitable result of greater motivation, awareness, access and acceptability was the greater use of contraception. The continuing fertility decline demonstrated that people from all classes and regions and ages were limiting family size. And the decline in abortion incidence during the 1920s demonstrates that more and more people were switching to modern contraceptives to achieve fertility control — an impression affirmed by the experience of counselling centres, where many of the patients sought to upgrade their contraceptive practices from coitus interruptus to something more convenient and more reliable.[25] By the end of the decade German couples were protected by more than fifty million condoms; more than one million diaphragms, cervical caps and IUDs; and more than three million chemical packages annually.[26] And women knew that abortion was always available should they ever need it; more than one hundred thousand women a year took advantage of the most reliable form of birth control, with a slight increase during the depression.[27]

The history of birth control is not unambiguously linear, however. Different methods were taken up by different people from different classes for different reasons at different times. Some made traditional techniques work; others eagerly responded to the security and

CONCLUSION

convenience of modern contraceptives; still others chose, or were compelled to rely on, abortion. Couples who knew what they wanted — for themselves, their family, or their children — more readily accepted the family planning outlook that is essential for long-term fertility control. Couples who acted only to prevent conception on occasion were more likely to fail, or to depend on abortion.[28] But between 1890 and 1930 modern birth control spread throughout German society, and between 1895 and 1935 German fertility fell by half.

NOTES

1. Ansley Coale, 'The demographic transition', International Union for the Scientific Study of Population, International Population Conference (IUSSP, Liege, 1973), p. 62; Michael Teitelbaum, *The British fertility decline: demographic transition in the crucible of the Industrial Revolution* (Princeton University Press, Princeton, 1984), p. 218; Lado Ruzicka and John Caldwell, *The end of demographic transition in Australia* (Australian National University Press, Canberra, 1977), p. 194.

2. Coale, 'Demographic transition', pp. 65-7; Etienne van de Walle and John Knodel, 'Europe's fertility transition: new evidence and lessons for today's developing world', *Population Bulletin*, 34 (1980) pp. 21, 32-4; Edward Shorter, John Knodel and Etienne Van de Walle, 'The decline of non-marital fertility in Europe, 1880-1940', *PS*, 25 (1971), p. 388; Teitelbaum, *British fertility decline*, pp. 218-19; Ronald Lesthaeghe, *The decline of Belgian fertility, 1800-1970* (Princeton University Press, Princeton, 1977), pp. 119, 224; Kenneth Lockridge, *The fertility transition in Sweden: a preliminary look at smaller geographic units* (University of Umeaa Press, Umeaa, 1983), p. 59; John Knodel, *The decline of fertility in Germany, 1871-1939* (Princeton University Press, Princeton, 1974), pp. 243, 250, 262; Massimo Livi-Bacci, *A history of Italian fertility during the last two centuries* (Princeton University Press, Princeton, 1977), p. 186; Massimo Livi-Bacci, *A century of Portuguese fertility* (Princeton University Press, Princeton, 1971), pp. 101, 107-8, 114.

3. Allgemeine Konferenz der Deutsche Sittlichkeitsvereine, *Die geschlechtlich-sittlichen Verhältnisse der evangelischen Landbewohner im Deutschen Reiche* ed. C. Wagner (2 vols, Reinhold Werther, Leipzig, 1895-6), vol. I, pp. 252, 255; vol. II, p. 313; Dr Jorns, 'Zur willkürlichen Beschränkung der Geburtenzahl', *ZMB*, 24 (1911) p. 53; B. Schlegtendahl, 'Die Empfängnis und ihre Verhütung', *ZMB*, 27 (1914), pp. 329-36; Carl Reissig, 'Geheimmittelschwindel und Geschlechtsleben in der Annonce', *Aerztliche Vereinsblatt Deutschland*, 36-8 (1909), pp. 1-29.

4. J. Moses, 'Zur Psychologie und Soziologie jugendlicher unehelicher Mutter', *ZSWSP*, 13 (1926), p. 170; Heidi Rosenbaum, *Formen der Familie: Untersuchungen zum Zusammenhang von Familienverhältnissen, Sozialstruktur und sozialem Wandel in der deutschen Gesellschaft des 19. Jahrhunderts* (Suhrkamp, Frankfurt, 1982), p. 459; Lawrence Stone, *The*

family, sex and marriage in England, 1500–1800 (Weidenfeld and Nicolson, London, 1977), p. 415; E.P. McCormick, 'Adolescence' in John Money and Herman Musaph (eds), *Handbook of sexology* (Excerpta Medica, New York, 1977), p. 628.

    5. J.T. Fawcett, *Psychology and population: behavioral research issues in fertility and family planning* (Population Council, New York, 1970), p. 44; John Scanzoni, *Sex roles, life styles and childbearing: changing patterns in marriage and the family* (Free Press, New York, 1975), pp. 10–12; Stone, *Family*, pp. 415–18; Van de Walle and Knodel, 'Europe's fertility transition', pp. 28–9.

    6. R. Spree, *Soziale Ungleichheit vor Krankheit und Tod: Zur Sozialgeschichte des Gesundheitsbereichs im Deutschen Kaiserreich* (Vandenhoek und Rupprecht, Göttingen, 1981), p. 90; Erich Brauer, *Die abnehmende Fruchtbarkeit der berufstätigen Frau: Ein Beitrag zur Untersuchung der sozialpsychologische Seite der Unfruchtbarkeit. Sexus* (Ernst Bircher, Leipzig, 1921), pp. 18, 22–6, 31, 34, 40; Lesthaeghe, *Decline of Belgian fertility*, pp. 41–2, 145, 228–30; Livi-Bacci, *Century of Portuguese fertility*, pp. 129–31.

    7. Allgemeine Konferenz, *Verhältnisse*, vol. I, pp. 32, 51–2, 119, 252, 255; vol. II, pp. 102, 121, 155, 158, 288, 368, 507; O. Polano, 'Beitrag zur Frage der Geburtenbeschränkung', *ZGG*, 79 (1917), p. 572; Hermann Gebhardt, *Zur Bäuerlichen Glaubens- und Sittenlehre*, 3rd edn (Gustav Schlossmann, 1895), p. 138; 'The Mittelstand in German society and politics, 1871–1914', *Social History*, 2 (1977), p. 426; Werner Blessing, 'Umwelt und Mentalität im ländlichen Bayern: Eine Skizze zum Alltagswandel im 19. Jahrhundert', *ASG*, 19 (1979), pp. 26, 28; Dr Haneld, *Zur Frage der Geburtenbeschränküng und Lebenshaltung in Beamtenfamilien* (Berlin, 1916); Joseph Banks and Olive Banks, *Feminism and family planning in Victorian England* (Schocken, New York, 1964), pp. 79–81; Eugen Weber, *Peasants into Frenchmen: the modernization of rural France, 1870–1914* (Stanford University Press, Stanford, 1976), pp. 229–30.

    8. Peter Stearns, *Lives of labor: work in a maturing industrial society* (Croom Helm, London, 1975), pp. 4–5, 13, 142, 200, 242, 270, 293.

    9. Roderick von Ungern-Sternberg, *The causes of the decline in birthrate within the European sphere of civilisation* (Eugenics Research Association, Cold Spring Harbour, 1931), pp. 46, 136; Berthold Polag, 'Die Berechtigung des künstlichen Abortus vom medizinischen, juristischen, und nationalökonomischen Standpunkte', PhD dissertation, University of Strassburg, 1909), p. 67; E.R. May, 'Zur Frage des Geburtenrückganges', *Schmollers Jahrbuch*, 40 (1916), p. 56; L. Gschwendtner, 'Über die Motive der Fortpflanzung bzw. der Geburtenverhütung', *ARGB*, 21 (1929), p. 268; Stearns, *Lives of labor*, pp. 28, 32–3, 60, 65, 70–1, 270–2, 274, 276; Peter Stearns, 'Adaptation to industrialization: German workers as a test case', *CEH*, 3 (1970), pp. 322, 326; L. Niethammer, 'Wie wohnten die Arbeiter im Kaiserreich?', *ASG*, 16 (1976), p. 69; Sandra Coyner, 'Class consciousness and consumption: the new middle class during the Weimar Republic', *JSH*, 10 (1977), p. 314. On the new role of women and its impact on family life see also Marie Bernays, *Untersuchungen über den Zusammenhang von Frauenfabrikarbeit und Geburtenhäufigkeit in Deutschland* (Möser, Berlin, 1916), and R. Hotstätter, *Die arbeitende Frau: ihre wirtschaftliche Lage,*

CONCLUSION

Gesundheit, Ehe und Mutterschaft (Perles, Vienna, 1929).

10. Franklin Mendels, 'Proto-industrialization: the first phase of the industrialization process', *Journal of Economic History*, 32 (1972), p. 253.

11. Max Marcuse, *Der eheliche Präventivverkehr: seine Verbreitung, Verursachung und Methodik* (Enke, Stuttgart, 1917), case nos 62, 40, 165, 105, 110 and 22, respectively; compare cases 60, 64, 100.

12. Brauer, *Abnehmende Fruchtbarkeit*, p. 26; Felix Theilhaber, *Das sterile Berlin* (Enke, Stuttgart, 1917), pp. 96-7; Oldenberg, 'Geburtenrückgang', p. 428; Mirko Kosic, 'Die soziologischen Grundlagen der Geburtenbeschränküng', *ASA*, 10 (1916-17), p. 447; Gschwendtner, 'Motive', p. 268; Ulrich Linse, 'Arbeiterschaft und Geburtenentwicklung im deutschen Kaiserreich von 1871', *ASG*, 12 (1972), p. 22.

13. Marcuse, *Eheliche Präventivverkehr*, case nos 65, 18, 175 respectively.

14. Ibid., nos 244, 225.

15. Polano, 'Beitrag', p. 572; Brauer, *Abnehmende Fruchtbarkeit*, p. 34; Stearns, *Lives of labor*, p. 286; Heinrich Gödde, 'Ist die Zahl der Vielgebärenden in den letzten 20 jahren zurückgegangen', PhD dissertation, University of Bonn, 1915.

16. Bumm, 'Zur Bevölkerungspolitik', *ZGyn*, 42 (1918), p. 619.

17. O. Krohne, 'Empfängnisverhütung, künstliche Unfruchtbarkeit und Schwangerschaftsunterbrechung vom bevölkerungspolitischen und ärztlichen Standpunkt', *ZAF*, 14 (1917), p. 344; O. Krohne, 'Künstliche Fehlgeburt und Künstliche Unfruchtbarkeit vom Standpunkt des Staatsinteresse' in Placzek (ed.), *Künstliche Fehlgeburt*, pp. 370-1, 378-9; G. Winter, 'Sollen wir Bevölkerungspolitik treiben?', *MGG*, 47 (1918), p. 356.

18. Allgemeine Konferenz, *Verhältnisse*, vol. I, pp. 51-2, vol. II, pp. 121, 313; Hans Ferdy, *Sittliche Selbstbeschränkung*, (Verfasser, Hildesheim, 1904) p. 136; Linse, 'Arbeiterschaft', pp. 218, 228. On men and therapeutic contraception for their wives see Marcuse, *Eheliche Präventivverkehr*, cases 1, 7, 10, 13, 24, 32, 33, 72, 96, 99, 102, 136; also Polano, 'Beitrag', p. 572.

19. Marcuse, *Eheliche Präventivverkehr*, p. 119; Jorns, 'Willkürlichen Beschränkung', p. 54; Robert Engelsmann, 'Die Ursache des Geburtenrückganges', PhD dissertation, University of Münster, 1937, p. 143; Renatte Brandt-Wyt, 'Der Wille zum Kinde beim Weibe: Ein Versuch zur Erklärung des Geburtenrückganges', *Dokumente der Fortschritt*, 6 (1913), pp. 24-5; Angus McLaren, *Birth control in nineteenth century England: a social and intellectual history* (Holmes and Meier, New York, 1978), p. 227.

20. A. Haberda, 'Gerichtsärztliche Erfahrungen über die Fruchtabtreibung in Wien', *VGMOS*, 56 (1914), pp. 64-5; Polag, 'Berechtigung', p. 71; Jahns, *Delikt*, p. 31; Max Hirsch, *Fruchtabtreibung und Präventivverkehr im Zusammenhang mit dem Geburtenrückgang* (Kabitzsch, Würzburg, 1914), p. 32.

21. Stearns, *Lives of labor*, pp. 274-5; Stearns, 'Adaptation', p. 326; A. Grotjahn, *Eine Karthothek zu Paragraph 218. Berichte aus eine Kleinstadtpraxis über 426 künstliche Aborte in einem Jahr* (Metzner, Berlin, 1932), p. 12.

22. Polano, 'Beitrag', p. 570; Marcuse, *Eheliche Präventivverkehr*, p. 126 and case nos 134, 161, 172, 180, 213; Fritz Meder, 'Die konzeptionsverhütung in der Hand des freipraktizierenden Arztes', *ZGyn*, 55 (1931), p. 2563; Engelsmann, 'Ursache', p. 143; Edward Shorter, *A history of*

women's bodies (Basic Books, New York, 1982), pp. 9, 15; Peter Stearns, *Be a man! males in modern society* (Holmes and Meier, New York, 1979), pp. 66-7. On miners see Hannes Pyszka, *Bergarbeiterbevölkerung und Fruchtbarkeit* (Birk, Munich, 1911).

23. Gschwendtner, 'Motive', p. 278. See also Marcuse, *Eheliche Präventivverkehr*, case no. 227; Grete Rettberg, 'Gerichtlich- medizinische Untersuchung von 133 Stratverfahren wegen Abtreibung in Landgerichtsbezirk Göttingen, 1930-1939', PhD dissertation, University of Göttingen, 1942, pp. 26-7; Spree, *Soziale Ungleichheit*, p. 90.

24. Ungern-Sternberg, *Causes*, p. 43; Marcuse, *Eheliche Präventivverkehr*, case no. 31; Marcuse, *Eheliche Präventivverkehr*, pp. 18-19; Konstantin Inderheggen, 'Das Delikt der Abtreibung im Landgerichtsbezirk Mönchen-Gladbach in der Zeit von 1908 bis 1938 (Fromman, Jena, 1940),p. 20; S. Peller, *Fehlgeburt und Bevölkerungsfrage. Eine medizinalstatistische und sozialbiologische Studie* (Hippokrates, Stuttgart, 1930), p. 97; R. Fetscher, 'Entwicklung der Eheberatung', *DMW*, 56 (1930), p. 2139.

25. Anton Hengge, 'Zum Geburtenrückgang', *MGG*, 46 (1917), p. 183; Peller, *Fehlgeburt*, pp. 100, 184; Andreas Friese, 'Fehlgeburt und Lebensalter', PhD dissertation, University of Berlin, 1935, pp. 23, 27-8, 30; Engelsmann, 'Ursache', pp. 87-9; Hofstätter, 'Heiratsaussichten', p. 383; A. Grotjahn, *Die Hygiene der menschlichen Fortpflanzung: Versuch einer praktischer Eugenik* (Urban and Schwarzenberg, Berlin, 1926), p. 310; Marcuse, *Eheliche Präventivverkehr*, p. 25; Gschwendtner, 'Motive', p. 280; Hans Nevermann, *Über Eheberatung* (Kabitzsch, Leipzig, 1931), p. 42; Fetscher, 'Entwicklung der Eheberatung', p. 2139; Fink, 'Wirkung der Verhütungsmittel', p. 335.

26. These figures are estimations extrapolated from data on contraceptives and abortion presented in Chapter 2 and Chapter 3.

27. Friese, 'Fehlgeburt', *passim*, and other sources in Chapter 3.

28. Marcuse, *Eheliche Präventivverkehr*, pp. 109-10; Haberda, 'Erfahrungen', p. 64; Schaeffer, 'Statistische Beitrag', p. 636; Peller, *Fehlgeburt*, p. 101.

Suggestions for Further Reading

FERTILITY DECLINE AND THE POPULATION QUESTION

The standard analysis of the German fertility transition is John Knodel, *The decline of fertility in Germany, 1871-1939* (Princeton University Press, Princeton, 1974). The German decline was part of the general western decline, which is summarised in Ansley Coale and Susan Watkins (eds), *The decline of fertility in Europe* (Princeton University Press, Princeton, 1986). Two national studies which are especially valuable for their discussion of social causes of fertility decline are: Ronald Lesthaeghe, *The decline of Belgian fertility, 1800-1970* (Princeton University Press, Princeton, 1977); and Lado Ruzicka and John Caldwell, *The end of demographic transition in Australia* (Australian National University Press, 1977). The best contemporary analysis of the fertility decline is Roderick von Ungern-Sternberg, *The causes of the decline in birthrate within the European sphere of civilization* (Eugenics Research Association, Cold Spring Harbor, 1931). An excellent recent discussion is presented by Manfred Stürzbecher, *Die Bekämpfung des Geburtenrückganges und der Säuglingssterblichkeit im Spiegel der Reichstagsdebatten, 1900-1933* (PhD thesis, Free University of Berlin, 1954). For contrasting assessments of the fertility decline and its social, economic, and political impact see Jean Bornträger, *Der Geburtenrückgang in Deutschland: seine Bewertung und seine Bekämpfung* (Kabitzsch, Würzburg, 1913); and Julius Wolf, *Der Geburtenrückgang: die Rationalisierung des Sexuallebens unserer Zeit* (Fischer, Jena, 1912).

BIRTH CONTROL: MEDICAL ASPECTS

The standard historical introduction to the methods of birth control is Norman Himes, *The medical history of contraception* (Gamut Press, New York, 1936; reprinted 1963). On patent medicines see Elmar Ernst, *Das 'industrielle' Geheimmittel und seine Werbung. Arzneifertigwaren in der zweiten Hälfte des neunzehnten Jahrhunderts in Deutschland* (Jal, Würzburg, 1975); James Young, *The toadstool millionaires: a social history of patent medicines in America before federal regulation* (Princeton University Press, Princeton, 1961); Sarah Stage, *Female complaints. Lydia Pinkham and the business of women's medicine* (Norton, New York, 1979). The best overview of contraceptive techniques is presented by Ludwig Fraenkel, *Die Empfängnisverhütung. Biologische Grundlagen, Technik und Indikationen, für Aerzte bearbeitet.* (Enke, Stuttgart, 1932). On abortion see Louis Lewin, *Die Fruchtabtreibung durch Gifte und andere Mittel. Ein handbuch für Aerzte, Juristen, Politiker, Nationalökonomen,* 4th edn (Stilke, Berlin, 1925); Georg Winter, *Der künstliche Abort. Indikationen, Methode und Rechtspflege für den geburtshilflichen Praktiker* (Enke, Stuttgart, 1926; Frederick Taussig, *Abortion: spontaneous and induced* (Mosby, St Louis, 1936).

BIRTH CONTROL: SOCIAL ASPECTS

Max Marcuse wrote an excellent social analysis of the practice of birth control: *Der eheliche Präventivverkehr: seine Verbreitung, Verursachung, und Methodik* (Enke, Stuttgart, 1917). For an equally comprehensive discussion of abortion see Sigismund Peller, *Fehlgeburt und Bevölkerungsfrage. Eine medizinalstatistische und sozialbiologische Studie* (Hippokrates, Stuttgart, 1930). For two recent interpretations of the practice of birth control in Germany see Ulrich Linse, 'Arbeiterschaft und Geburtenentwicklung im deutschen Kaiserreich von 1871', *ASG*, 12 (1972), pp. 205-72; and Robert Neuman, 'Working class birth control in Wilhelmian Germany', *CSSH*, 20 (1978), pp. 408-28. On the practice of birth control elsewhere see: Linda Gordon, *Woman's body, woman's right. A social history of birth control in America* (Grossmann, New York, 1976); James Mohr, *Abortion in America. Origins and evolution of national policy, 1800-1900* (Oxford University Press, New York, 1978; Angus McLaren, *Birth control in nineteenth century England: a social and intellectual history* (Holmes and Meier, New York, 1978); Angus McLaren, 'Abortion in France: women and the regulation of family size, 1800-1900', *French Historical Studies*, 10 (1978), pp. 461-85.

IDEOLOGY AND POLITICS OF BIRTH CONTROL

Three social movements supported birth control in Germany: see Richard Evans, *The feminist movement in Germany, 1894-1933* (Sage, London, 1976); Robert Neuman, 'The sexual question and social democracy in Imperial Germany', *JSH*, 7 (1974), pp. 271-86; Atina Grossmann, 'Satisfaction is domestic happiness: mass working class

Sex Reform organizations in the Weimar Republic', in Michael Probkowski and Isidor Wallman (eds), *Towards the holocaust, the social and economic collapse of the Weimar Republic* (Greenwood, Westport, 1983), pp. 265-93. Two contemporary works which argue the pros and cons of 'liberated' sexuality, respectively, are: Julius Wolf, *Die neue Sexualmoral und das Geburtenproblem unserer Tage* (Fischer, Jena, 1928); and August Mayer, *Gedanken zur modernen Sexualmoral* (Enke, Stuttgart, 1930). On the politics of birth control elsewhere see: Rosanna Ledbetter, *A history of the Malthusian league, 1877-1927* (Ohio State University Press, Columbus, 1976); Richard Soloway, *Birth control and the population question in England, 1877-1930* (University of North Carolina Press, Chapel Hill, 1982; James Reed, *From private vice to public virtue. The birth control movement and American society since 1830* (Basic Books, New York, 1978).

SOCIAL CHANGE AND BIRTH CONTROL

Birth control represented an adaptation to changing social, economic, and familial circumstances. On this larger context see: Heidi Rosenbaum, *Formen der Familie. Untersuchungen zum Zusammenhang von Familienverhältnissen, Sozialstruktur und sozialem Wandel in der deutschen Gesellschaft des 19. Jahrhunderts* (Suhrkamp, Frankfurt, 1982); Peter Stearns, *Lives of labor: work in a maturing industrial society* (Croom Helm, London, 1975); Eugen Weber, *Peasants into Frenchmen: the modernization of rural France, 1870-1914* (Stanford University Press, Stanford, 1976); Michael Phayer, *Sexual liberation and religion in nineteenth-century Europe* (Croom Helm, London, 1977); Edward Shorter, *The making of the modern family* (Fontana, London, 1977).

Index

abortifacients 16-18, 20-3, 32n52, 75, 90, 99-100
abortion 16, 21-2, 55-7, 68-80, 89-105, 121-3, 126, 140, 142, 144-9, 151
   complications 43, 75-6
   criminal 70, 75,79, 90, 101-5, 143
   febrile 43, 75, 78, 85-6n30
   incomplete 74-5, 96
   legal status 56, 71-2, 133-4, 146-7, 153-4
   modern 4, 43, 90-3, 96-9, 167
   mortality 76-7
   self-induced 90
   spontaneous 70-1, 73, 78, 104
   therapeutic 71-4, 78, 85n26, 143
   traditional 15-23, 97-100
abortionists 16, 22, 70, 75-6, 78, 89-93, 95, 97, 100, 104
abstinence 7-8, 40
advertising 20-2, 48-50, 91-2, 95, 100, 114, 144
   regulations 112-13, 137-9, 144, 149, 154
Albrecht, Hans 134
Amberley, Viscount 156n15
amenorrhea 9
anal intercourse 10-11
apiol 18
army 50-1

baths 15, 100, 143
   see also abortion, traditional
Berlin 69-73, 98-9, 116, 120-1, 124, 135-9, 145, 149
Bilfinger, Eugen 54
Bilz, Friedrich 14
birth control 51, 56-7, 112, 124-7, 137, 141-3, 148-9, 152-3, 163
   and politics 77, 118, 133-7, 141-7
   Center Party 55, 138, 141, 147
   Social Democrats 54-5, 141-2, 145, 147
   modern 3-4, 163-70
   popular attitudes 11-12, 23-4, 164-70
   of Catholics 7, 14, 148
   of men 39, 44, 90
   of women 56-7, 100-1, 105, 167-8
   traditional 4, 7-8, 23-4, 164-5
'Birth Strike' 55, 145
Bornträger, Jean 142, 155
Bradlaugh-Besant trial (England) 37
breast feeding 9
Breslau 69, 95
Bumm, Ernst 70
Bund für Mutterschutz see League for the Protection of Motherhood
Buttenstedt, Carl 9-10

caesarian section 41, 72-3
Capellmann, Carl 40
Carlile, Robert 37
'Casti Conubbii' (encyclical) 148
cervical caps 41, 57, 114, 122
civil servants, and birth control 8, 23, 70, 122
coitus interruptus 11-12, 35n80, 122
coitus reservatus 11
coitus saxonicus 11
condoms 37-9, 49-51, 57, 59n12, 112-14, 121-2, 149, 167
contraception 12-13, 23-4, 36, 38-41, 50, 53, 56-7, 104-5, 112, 114, 126, 140, 142-4, 148, 169-70
   chemical 40-5, 51, 57,

177

115-17, 122-3, 142
  hormonal 116-17
  mechanical 37-43, 49-51, 57,
    112-15, 121-2, 142-3
    see also cervical caps,
    condoms, diaphragm,
    intra-uterine devices,
    tampon
  traditional 7-15
contraceptives, brand names 39,
  43, 114-16, 122
contraceptives, marketing 39,
  42, 44, 48-50, 57, 113-14,
  163-4
contraceptives, regulations
  49-50, 138-9, 142, 144, 149,
  154, 159n39
contraceptives, testing 44-5,
  115-16
counselling centres, marital
  118-21, 125, 152
counselling centres, sexual 121-3
curettage 74, 96-7, 143

'Diachylon' 16
diaphragm 38-41, 49-51, 57, 79,
  114, 122
doctors, and abortion 71-2,
  76-80, 88n52, 91, 95-7, 99,
  146-7
doctors, and birth control 77,
  125-6, 144, 151-2
doctors, and contraception 7, 12,
  40-5, 51-3
doctors, and quacks 140-1
domestic servants, and birth
  control 40, 51, 70
douching 13-14, 37, 40-1
druggists, and birth control 39,
  42, 49-50, 94, 142
Drysdale, Charles 36, 38
'Dublosan' 113
Duisburg 100

East Prussia 17, 49, 90, 99
Ebell Irrigator 13
Ergot 17
Eugenics 117-21, 152-4

false pregnancy 89-90

farmers, and birth control 8, 10,
  23, 70
female complaints 18-22
  see also menstrual
  irregularity
feminism 55-6, 126, 134
fertility decline 1-3, 133-4, 142,
  148, 154-5, 163
Fraenkel, Ludwig 117, 125-6
Fraenkel, Manfred 45
Frankfurt/Main 120-1, 123
Freudenberg, Karl 77
frigidity 11

Gauss, C.J. 154-5
'Gebärstreik' see 'Birth Strike'
Geburtenrückgangsfrage 77, 145
Geheimmittell see patent
  medicines
German Gynaecological Society
  99, 125-6
German Medical Association 79,
  140, 147, 150, 152
German Society to Combat
  Venereal Disease 8, 141
'Glücksehe' see Buttenstedt, Carl
Goldstein, Ferdinand 133
Göttingen 90, 96
Gräfenberg, Ernst 42, 114, 122
  see also intra-uterine devices
Grotjahn, Alfred 133, 152-3
Günther, Gustav 44

Haberda, A. 47
Haberlandt, Ludwig 117
Haire, Norman 116
Hanssen (Dr) 13
Hausmeister, Max 54
health insurance programme 4,
  14, 19, 40, 53-4, 57, 68, 70,
  79, 96, 98, 121-3, 140, 149,
  153n28, 167
Hegar, August 47
Heiser, Paul 98, 124, 145-6
Hinz, Friedrich 14-15
Hirsch, Max 71, 143
Hirschfeld, Magnus 10, 121, 146
Hirtsiefer (Prussian Minister of
  Welfare) 120
Hodann, Max 121

Hohenlohe (Chancellor) 138
Hohlweg (Dr) 42
Horch (Dr) 10
hospitals, and abortion 68, 72, 74-5, 96
hospitals, and sterilisation 123, 150-1

Imperial Ordinance on Trade with Medications 22, 94, 137
International Hygiene Exhibition (Dresden) 8
International Medical Congress (Amsterdam) 12, 38
International Neo-Malthusian Congress (Dresden) 54
intra-uterine devices 41-3, 51, 57, 97, 114-15, 122, 142-3
Irrigator 13

Kafka, Karl 41
Karezza 11
Kienle, Else 149
Kirchmann, Julius von 135-7
Klyso-pump 14
Knaus and Ogino (drs) *see* rhythm
Knowlton, Charles 13, 37
Krey, Franz 149
Krohne, Otto 48

lead, and abortion 16
League for the Protection of Motherhood 55-6, 121, 123, 146
Leunbach, Jonathan 99
Levy-Lenz, Ludwig 13
Lex Heinze 49-50, 138-9, 141

male continence 11
Malthus, Thomas 36-7
Malthusian League 37
Marcuse, Julian 126
Marcuse, Max 8, 11, 13-14, 51
massage, and abortion 15, 93, 143
masturbation 7, 10
Mayer, August 152
Mensinga, Wilhelm 4, 38-40
menstrual irregularity 19, 99, 137, 142
package preparations 17-18, 100
Merck (Dr) 150-1
midwives and abortion 68, 79-80, 91-2, 94-7, 99, 144
midwives and contraception 42-4, 49, 51
Mill, John Stuart 36, 136
Mönchen-Gladbach 100, 154
Monist League 117-18
Munich 69-70
Musczynski (abortionist) 20-2, 99, 102

Näcke, Paul 10-11
National Socialists, and birth control 153-4
naturopaths, and birth control 42, 92-4, 140-1, 144
neo-malthusianism 4, 36-8, 54, 134-5, 163
Nürnberger, Ludwig 77

Obturator *see* intra-uterine devices
Offenburg 150-1
oral sex 10
Otto, H. 40
ovulation 8-9
Owen, Robert Dale 37

patent medicines 4, 18-22, 31n50, 94, 105, 137, 141-2
pedlars 42, 49-50, 142
pharmacists, and birth control 18, 22-3, 49-50, 94, 137, 142
 see also Imperial Ordinance on Trade with Medications
phosphorus, and abortion 16
Place, Francis 13
Polano, Otto 11
prostitution 7, 10, 39, 41
Prussian Health Council 73
Prussia 69, 77, 137
Pust (Dr) 114, 122

quacks *see* doctors and quacks, naturopaths

INDEX

quinine 17

'Ramses' (diaphragm) 114, 122
rape, and abortion 74, 104
Reichsbund der Kinderreichen Deutschlands 153
Reichsgericht 46, 50, 72
Reichstag 135, 138, 145-8, 153
Rendell (pharmacist) 38, 43
rhythm 8-9
Rodecurt, M. 116
Roeren, Hermann 141
Ruhr 42, 90-2, 100, 102, 104
Rümelin, Gustav 37

Sachs (Dr) 99
Saxony 121, 124, 140, 148
Schleswig-Holstein 13, 99
Schmerz (Dr) *see* sterilisation, male
Sellheim, Hugo 98-9
sex reform organisations 56, 92, 117, 123-5, 148-9
sex reform periodicals 56, 124
Silesia 90
Social Harmony Union 54
Steinhäuser, Willi 115
Steriletts 42, 122
   see also intra-uterine devices
sterilisation 45-8, 51, 117, 122-3, 144, 150-4
   legal status 46, 150-1, 154
   male 45-6, 48, 117, 150-1
   medical attitudes 63n47

therapeutic 46-8, 123, 150-3
   USA 47, 154
sterility 76
Stöcker, Helene 56, 146
suppositories 38, 43-4, 79
   see also contraception, chemical
syringes 13, 75, 96-108, 141, 143

tampon 13, 37
Theilhaber, Felix 148
Thuringia 40, 90-2, 99-100, 102, 124

Uhden, Karl von 137
usus equae 11

vasectomy *see* sterilisation, male
venereal disease (VD) 7-8, 10-11, 39, 51, 55, 70, 94, 112-13, 121, 149
Venus Apparatus 14-15

Wartenburg, Alma 55
Weisse Kreuz 7
Wilde, Friedrich 41
Winter, Georg 72, 74, 77, 117
Wolf, Friedrich 149
workers, and birth control 10, 70, 122, 150

Zacharias, Otto 38

For Product Safety Concerns and Information please contact our EU
representative GPSR@taylorandfrancis.com
Taylor & Francis Verlag GmbH, Kaufingerstraße 24, 80331 München, Germany

www.ingramcontent.com/pod-product-compliance
Lightning Source LLC
Chambersburg PA
CBHW061448300426
44114CB00014B/1882